Joseph F. Loubat

Narrative of the Mission to Russia, in 1866

Joseph F. Loubat

Narrative of the Mission to Russia, in 1866

ISBN/EAN: 9783337299422

Printed in Europe, USA, Canada, Australia, Japan

Cover: Foto ©ninafisch / pixelio.de

More available books at **www.hansebooks.com**

NARRATIVE

OF THE

MISSION TO RUSSIA, IN 1866,

OF THE

HON. GUSTAVUS VASA FOX,
ASSISTANT-SECRETARY OF THE NAVY.

FROM THE JOURNAL AND NOTES

OF

J. F. LOUBAT.

EDITED BY

JOHN D. CHAMPLIN, JR.

NEW YORK:
D. APPLETON AND COMPANY,
549 & 551 BROADWAY.
1873.

ENTERED, according to Act of Congress, in the year 1872, by
J. F. LOUBAT,
In the Office of the Librarian of Congress, at Washington.

TO THE

HONORABLE G. V. FOX.

My dear Sir:

Permit me to dedicate to you this book, a memorial of that important and unique mission, in which I had the honor to act as one of your secretaries.

Yours, sincerely,

J. F. LOUBAT.

New York, May, 1873.

CONTENTS.

CHAPTER I.
Introductory, ... Page 10

CHAPTER II.
Crossing the Atlantic, ... 22

CHAPTER III.
Ireland—France—England, ... 36

CHAPTER IV.
Copenhagen—The King's Visit—The Royal Dinner—Hospitalities—The Stonewall—Thorvaldsen—The Museums, ... 54

CHAPTER V.
In the Baltic—Sweaborg—Helsingfors—Gulf of Finland—Cronstadt, . 69

CHAPTER VI.
Peterhof—The Imperial Audience—The Resolution of Congress—At the Forts—The Naval Banquet, ... 86

CHAPTER VII.
Cronstadt—The Arsenal—The Steamship-Works—The Municipal Banquet, ... 115

CHAPTER VIII.

St. Petersburg—St. Isaac's—The Fête of the River Yacht Club—Czarskoë-Selo, ... Page 126

CHAPTER IX.

The Admiralty—Imperial Library—Winter Palace and Hermitage—Dinner to the Crews, ... 141

CHAPTER X.

The Nevsky Prospect—Alexander Nevsky—Steel-gun Foundery—Exchange and Academy of Sciences—The Merchants' Dinner, . . . 151

CHAPTER XI.

Krasnoë-Selo—Manœuvres—Honorary Citizenship—Cathedral of Peter and Paul—Mining Institute, ... 165

CHAPTER XII.

Dinner of the Good-Birth Society—Poem of Oliver Wendell Holmes, . 175

CHAPTER XIII.

Receptions on the Miantonomoh—Presentations at Court—Races at Czarskoë-Selo—Dinner of Merchants' Society of Mutual Assistance, . . 185

CHAPTER XIV.

Review at Krasnoë-Selo—Mr. Gromoff's Fête—Naval Review—The Imperial Dinner—Ball at the English Palace, ... 195

CHAPTER XV.

From St. Petersburg to Moscow—The Nicholas Railway—Great Novgorod—The Kremlin—Temple of the Saviour, ... 208

CHAPTER XVI.

Prince Dolgorouky's Dinner—Fête at the Zoological Gardens—The Bazaar—Church of Kazan—Agricultural Academy—Review of Troops—Novo Dievitchy Convent 220

CONTENTS.

CHAPTER XVII.

Banquet of the Municipality of Moscow . . . . . PAGE 241

CHAPTER XVIII.

Kuzminki—Prince Galitzine's Fête—The Foundling Asylum—The Romanoff House—Sokolniki Park, ... 262

CHAPTER XIX.

Troitza Monastery—St. Sergius—The Russo-Greek Church—The Metropolitan Philaret—Amerikanskaïa Avenue—Diploma of Honorary Citizenship—Nijny-Novgorod, ... 271

CHAPTER XX.

Official Visits—Tomb of Minin—View from the Kremlin—The Great Fair—The Volga—The Tea-Trade—The Merchants' Dinner—Russian Gypsies, ... 285

CHAPTER XXI.

The Volga Steamers—A Peasant-Welcome—Departure from Nijny-Novgorod—Ship-building on the Volga—Kostroma—The Czar Michael—Susanin—A Lady's Welcome, ... 300

CHAPTER XXII.

An Embarrassing Honor—The Banquet at Kostroma—Reception by Ladies—Mr. Fox an Honorary Citizen of Kostroma—Ribinsk, . . . 314

CHAPTER XXIII.

Uglitch—Kemra—Kortcheva—Reception at Tver—A Soldier of Borodino—St. Petersburg Bazaar—The Great Theatre—Breakfast at the Grand-duchess Constantine's, ... 324

CHAPTER XXIV.

Banquet of the English Club—Speech of Prince Gortchakoff, . . 339

CONTENTS.

CHAPTER XXV.

Imperial Presents—Mr. Jukoff's Fête—Farewell to the Emperor—Prince Gortchakoff's Dinner—Alexander Nevsky—The Alexander Institute—The Beauharnais Palace, ... PAGE 359

CHAPTER XXVI.

Rifled Guns and Targets—The Commemorative Chapel—Cronstadt Citizenship—Farewell Breakfast—Peasant Deputation—The Emancipation Medal—The Departure, ... 372

CHAPTER XXVII.

In the Baltic—The Approach to Stockholm—Official Courtesies—Gustavus III.—Skokloster—Jefferson—Presentation at Court—Royal Visit to the Ships—The Djurgård, ... 387

CHAPTER XXVIII.

Riddarholm—Birjer Jarl—The Mosebacken—Ulriksdal—The Royal Dinner—Haga—Rosendal—Drottingholm—Queen Dowager Josephine—Departure—Kiel—Prince Adalbert of Prussia—Parting Salutes, . . 400

CHAPTER XXIX.

Official Correspondence, ... 418

APPENDIX.

A. Dispatch from Prince Gortchakoff to M. de Stoeckl, . . . 425
B. Names of United States Men-of-War, ... 428
C. Miantonomoh Galop, ... 434
D. Speech of Prince Gortchakoff, ... 436
E. Grand-duke Alexis's Visit to Mr. Fox, ... 440

LIST OF ENGRAVINGS.

	ENGRAVER.	PAGE.
1. ALEXANDER II., Emperor of Russia	J. C. Buttre	Front.
2. HON. G. V. FOX	H. B. Hall	16
3. "MIANTONOMOH"	J. C. Buttre	52
4. CHRISTIAN IX., King of Denmark	H. B. Hall	56
5. PRINCESS DAGMAR	J. C. Buttre	64
6. ADMIRAL LESSOVSKY	H. B. Hall	80
7. ADMIRAL CRABBE	J. C. Buttre	108
8. OLGA, Queen of Wuerttemberg	do.	144
9. MARIE, Empress of Russia	H. B. Hall	190
10. ALEXANDER ALEXANDROVITCH, Czarevitch	J. C. Buttre	256
11. GRAND-DUKE CONSTANTINE	do.	284
12. ALEXANDER, PRINCE GORTCHAKOFF	do.	302
13. CHARLES XV., King of Sweden and Norway	do.	304

FOX'S MISSION TO RUSSIA.

CHAPTER I.

INTRODUCTORY.

ON Monday, the 16th day of April (the 4th of the Russian calendar), 1866, the life of Alexander II., Emperor of Russia, was saved providentially from the attack of an assassin.

In the morning of that day, a young journeyman cap-maker, one of the newly-emancipated serfs, Ossip Ivanovitch Komissaroff by name, left his house to perform the customary act of thanksgiving for his recovery from sickness. He started with the intention of going to the little chapel that has long been established in the log-house, built for his own use by Peter the Great, on an island in the Neva, when about to found the new capital. When Komissaroff reached the river's bank, he discovered that the movable bridge leading to the island had been taken away, in anticipation of the imminent annual break-up of the ice. To this fact, trivial in itself, was due the preservation of the Emperor's life.

His visit to the chapel being thus prevented, Komissaroff turned his steps to the palace quay. On approaching the Summer Garden, a favorite place of resort in the spring, he saw one of the imperial carriages standing by the gate, and, hoping to get a sight of his liberator, whom he had never seen, he joined the crowd of people who were waiting for the Emperor to pass. While trying to secure a favorable position, his attention was attracted by a large man, who evidently was determined to force his way to the front, and Komissaroff, who is of small stature and slight frame, followed him closely. He observed nothing peculiar in the stranger's appearance, except that he kept his right hand constantly in his coat pocket.

The Emperor soon appeared, accompanied by his nephew and his niece, their Imperial Highnesses the Duke of Leuchtenberg[1] and the Princess of Baden. Before getting into the carriage, he stopped to put on an overcoat, when the man beside Komissaroff suddenly drew a pistol from his pocket and aimed it at his Majesty. He stood so near that the shot must inevitably have proved

---

[1] Nicholas Maximilianovitch, Prince Romanovski and Duke of Leuchtenberg, a major-general in the suite of the Emperor of Russia. He is the second child and eldest son of the late Duke Maximilian of Leuchtenberg, Prince of Eichstaedt, and of the Grand-duchess Marie Nicholaëvna, the eldest daughter of the late Emperor Nicholas. Maximilian, his father, was the son of Prince Eugene Beauharnais. The Princess of Baden, Marie Maximilianovna, is the first child and elder daughter of Duke Maximilian. She married, February 11, 1863, Prince Louis William August, of Baden. It is a singular fact that the Duke of Leuchtenberg, who was with the Emperor when Karakozoff made the attempt on his life, was also in the carriage with him and Napoleon III. when the Czar was fired at in Paris, in 1867, by the Pole Berezowski.

fatal, had not Komissaroff, by a well-aimed blow, struck up his arm and caused the discharge of the weapon in the air.

The indignant people fell upon the assassin with cries of fury, and, but for the interposition of the Emperor, would have torn him to pieces. His Majesty, who had remained calm and self-possessed during the exciting scene, called out, "Let him alone, children!" At once every hand fell, and the police secured their prisoner.

Making his way through the crowd, the Emperor confronted the baffled murderer, and asked:

"Who art thou?"

"A Russian."

"A Russian! Why, then, do you want to kill me?"

"Because you have deceived us, and given us an illusory liberty and emancipation without land."

This attempt to personate a dissatisfied serf was unsuccessful. Under the red shirt which he wore was another of fine linen, and in his pocket were papers that proved his connection with an infamous secret organization known as the "Nihilists." These papers led to the arrest of several hundred other members.

The Emperor drove at once to the Kazan cathedral to return thanks for his safety, and thence to the Winter Palace, where he received the congratulations of the council. All the imperial family and the officers of state then accompanied his Majesty to the cathedral, where a solemn *Te Deum* was sung, and thanks were again given to God for his preservation. An impromptu reception was afterward held at the palace, where all who had the *entrée* hastened to tender their congratulations in person. As soon as the demonstrations of loyalty had somewhat subsided, the Emperor asked for his preserver. General Todtleben, one of his Majesty's aide-de-camp generals, the hero of Sevastopol, had brought Komissaroff in his carriage, and now led him forward into the presence. The Emperor, much affected, embraced and kissed the bewildered young man, who could scarcely believe his good fortune, thanked him in broken words for his loyalty and devotion, and pronounced him a noble from that hour, amid the acclamations of all present.

Komissaroff was then invited to tell his own story, which he did with much self-possession, notwithstanding the strangeness of his surroundings. The assemblage was thrilled to hear that he was a native of Kostroma, the birthplace of Ivan Susanin, who, in 1613, by a noble act of self-sacrifice, saved the life of the founder of the house of Romanoff. This remarkable coincidence made a deep impression on all classes of people, and it was universally regarded as additional evidence of the direct interposition of Providence in behalf of the liberator.

Komissaroff, in consideration of his eminent service to his country, in addition to the nobility conferred upon him by the Emperor, was authorized to add to his name that of Kostromsky, derived from his native town Kostroma, to distinguish him and his descendants forever. Honors and decorations were showered on him by different sovereigns, lands, houses, and contributions of money were given him by his grateful countrymen, and the principal towns and cities presented him their freedom. He was made the hero of the hour; his portrait was everywhere, and he could not appear without exciting enthusiasm. Indeed, so many were the receptions and *fêtes* given in his honor, and so overwhelmed was he with invitations, that the only question was to whom he should deny himself.

The baffled assassin proved to be a Russian, named Dmitry Karakozoff, the son of a small landed proprietor of the government of Saratov. He was but twenty-four years of age, and had been successively at the school of Penza, the University of Kazan, and the University of Moscow, from the last of which he had been dismissed for not paying his fees. Of a gloomy and hypochondriacal disposition, he soon found fitting associates in the latter city among the Nihilists, whose organization bore the significant and appropriate name of "Hell." Nihilism in Russia is the quintessence of radicalism and revolution, the bitter product of social corruption and moral chaos. Its converts, or rather perverts, are found chiefly among the reckless and disappointed, among those who prefer the uncertainties of an unknown future to what they consider the ills of the present. To overturn the government is to them the first stepping-stone to liberty and to a new order of things. The Nihilists found Karakozoff a willing tool, and on him fell by lot the business of assassinating the Emperor, which was to be the signal for a general revolution. That he failed was certainly not his fault.

On his trial he claimed to be a nobleman, but he was not recognized as such by the proper tribunal, and the court sentenced him to be degraded from his civil rights and to suffer death by hanging. The sentence was executed on the following 15th of September.

The attempt of Karakozoff created a profound impression among the Russian people. As soon as the news spread, an extraordinary and indescribable enthusiasm seized upon all, high and low, rich and poor. Processions filled the streets, living masses thronged about the palace, and the national hymn was sung everywhere. It seemed as if the people could not testify sufficiently their love for their sovereign and their gratitude for his escape.

Mr. Clay, our minister to Russia, in a dispatch to Mr. Soward, under date of April 22, 1866, says:

"Thousands of the people at once assembled at the Winter Palace, and hurrahed till his Majesty showed himself again and again on the balcony. There they camped all night and the next day, renewing the demand to see the Emperor, and, as fast as one vast multitude saw their much-loved ruler, another succeeded. Twice I drove to the neighborhood of the palace. I never before saw a larger mass of people together, all intensely silent at the time, and looking steadily toward the balcony where the Emperor was expected to appear. And so continued the excitement among all ranks, till I suppose, successively, every man almost in St. Petersburg, from the Emperor's brothers to the lowest workman, had seen their illustrious sovereign."

Mr. Clay concluded his dispatch as follows: "Addresses of congratulation have come in from all Russia and all Europe by telegram and post. The different 'colonies' of foreigners here, and the Americans among others, have sent in their addresses to his Imperial Majesty, and all have been gratefully and graciously received and answered.

"I expect to hear from our own land, which owes so much to Alexander II., and shall wait impatiently to be the bearer of the words of emotion which fill the hearts of the millions of the great republic."

Mr. Seward, as soon as he had received official notification of the attempted assassination, through Mr. Edward de Stoeckl, the Russian minister at Washington, sent a dispatch to Mr. Clay, expressing the President's desire that he should seek a personal interview with the Emperor, congratulate him in the name of the United States upon his escape, and assure him of the sincere respect, affection, and friendship of the American people.

On the 29th of May, Mr. Clay delivered his address of congratulation to the Emperor, at a special audience at the Winter Palace; and the Emperor returned his thanks for the same to the President and People of the United States.

In the mean time, the leaders of the Republican party in Congress, believing that something more than a mere formal message of congratulation was due to the nation that had given us its warmest sympathies in our hour of peril, asked on the 4th of May, through the Honorable Thaddeus Stevens, of Pennsylvania, the "unanimous consent of the House of Representatives to introduce a joint resolution relative to the recent attempted assassination of the Emperor of Russia." The resolution was passed and sent to the Senate, where it was also passed, after a slight amendment, on the 8th of May. Two days afterward the House concurred in the amendment, and on the 16th it was approved by President Johnson:

JOINT RESOLUTION RELATIVE TO THE ATTEMPTED ASSASSINATION OF THE EMPEROR OF RUSSIA.

Be it resolved by the Senate and House of Representatives of the United States of America, in Congress assembled, That the Congress of the United States of America has learned with deep regret of the attempt made upon the life of the Emperor of Russia by an enemy of emancipation. The Congress sends greeting to his Imperial Majesty, and to the Russian Nation, and congratulates the twenty million of serfs upon the providential escape from danger of the sovereign to whose head and heart they owe the blessings of their freedom.

SEC. 2. *And be it further resolved,* That the President of the United States be requested to forward a copy of this resolution to the Emperor of Russia.

Approved *May* 16, 1866.

To give additional significance to this solemn act of Congress, it was resolved to send a special envoy in a national vessel to carry the Resolution to the Emperor of Russia. For this delicate mission, Congress selected the Honorable Gustavus Vasa Fox, the Assistant Secretary of the Navy, a gentleman whose efficient administration of his branch of the service during the war had won recognition both at home and abroad. It was determined also, at his own request, to send him in a monitor,

G. V. Fox.
Asst. Secy of the Navy
1861-66

a class of vessel which had never yet crossed the Atlantic, but in whose seaworthiness Mr. Fox had implicit confidence. The Miantonomoh, a two-turret monitor, was chosen for this service, and the Augusta and Ashuelot, two wooden men-of-war, were selected to accompany her.

The following letter of instructions, addressed to Commander Alexander Murray, explains itself:

NAVY DEPARTMENT,
WASHINGTON, May 22, 1866.

SIR: Mr. G. V. Fox, Assistant Secretary of the Navy, has been selected by the Government to bear to the Emperor of Russia the Resolution of Congress congratulating him on his recent escape from assassination.

The Department places at the service of Mr. Fox, to convey him to Cronstadt, the Miantonomoh, which vessel is to be accompanied by the Augusta. The Ashuelot has been ordered to report to you, at St. John's, N. F., for the purpose of accompanying the Miautonomoh a portion of the way across the ocean, and all the way, if you deem her presence necessary. When you no longer need her, you will allow her to pursue her course to the Asiatic Squadron, in accordance with orders in the possession of Commander Febiger.

Such aid and assistance will be extended by you to Mr. Fox as may be conducive to the success of his mission. He will notify you when he has no further need of the Miantonomoh or Augusta, and when he shall have done so you will visit three or four of the principal ports of Europe, where our commerce extends, and from which emigration to this country proceeds, north of Portugal. You will, after Mr. Fox notifies you that you are at liberty to direct your own movements, take the earliest occasion to report by letter to Rear-Admiral L. M. Goldsborough, enclosing him a copy of these instructions, and will join him, within a reasonable time, at Lisbon, unless he shall instruct you to meet him elsewhere or proceed otherwise.

Very respectfully, etc.,

(Signed)   G. WELLES,
Secretary of the Navy.

Commander A. MURRAY,
Commanding U. S. Steamer Augusta, St. John's, N. F.

The following was addressed to Mr. Fox, by the Honorable Mr. Welles, Secretary of the Navy:

NAVY DEPARTMENT,
WASHINGTON, May 26, 1866.

Hon. G. V. Fox, *Assistant Secretary of the Navy.*

SIR: Congress having signified its wish that you should convey to the Emperor of Russia the congratulatory resolution of that body upon his escape from assassination, the President has been pleased, in conformity with the wishes thus indicated, to appoint you Assistant Secretary of the Navy, for that purpose; you will, therefore, proceed to the discharge of that duty before entering upon the special employment assigned to you by this Department. For that purpose you are authorized to take passage in the U. S. steamer Ashuelot, now at Boston, preparing to cross the Atlantic. This vessel will convey you to St. John's, N. F. At that place you will find the U. S. steamer Augusta and U. S. turreted ironclad Miantonomoh, which are destined to form a part of the European Squadron. On your own request, you will take passage in the Miantonomoh to Cronstadt, Russia, and, after executing the mission intrusted to you, under the direction of the Secretary of State, you will proceed to carry into effect the wishes of this Department in collecting information for national purposes, by visiting the most important naval stations of Europe. It is desirable that you should obtain all information that is attainable relative to the means which are possessed by the principal naval powers for building, repairing, and laying-up naval vessels, and whatever may be useful in regard to their navy yards and navy establishments. It is important that you should also examine some of the more modern-built naval vessels abroad; and, availing yourself of your experience, you will be able to institute comparisons between the present naval appliances and improvements of your own country and those of Europe. You will consider it your duty to procure all the information which you can obtain relative to naval matters, and will, from time to time, as you may find convenient, communicate the same to the Department, making your final and complete report on your return.

Your absence will not be extended beyond six months. Wishing you a pleasant and useful tour,

I am very truly, your friend,

GIDEON WELLES,
Secretary of the Navy.

The following was addressed by the State Department to the diplomatic representatives of the United States in Europe:

DEPARTMENT OF STATE,
WASHINGTON, *April*, 1866.

To the Diplomatic and Consular Officers of the United States in Europe.

GENTLEMEN: This will be presented to you by Gustavus V. Fox, Esquire, Assistant Secretary of the Navy. It is universally acknowledged that the professional experience and abilities of this gentleman have materially contributed to the recent triumph of our arms in his branch of the service, and to the improvement and development of our naval force. As he also has eminent qualities of character, I commend him to your regard and to any attentions which may serve to make his abode in your vicinity agreeable.

I am gentlemen, your obedient servant,
WILLIAM H. SEWARD.

The friendship which has existed between Russia and the United States ever since we became a nation was cemented anew when our ancient ally, alone of all the governments of the old world, sent to us words of sympathy when we were believed by our enemies to be in the throes of dissolution.[1] That act sunk deep into our hearts, for it proved to us that we had one friend on whom we could rely even in our darkest hour. Soon after, Admiral Popoff visited San Francisco, and we endeavored to show our gratitude by offering what courtesies were in

[1] Appendix A.

our power to him and his officers. The following year, Russia gave emphasis to her declarations by sending into our waters a powerful fleet, which visited our principal seaports and added moral weight to our cause. The joy with which Lessovsky and his gallant comrades were received in our cities is matter of history. We welcomed them as friends and allies, and tried to prove by deeds all that our words expressed. A year after they left our shores, President Lincoln was struck down by the hand of an assassin, and again the great Empire of the East was prompt in sending her condolence and sympathy to us in our sorrow. These evidences of friendly feeling were not lost upon us; and, when we heard that Alexander II. had been saved providentially from a similar death, we were moved to give utterance in the most solemn manner to the sentiments which affected the nation as one man.

The Resolution of Congress, the selection of an officer of the government to deliver it, and the sending of one of our most powerful men-of-war to bear it across the ocean, were fitting expressions of those sentiments.

The act was unique in our history. Never before was such a resolution voted by the Congress of the United States. Never before was such a mission sent in such an unexampled manner by the American people.

CHAPTER II.

CROSSING THE ATLANTIC.

MR. FOX left Washington on Wednesday, May 23d, for Boston, intending to sail thence for St. John's, Newfoundland, where the monitor Miantonomoh had preceded him. On Tuesday, May 29th, the dispatches of the State Department and the Resolution of Congress to be presented to the Emperor of Russia were brought from Washington and delivered to him by Mr. Berdan. On Wednesday, May 30th, at one o'clock P. M., Mr. Fox, in company with Captain John Bythesea, of the English Royal Navy, naval *attaché* to the British embassy at Washington, who had been invited to cross the Atlantic in the Miantonomoh with him, set sail for Newfoundland on board the double-end steamer Ashuelot, Commander J. C. Febiger.

On Sunday, June 3d, at forty minutes past midnight, Cape Pine Light was made, and, ten minutes after, Cape Race Light was seen, E. ¼ N., distant twenty miles. At a quarter-past two A. M., made the land about Cape Race. It is one hundred feet high, sloping gradually toward the north, and is bare of trees and vegetation. Snow was seen lying in streaks on the hills. In running up the coast of Newfoundland, which is bare, rugged, and precipitous, the most elevated points being about one thousand feet high, many icebergs were seen, some grounded and some floating. The largest were about two hundred feet in height and two thousand feet in length. At a quarter-past twelve P. M., after a passage of three days and twenty-two hours, the Ashuelot cast anchor in St. John's Bay, Newfoundland.

St. John's, which is the easternmost seaport of North America, has an excellent harbor, with a very narrow entrance, capable of being defended easily, though the present fortifications are inadequate against modern artillery. The hills surrounding the harbor are from three hundred to seven hundred feet in height. The city, which contains about thirty-five thousand inhabitants, is built on the slope of these hills and consists mainly of one long, irregular street, with lanes running from it. The houses are generally of wood. Among the public buildings are the Government-house, the House of Assembly, the custom-house, and a hospital. There are nine or ten churches, among which the Roman Catholic cathedral is conspicuous for its size. One of the features of the town are the wharves and stages for drying codfish, which line the shore. St. John's exports annually from five hundred thousand to a million quintals of codfish, besides large quantities of salmon, herring, cod-liver oil, seal and whale oil, and sealskins. It was founded in 1583 by Sir Humphrey Gilbert.

The island of Newfoundland has an area of about thirty-six thousand square miles, and contains a population of nearly one hundred and fifty thousand. It was discovered in 1497 by Sebastian Cabot, and named by him "Baccalaos," the Indian word for codfish. The interior has been but little explored, but it is estimated that at least one-third of the island is covered with fresh water. The hills, none of which are more than fifteen hundred feet above the level of the sea, are almost destitute of soil, and are covered with a stunted growth of firs and other small trees and shrubs. Coal-beds exist in the western part of the island, and copper and lead are found in considerable abundance, but little effort has been made to develop the mineral resources. The inhabitants, mostly English, Irish, and Scotch, and their descendants, are engaged chiefly in the fisheries, agriculture receiving but little attention.

Mr. Fox found the Augusta and the Miantonomoh awaiting him at St. John's, the squadron being under the orders of Commander Alexander Murray. The officers of the two ships were as follows:

AUGUSTA.

Commander, Alexander Murray.
Lieutenant Commander, James M. Prichett.
Lieutenant, J. D. Graham.
Acting Volunteer Lieutenant, James R. Wheeler.
Acting Masters, Z. S. Tanner, M. W. McEntee.
Acting Ensign, James H. Delano.
Mates, David Fader, O. F. O'Neill, A. H. Lewis, C. H. Venable.
Surgeon, W. K. Scofield.

THE OFFICERS OF THE SHIPS. 25

Passed Assistant Surgeon, H. S. Pitkin.
Paymaster, Judson S. Post.
Acting Chief-Engineer, James M. Adams.
Acting First Engineer, C. H. Glack.
Acting Second Engineers, J. E. Hilliard, J. Matthews, George C. Castell.
Acting Third Engineers, C. H. Pennington, William G. Hughes.
Boatswain, George Smith.
Paymaster's Clerk, John H. Fancher.

MIANTONOMOH.

Commander, John C. Beaumont.
Lieutenant Commander, John J. Cornwell.
Lieutenant, M. S. Stuyvesant.
Acting Master, J. F. Alcorn.
Acting Ensigns, J. F. Blanchard, Daniel McKay, Joseph S. Young.
Mates, John McManus, E. E. Bradbury.
Surgeon, William E. Taylor.
Assistant Surgeon, Charles L. Green.
Acting Assistant Paymaster, F. C. Imlay.
Acting Chief-Engineer, William A. R. Lattimer.
Acting First Assistant Engineer, George B. Orswell.
Acting Second Assistant Engineers, R. D. Giberson, T. W. Hineline, H. K. Steever, A. J. Doty.
Acting Third Assistant Engineers, R. B. Dick, John E. Edwards, James McNabb, J. A. Frank.
Captain's Clerk, John B. Collings.
Paymaster's Clerk, George W. Thompson.

As every thing connected with this first trip ever made by a monitor across the Atlantic is of interest, the reports of Commander Beaumont to the Navy Department of the passage from New York to Halifax, and from Halifax to St. John's, are given from the Report of the Secretary of the Navy for 1866.

United States Steamer Miantonomoh (3d rate),
Halifax, Nova Scotia, *May*, 1866.

Sir: I have the honor to inform the Department that, during the passage of this vessel from New York to this place, we expended one hundred and nine (109) tons of coal, only ten (10) tons of which were taken from the bunkers. When steaming, our average speed was six and six-tenths ($6_{\tfrac{6}{10}}$) knots. The conduct of the vessel in the rough weather we experienced on the 10th and 11th instant confirms me in the opinion already expressed to the Department in a previous communication, that she is an excellent sea-boat, as safe as and more comfortable than any vessel I ever served in. It was only on my arrival at this place, on the 10th instant, that I learned from Commander Murray, of the Augusta, that we had experienced heavy weather. When leaving New York on the 6th instant, the draught of the vessel was fifteen feet eight inches (15.8) forward, fifteen feet and three inches (15.3) aft, at which time we had on board four hundred and fifteen tons of coal. I would advise not taking more on board, unless it is absolutely necessary to make a passage of more than two thousand miles. The turret and weather curtains, the means of battening the hatches and turrets, and the lookout tower erected on the after-part of the hurricane-deck, have all proved of the utmost utility.

The tower serves both as an admirable lookout station and rest for the standard-compass, which, at an elevation of nineteen (19) feet above the hurricane-deck, is scarcely, if at all, affected by local attraction.

Since our arrival here, we have been visited by the civil, military, and naval authorities, all of whom have manifested in strong terms their admiration of the vessel.

I have the honor to be, very respectfully,
Your obedient servant,
J. C. BEAUMONT,
Commander.

Hon. GIDEON WELLES,
Secretary of the Navy, Washington, D. C.

UNITED STATES STEAMER MIANTONOMOH (3D RATE),
ST. JOHN'S, NEWFOUNDLAND, *May* 24, 1866.

SIR: It is again my pleasure to be able to inform the Department of the excellent conduct of this vessel at sea during our late passage from Halifax, Nova Scotia, to this place, between the 18th and 23d instant.

I have seen no reason to change the opinion I have already given regarding her good qualities. The engines worked perfectly during the whole passage, not occasioning the slightest trouble or delay. In fitting vessels of this class for sea, I respectfully suggest the propriety of placing the sea-wheel abaft instead of forward of the pilot-house, in order that the helmsman may have the compass immediately before him; and also, from his increased distance from the stem, enable him sooner to detect the sheer of the vessel. I would also suggest that the bottom of the temporary coal-crib be raised at least three (3) feet above the deck, in order to allow a free passage of the water. The one on deck is only sixteen inches above it, and is therefore considerably washed in a rough sea.

I have the honor to be, very respectfully,
Your obedient servant,
J. C. BEAUMONT,
Commander.

Hon. GIDEON WELLES,
Secretary of the Navy, Washington, D. C.

Commander Murray was the only officer acquainted with the fact that the Miantonomoh was to cross the Atlantic, until the squadron had rendezvoused at St. John's. When the Assistant Secretary of the Navy arrived, and it became known that he was to go on the monitor, there was some surprise and not a little anxiety expressed; but there was no disposition shown to hold back, notwithstanding that the officers and crews of the sealing-vessels, engaged in a much more perilous duty, freely expressed their opinion that it was dangerous to go to sea in such a ship as the Miantonomoh. Previous to this, it had been the general opinion of the public that the monitors were fit only for harbor defence and coast duty; and, although the Monadnock, of similar construction to the Miantonomoh, had safely doubled Cape Horn, their sea-going qualities had not yet been tested by a voyage across the Atlantic. It was not strange, therefore, that there should be some apprehension as to the

result of such a trip, with no chance to make a harbor in case of extraordinarily bad weather.

The Miantonomoh was a monitor of the two-turret class, built at Brooklyn, in 1864–'65. She was two hundred and fifty-nine feet and two inches in length, fifty-two feet and ten inches beam, and fourteen feet and nine inches depth of hold. She drew fourteen feet and nine and a quarter inches, and her deck was thirty-one inches above water on the side. Her tonnage was twelve hundred and twenty-five, new measurement, and she carried three hundred and fifty tons of coal. Her hull was of wood, covered with seven-inch side-armor and two-and-a-quarter-inch deck-armor. Her turrets were ten inches thick, and had a diameter in the clear of twenty-one feet. Her engines were back-action, with four cylinders, of thirty inches diameter and twenty-seven inches stroke. She had two propellers, each of ten feet and six inches diameter. Her battery consisted of four fifteen-inch Dahlgren guns.

The Miantonomoh was named after the celebrated chief sachem of the Narragansett tribe of Indians, in Rhode Island, who was captured and slain by Uncas, chief of the Mohegans, in 1643, during a raid which Miantonomoh made into his country. Sachem's Plain, the place of his execution, is in the town of Norwich, Connecticut. The site of his grave is still shown.

June 5th.—On Tuesday evening, at eight o'clock, Mr. Fox, accompanied by Captain Bythesea, went on board of the Miantonomoh, and at nine P. M. the squadron got under way. In passing out of the harbor, the Ashuelot unfortunately sunk a brig, but without damage to herself, and without causing any detention. At eleven o'clock the ships left the coast and steered for the south point of Ireland. At half-past three o'clock on the morning of Saturday, June 16th, the southeast coast of Ireland was made, and at four P. M. the squadron came to anchor in Queenstown harbor.

Commander Murray's report, to the Navy Department, of the voyage from St. John's to Queenstown, is as follows:

UNITED STATES STEAMER AUGUSTA (3D RATE),
QUEENSTOWN, IRELAND, June 16, 1866.

SIR: I have the honor to report the arrival of this ship, the Miantonomoh, and Ashuelot, at this port, having performed the trip across the Atlantic in ten[1] days and eighteen hours, without accident of any kind.

Our progress was uniform, the longest day's run being 176 miles, and the shortest 137; average 168.

A great portion of the way (1,100 miles) the Miantonomoh was in tow of the Augusta, as a matter of convenience and precaution more than necessity, the Miantonomoh consuming a fair proportion of coal.

I think she could have crossed over alone. The weather generally was very good, the only strong winds being from the westward. Heavy weather does not appear to materially affect the speed or rolling of the monitor, for, while the other vessels were lurching about, and

---

[1] Apparent time; the true time would be four hours less, or ten days and fourteen hours.

their progress checked by heavy seas, she went along comparatively undisturbed or unchecked.

I thought it inexpedient to part with the Ashuelot, the Augusta's engines showing signs of weakness, which once or twice occasioned vexatious stoppages. The Ashuelot will coal here, and proceed without further delay, in obedience to last orders of the Department.

I have the honor to be, very respectfully, your obedient servant,

A. MURRAY, *Commander.*

Hon. GIDEON WELLES,
   Secretary of the Navy, Washington, D. C.

The following report of the passage across the Atlantic, made to Secretary Welles by Assistant Secretary of the Navy Fox, and the log appended, give all the material facts of the voyage:

UNITED STATES STEAM MONITOR MIANTONOMOH,
QUEENSTOWN, IRELAND, *June* 16, 1866.

SIR: The United States side-wheel steamer Augusta (third rate), 1,310 tons (old measurement), Commander A. Murray, senior officer; United States monitor ironclad Miantonomoh (third rate), 1,225 tons, Commander J. C. Beaumont; and United States side-wheel steamer Ashuelot (third rate), double-ender, 786 tons, Commander J. C. Febiger, left St. John's, Newfoundland, Tuesday, June 5th, at 10 P. M., and the two former arrived at Queenstown, Ireland, Saturday, the 16th instant, at four P. M., after a pleasant trip across the Atlantic of ten days and eighteen hours. The Ashuelot kept on to Portsmouth.

The material facts of the passage are placed in the form of an abstract log, attached to this letter.

There remains but one question to discuss concerning the monitor type of iron-clads invented by Captain Ericsson: Can they be constructed so as to make them efficient fighting, sea-going cruisers? If not, then we must adopt the European models, abstain from any further attempts at progress, and content ourselves with a naval force for defensive purposes only, or invite new schemes. The facts with regard to the behavior of this vessel in a moderate gale of wind and heavy sea, when a frigate would find it impossible to use her battery, are as follows: Head to the sea, she takes over about four feet of solid water, which is broken as it sweeps along the deck, and after reaching the turret it is too much spent to prevent firing the fifteen-inch guns directly ahead. Broadside to the sea, either moving along or stopped, her lee guns can always be worked without difficulty, the water which passes across the deck from windward being divided by the turrets, and her extreme roll so moderate as not to press her lee guns near the water. Lying in the same position the fifteen-inch guns can be fired directly astern without interference from water, and when stern to the sea, the water which comes on board is broken up in the same manner as when going head to it. In the trough of the sea her ports will be liable to be flooded, if required to use her guns to windward. This, therefore, would be the position selected by an antagonist who designed to fight a monitor in a seaway. An ordinary vessel, high out of water and lying in the trough of the sea broadside-to, is attacked by a wave which climbs up the side, heels her to leeward, and, passing underneath, assists in throwing her back to windward, when another wave is met and the heavy lee lurch repeated. A wave advancing upon a monitor, in a similar position, finds no side above the water to act against; it therefore climbs aboard without difficulty, heels the vessel a few degrees to windward, and passes quickly to leeward, underneath. The water which has got on board, having no support to push it on, and an inclined deck to ascend, becomes broken water, a small portion going across the deck and off to leeward, but the largest part tumbling back to windward, overboard, without sending against the turret any thing like the quantity which first got on deck. The turret-guns thus occupy a central position, where, notwithstanding the lowness of the vessel's hull, they are more easily and safely handled in a sea-way than guns of the same height above the water in a broadside vessel.

The axis of the bore of the fifteen-inch guns of this vessel is six and one-half feet above the water, and the extreme lurch observed when lying broadside to a heavy sea and moderate gale was seven degrees to windward and four degrees to leeward, mean five and one-half degrees, while the average roll at the same time of the Augusta—a remarkably steady ship—was eighteen degrees, and the Ashuelot twenty-five degrees, both vessels being steadied by sail. A vessel which attacks a monitor in a sea-way must approach very close to have any chance of hitting such a low hull, and even then the monitor is half the time covered up by three or four feet of water, protecting herself and disturbing her opponent's fire. From these facts, not unknown to monitor-men, and the experience we have derived from the use of such vessels during the war, we may safely conclude that the monitor type of iron-clads is superior to the broadside, not only for fighting purposes at sea, but also for cruising. A properly-constructed monitor, possessing all the requirements of a cruiser, ought to have but one turret, armed with not less than twenty-inch guns; two independent propellers; the usual proportion of sail; and should be constructed of iron. The comforts of this monitor to the officers and men are superior to those of any other class of vessels in the navy, arising chiefly from her steadiness, ample accommodations, artificial ventilation, and the great quantity of light afforded by having the bull's-eyes overhead instead of at the side. The commander and lieutenant-commander, and several of the officers, are old monitor-men, and acquired confidence in this form of vessel off Charleston; nevertheless the officers and men deserve to share with their comrades in the Pacific the credit which attaches to extending the voyages of ships embracing so many novelties.

I have the honor to be, with great respect, your obedient servant,

G. V. Fox,
Assistant Secretary of the Navy.

Hon. Gideon Welles,
Secretary of the Navy, Washington, D. C.

35 A

...John's, Newfoundland, to Queenstown, Ireland, J. C. Beaumont,

Date	Latitude N.	TEMPERATURES											BAROMETER		Total number of persons on board.	Total number sick.
		Deck.		Cabin.		Ward room.		Berth deck.		Engine-room.	Fire-room.	Water.					
		Noon.	Midnight	Noon.	Midnight	9 A.M.	6 P.M.	9 A.M.	6 P.M.			Noon.	Midnight	Noon.	Midnight		
...day, ...		....	82	65	67	....	....	....	....	....	....	....	41	....	80.80	149	5
...day, 1		48	58	67	69	82	....	62	61	97	108	89	88	80.58	29.93	149	5
...day, 4		46	40	64	68	60	63	68	66	96	106	41	41	29.90	29.90	149	5
...day, 3		50	50	63	67	63	82	64	74	94	118	46	55	29.75	29.75	149	4
...day, 5		62	62	67	68	68	66	68	69	94	111	53	57	29.70	29.93	149	4
...day, 1		56	63	64	65	65	66	70	72	65	140	54	58	80.20	30.05	149	3
...day, 4		56	54	62	64	66	69	72	72	99	110	55	62	80.00	80.04	149	4
...day, 5		60	60	65	68	66	72	73	73	99	110	56	56	80.45	80.50	149	4
...day, 5½		57	59	65	68	72	70	73	72	100	110	57	76	80.42	80.29	149	5
...day, 5½		65	54	66	67	69	70	72	78	103	109	57	54	80.15	80.00	149	5
...day, 4		64	....	67	70	70	69	72	71	105	115	56	53	80.25	80.20	149	5
...day, 8		....	....	67	....	....	....	....	....	112	....	56	....	80.00	....	149	5

...th-deck thermometer is hung from N. D. beams, near the middle of the deck, away from galley

8 A. M. Average blowing, twice in four hours.

work.

under all sail, rolling 10°; Ashuelot, 20°.

UNITED STATES STEAMER AUGUSTA (3D RATE),
PORTSMOUTH, ENGLAND, *June* 23, 1866.

SIR: I have the honor to report that this ship and the Miantonomoh (third rate) arrived at this port this morning, two days from Queenstown. The Ashuelot (third rate) was coaling when we left, and was to sail in a few days for Lisbon in the execution of her original "sailing-orders."

I am, very respectfully, your obedient servant,

A. MURRAY,
Commander and Senior Officer.

Hon. GIDEON WELLES,
Secretary of the Navy, Washington, D. C.

CHAPTER III.

IRELAND—FRANCE—ENGLAND.

WHILE on the voyage, Mr. Fox threw overboard each day, at noon, a bottle containing the date, the latitude and longitude, and a request that the finder would indorse the date and place of discovery on the paper and forward it to the nearest government official. The contents of three of these bottles, picked up on the coast of France, after drifting more than a thousand miles, were sent afterward by the United States minister at Paris to the State Department at Washington. One, thrown overboard June 12, 1866, in latitude 49° 57' N., longitude 27° 03' W., was found January 23, 1867, near Omanville, arrondissement of Cherbourg. The second, thrown over June 13, 1866, in latitude 50° 14' N., longitude 22° 26' W., was picked up February 1, 1867, near the town of Sables d'Olonne, in the department of La Vendée. The third, thrown over June 15, 1866, in latitude 50° 37' N., longitude 13° 13' W., was found near the middle of October, 1866, close to the port of Cherbourg.

Queenstown, formerly the Cove of Cork, is situated on an island, on the north side of Cork Harbor, about nine miles southwest from the city of Cork. Its name was changed from Cove of Cork to Queenstown, in 1849, in honor of Queen Victoria's visit there in that year. The harbor is famous for its capacity and safety. The town is supported chiefly by the naval and military establishments in its vicinity.

The Miantonomoh came to anchor between the two splendid English broadside iron-clads, the Achilles and the Black Prince. They were fine types of their class, and the monitor looked insignificant in comparison with their immense hulks; but she could undoubtedly have sunk both of them with ease.

Mr. Fox and Commander Murray called, in company with the United States consul at Cork, on the admiral in command of the station, whose residence overlooked the roads. They found him, spy-glass in hand, examining the monitor from the bluff. At that distance, only her turrets were visible, while her neighbors, the English ships, looked like three-deckers. After interchanging salutations, the admiral asked Mr. Fox, somewhat abruptly, "Did you cross the Atlantic in that thing?" On Mr. Fox's replying that he did, the admiral said with much emphasis, "I doubt if I would!"

Such a conclusion was not a strange one to arrive at, when viewing the Miantonomoh from such a distance; for, with none of her hull in sight, she did not look as substantial as even the traditional "cheese-box on a raft," to which the original monitor was likened when she first made her appearance in Hampton Roads.

Mr. Fox left the Miantonomoh at Queenstown, and,

after visiting Dublin, crossed the Channel by steam to Holyhead, to collect information concerning the speed of the packets on that line, which were considered at the time to be the fastest sea-going vessels of their kind in the world. The Ulster, on which he took passage, was a side-wheel steamer, two hundred and sixty-five feet in length, thirty-four feet beam, and thirteen feet draught. Her wheels were thirty-six feet in diameter. She made the crossing to Holyhead, a distance of sixty-four statute miles, in three hours and twelve minutes, consuming twenty tons of coal per hour. This is equal to seventeen knots per hour; but deducting one knot to allow for a favorable tide, it shows an actual speed of sixteen knots or a little less than eighteen and a half statute miles per hour. This was then the best time ever made at sea, but it has since been exceeded by the extraordinary performance of the U. S. steamer Wampanoag, a first-class vessel, of two thousand one hundred and thirty-five tons, built, together with her engines, by the U. S. Navy Department in 1864–'67. According to the report of Captain J. W. A. Nicholson, U. S. N., commander of the vessel during her trial-trip in February, 1868, the Wampanoag, without sail, in a moderate breeze and irregular sea, steamed $727\frac{84}{100}$ statute miles in thirty-eight hours, which is equal to $19\frac{14}{100}$ statute miles each hour. During twelve hours, she averaged $19\frac{171}{1000}$ statute miles each hour, and her greatest speed for one hour was $20\frac{481}{1000}$ statute miles. The coal consumed during this trial was 12,690 lbs. per hour.

The length of the Wampanoag is three hundred and

forty-two feet, breadth forty-five feet and two inches, and draught of water nineteen feet. Her propeller has four blades, and is nineteen feet in diameter.

In London a dinner was given to Mr. Fox by the American minister, the Honorable Charles Francis Adams, and Mrs. Adams, at which the most distinguished officials were present. At a ball at Buckingham Palace, Mr. Fox was specially presented to the royal family. A breakfast was given him to meet John Bright, and dinners by the Russian ambassador, Baron de Brunnow, and by the English Admiralty, and other officials. He received, also, many courtesies from the English Government. Officers were detailed to show him the dock-yards and to give him all the information he required; and copies of official naval publications were furnished to him for the use of the Navy Department.

Meantime, the Miantonomoh and the Augusta had left Queenstown for Portsmouth, where they arrived on Saturday, the 23d of June. The Ashuelot did not accompany them, but sailed for Lisbon, in the execution of her original sailing-orders.

The following telegram, published in the London *Times* of Saturday, June 23, 1866, announced the coming of the squadron:

"Plymouth, Friday evening. (By telegraph.) Two American ships-of-war passed up Channel, five miles south of the Eddystone, under half-steam, at eleven o'clock this morning; wind, south-southwest, light. Sea smooth. One of them, a monitor, appeared to be not more than a foot above the water's edge. The only man visible was aft, near the flag-staff, and he looked as if standing in the water. The other was a very large two-masted ship, which slackened her speed for a short time to communicate with a pilot-cutter. They are, it is said, bound for Portsmouth."

The following extracts from the English journals at this time are interesting, as showing the impression created by the appearance of the Miantonomoh in their waters:

"A strange vessel, with a strange figure and still stranger name, now lies anchored at Spithead. It was once actually mentioned as an official difficulty in an Admiralty report that names could not be conveniently discovered for our new ships-of-war; but the Americans have multiplied their frigates fiftyfold without incurring any such embarrassment. They call their ships after the rivers of their country; and, as rivers in all regions retain the designations given by the earliest settlers, the American cruisers are christened in the language of the red Indians.[1] What the Miantonomoh may actually signify in that tongue, we shall not proceed to inquire; what she represents is a matter of very great importance indeed. She is a real, genuine monitor—a true specimen of that singular fleet on which the Americans rely for their position on the seas. As these vessels resemble no other floating things, it follows almost inevitably that, if the American ship-builders are right, ours must be wrong, and it is our imperative duty to investigate the subject without prejudice or delay."

"It is said that the present war actually originated in a new fire-arm. Count Bismarck thought the needle-gun

[1] Appendix B.

would render the Prussian army irresistible, and so he seized the opportunity of breaking up the old system of Europe to reconstruct it afresh. The presumption may be a little overstrained, but Marshal Benedek alludes to it in his address to his soldiers, and there is truth enough in the idea to fix our attention on the great questions at issue. Muskets and cannon now constitute the reliance of nations, and the Prussians have developed one of these instruments and the Americans the other. A Prussian battalion is said to be a match, by means of its needle-gun, for three battalions armed with the ordinary musket, and an American monitor is expected to be superior to any other fighting-ship in the world. On one of these points it is but too likely that we shall soon have evidence in abundance, and on the other we know more than we did, for a real monitor has just crossed the Atlantic, and is now lying in British waters."

"The American monitor is literally a floating gun-carriage, and nothing more. She has not the least resemblance to any ordinary man-of-war either in shape or arrangements, but she does carry guns—enormous ones too —and the Miantonomoh has carried them across the Atlantic. These guns weigh upward of 20 tons, they have a bore of 15 inches, and they throw a 480-pound shot. The monitor has two turrets, and two of these guns are carried in each. Now, if the calibre of a gun is to decide the advantage in an action, we have certainly nothing to match the battery of the Miantonomoh. In our latest and most successful specimen of a fighting-ship we have got just half-way to the point reached by the Americans.

The Bellerophon carries guns weighing upward of twelve tons, and throwing 250-pound shot. Those are our heaviest and most powerful cannon, whereas an Italian iron-clad has just sailed for the Adriatic carrying 600-pounders, and the Americans, we are told, have already cast guns more than twice as big as those of the Miantonomoh. Either, then, the advantage does not belong exclusively to the largest gun, or that advantage does not belong to us."

"But there is another feature of the American specimen deserving attention. This monitor, though carrying 450-pounders, is but of 1,500 tons burden. Now, our newest model of a light cruiser is the Pallas—Mr. Reed's vessel—and she is of 2,400 tons burden, though her guns are only a quarter as big as those of the Miantonomoh. Even Captain Cowper Coles has not yet proposed to build a two-turret vessel of less burden than 3,000 tons, or double that of the monitor. Consequently, the Americans are far ahead of us in combining light tonnage with heavy armament. Of course, there are other points for consideration, where the monitor might not appear to so much advantage. The speed of the Miantonomoh, for instance, in her voyage across the Atlantic, was but seven knots an hour, and her *maximum* is only put at nine. Either the Warrior or the Achilles, therefore, would run round her with ease. Then her enormous guns are of a very peculiar pattern and capacity. They are made to throw very heavy shot with a very low velocity, a principle not approved by artillerists in this country. In fact, we have no evidence of the actual power of the Dahlgren gun against really good armor-plating, nor is it certain that the 300-pounders of the Bellerophon, if tried against the Hercules target, would not prove as effective as the 450-pounders of the Miantonomoh. What the Americans have shown is this, that they can send 450-pound guns to sea in a 1,500-ton vessel."

On Friday, June 29th, Mr. Fox, accompanied by the Duke of Somerset, the Comptroller-General of the Navy, Rear-Admiral R. S. Robinson, and several other high officials connected with the Admiralty, went to Portsmouth to visit the Miantonomoh. The vessel was thoroughly inspected, and the great guns were fired. The Duke of Somerset, who was the Chief Lord of the Admiralty, remarked to Mr. Fox that he did not think any cast-iron made in England could endure such charges of powder.

At half-past nine o'clock the same evening, Mr. Fox started for Cherbourg in the Miantonomoh, having with him on board the Hon. John Bigelow, United States minister to France, and his son. The vessels came to anchor in Cherbourg harbor at one o'clock, P. M., the following day. The monitor lay in the midst of the French iron-clad fleet, where a comparison of our system of ships, with low free-board and immense smooth-bore guns, and the French broadside system, with small rifles, was easily made, and by no means to our disadvantage.

Mr. Fox left Cherbourg at 5 P. M. for Paris. On the following Tuesday, July 3d, he had an interview with the Emperor Napoleon III., at the Tuileries. This was the day of the great battle of Sadowa, or Königgratz, in which the Austrians, under Field-Marshal Benedek, met with such a decisive defeat from the Prussians. His Majesty received dispatches in relation to the battle, while conversing with Mr. Fox.

The following report of the interview was sent by Mr. Fox to his Government on the same day that it occurred:

PARIS, FRANCE, July 3, 1866.

Hon. GIDEON WELLES, *Secretary of the Navy.*

SIR: Through the courtesy of the minister of the United States at this court, Hon. John Bigelow, I was received to-day at a private audience by Napoleon III. He expressed pleasure at seeing me, and invited me to be seated. He then inquired very particularly about the monitor and her passage across the Atlantic. I explained to him the principles on which she was constructed, the draught of water, the thickness of her defensive armor, the size of her guns, and the smallness and cheapness of the vessel, in comparison with the broadside system. He asked about the thickness of the deck-armor and the twin screws, but seemed most struck with the fact that she had crossed the Atlantic floating only two feet out of water. I told him that I had crossed sixty-four times, but never so comfortably nor with such a sense of security as in this monitor. He said that it was wonderful, but we were a people of great ingenuity and resource. I told him we were forced into another system from the Gloire and Warrior, as that system could not be operated in our Southern waters. He replied that his ministers would go and look at the vessel, and regretted that he could not (news of a great Prussian victory had just been received).

He then asked what the feeling was in the United States about his expedition to Mexico, and immediately added, "You are all against me."

I answered that the people of the United States were trying to remember only the ancient friendship which existed between the two countries. He then said: "Mexico was in anarchy. I desired only to establish a stable government, and thus prevent further expeditions; and, now I am about to withdraw, I presume it will be overrun by your people."

I replied that I did not believe that our emigration would take that direction; that we had an immense and valuable country that would not be crowded until a hundred millions of people had settled in it.

He said Mexico was very rich, and, away from the coast, healthy. He then remarked that our debt was very large.

I answered that before the war it would have appeared so, but that the war had developed our resources to such a degree that we felt no anxiety in regard to it; that we possessed a thousand square miles of land that bore gold and silver in very extraordinary quantities; and that to these were to be added coal, iron, copper, and agricultural products without parallel; that the northern section of the United States had not only grown richer during the war, but the debt was already under the process of extinguishment by that portion of the country.

He said that General Beauregard, whom he had seen

a few days since, had also remarked on the increased development of the North. The Emperor then spoke of the great vitality of the people of the United States. He asked about petroleum, and inquired if I thought we could use it for fuel. I told him of our experiments. He asked what I thought of the feeling South. I said that those who had done the fighting there, acquiesced the most readily in the result. He said that was always so; and I added that a majority of the Southern people followed their lead, and that trade would ultimately allay the feelings engendered by the contest.

He then explained the use he had made of the telegraph in his Italian campaign; asked what communication we had with California overland, which I answered, and what field-gun we had found the best; and, when I said the Napoleon smooth-bore, he said they had gone too far with rifles.

He then asked how long I should remain in Paris, which I answered, and immediately withdrew.

I am, with great respect, your obedient servant,

G. V. Fox,
Assistant Secretary.

On the following Friday, July 6th, Mr. Fox had an interview with Prince Napoleon in the presence of Mr. Bigelow, our minister at Paris. In the course of the conversation, the prince said to Mr. Fox:

"Do not be too friendly with Russia."

Mr. Fox replied:

"Russia and America have no rival interests. Russia

has always been friendly to America, and we reciprocate the feeling."

" But you can stand alone," said the prince. " You do not want friends."

Mr. Fox answered :

" When it was doubtful whether we should ever stand again, at a time when the most powerful nations menaced us, Russia felt and expressed her sympathy for us, and America never will forget it."

" Russia is for herself alone," said the prince, after a few moments' silence ; and the subject was changed.

After this interview, Mr. Fox returned to Cherbourg. He was accompanied by the Marquis de Chasseloup-Laubat, the Minister of the Navy ; by M. Dupuy de Lôme, the Director of Naval Construction ; and by General Frébault, the Director of the Artillery Department of the Navy. These gentlemen, together with the authorities of Cherbourg, visited the Miantonomoh, by invitation of Mr. Fox, and examined the vessel very critically.

Before Mr. Fox left London, the Prince of Wales and the Duke of Edinburgh had expressed a desire to see the Miantonomoh in the Thames. Mr. Fox, anxious to please their Royal Highnesses, and also to give the inhabitants of the world's metropolis an opportunity to see the monitor, sent her with her consort back to England as soon as the French official visit was over. She accordingly started for the Thames at five o'clock P. M., July 6th, Mr. Fox himself returning to Paris.

The Miantonomoh and the Augusta cast anchor at Sheerness, at the junction of the Thames and the Medway, in the afternoon of Saturday, July 7th, having made the run from Cherbourg in twenty-four hours. On the following day, Sunday, she changed her anchorage to the Nore. On Monday, Sir Baldwin W. Walker, the vice-admiral commanding at the Nore, with a numerous suite, visited her. On the same day she was thrown open to the public, and was visited by great numbers of people. Tuesday noon, July 10th, she entered the port, under steam, and anchored alongside of the iron-clad Lord Warden, then building on the Reed system. In comparison with this enormous specimen of naval architecture, the monitor looked almost insignificant.

On Saturday, July 14th, their Royal Highnesses the Prince of Wales and the Duke of Edinburgh, accompanied by their suites and by a number of other distinguished persons, visited the Miantonomoh. The Augusta saluted as they boarded the monitor, and they were received by the officers and by the Hon. Charles Francis Adams, the American minister at the court of St. James, with the customary honors. The ship and her machinery were shown to them in all their details, apparently to their great satisfaction.

During the stay of the Miantonomoh in the Thames, she was thronged daily by people who came down from London to see her, all appearing to take great interest in the new naval wonder. An article from the London *Times*, of July 17th, illustrates well the feeling which this new evidence of American skill and power aroused in England:

"The royal visitors at Sheerness on Saturday, as well

as the numerous pleasure-parties flocking thither on the same errand, saw a very extraordinary, and—we wish we could not feel it—a portentous spectacle. They saw a fabric, something between a ship and a diving-bell—the Romans would have called it a tortoise—almost invisible, but what there was of it ugly, at once invulnerable and irresistible, that had crossed the Atlantic safely, and was anchored in our waters, with the intention of visiting Russia. Round this fearful invention were moored scores of big ships, not all utter antiquities, but modern, for there were among them steamships, generally screws, and therefore none of them more than twenty years old. These ships form a considerable portion of the navy of this great maritime power, and there was not one of them that the foreigner could not have sent to the bottom in five minutes, had his errand not been peaceful. There was not one of these big ships that could have avenged the loss of its companion, or saved itself from immediately sharing its fate. In fact, the wolf was in the fold, and the whole flock was at its mercy. No human accountant will ever ascertain the cost of all these ships, of all sorts and sizes, that were once launched on the deep with a glorious career of destruction before them, and that are now laid up, many of them at their last anchorage, and painted that dirty yellow which is universally adopted to mark treachery, failure, and crime. But, to an enormous original expense, and to further cost in alterations and repairs, is still added the cost necessary to retard the sure process of decay, and to save these poor ne'er-do-wells from settling down at their moorings or blocking up the difficult channel. The authorized list of the steamships and vessels of the Royal Navy, and of sailing-ships in commission, mounts up to the important figure of 735. What the list includes, and what it does not include, we would rather not say hastily, for it is impossible to approach the royal harbors without seeing whole lines of unwieldy vessels that can hardly be included in any useful enumeration. But, whatever sentiments of veneration or regret may be roused at the sight of an old three-decker that has merely swung with the tide for thirty years, it is still sadder to read through a long list of ships of a tonnage and weight of metal unknown to our fathers, with first-rate machinery, many with accomplished officers and brave crews, which are all superseded by the last invention, and can only come under fire to be either sunk or burnt.

"The present is the time for a naval review of a much more modest and useful character than either of the spectacles we saw before and after the Russian War. We have a new naval administration, and it consists of men who have expressed their opinions freely on that side of the House which is most favorable to criticism. One of them, indeed, only last week, improved the disastrous collision in the Channel with laudable promptitude, and without sparing the feelings of his predecessors. That administration may itself handle the broom that sweeps clean, but there are those who think no administration proper to be intrusted with a work of inquiry, and who would rather see a commission for the purpose. If, as is alleged, our government, by parties and frequent change of ministers, is not favorable to a continuous and consistent policy, it should at least give us the compensation of new and unbiassed opinions. When a private establishment remains long in the same hands, and there happens to be no stint of money, accumulation becomes the law of every department. The place is burdened and filled with useless servants, useless horses and carriages, useless furniture, useless books, and all sorts of persons and things that it would be a charity to pension, to sell, or to destroy, as the case may happen to be. Of course, the old folks will never see this, and it is not till a new occupant has brought the common standard of the outer world to bear on the place that any change can be tolerated. Now, it is quite clear, and cannot be disputed, that every item in the list before us, from the Victoria, now in the Mediterranean, with her 102 guns, her 4,127 tons, and her 1,000 horse-power—nay, from the armor-plated Warrior, with 32 bigger guns, 6,109 tonnage, and 1,250 horse-power, down to the fleet of screw steam gunboats, has suffered a certain depreciation by the fact of the Miantonomoh, and the forthcoming fleet of monitors, of which she is the precursor. The value of any weapon and any engine of war depends upon the existing state of the art of war, and the existing means at the service of the foe. Just as the artillery of the Normans was rendered ineffective by that of the Plantagenets, and just as the muzzle-loader has been reduced to a mere fraction of its value by the invention of breech-loaders, the ships which, twenty years ago, were said to make England impregnable, and to console us for the want of unlimited armies, are now found to be useless against a ship that hardly shows itself above the water, and that can discharge with perfect steadiness and accuracy a projectile which even our best armor-plating is not quite proof against. But, if even our best and latest ships have now to consider how they may fare in the hands of this new antagonist, what hope is there for the swarms of obsolete curiosities now encumbering our anchorages?

"It is almost oppressive to think of the immense amount of resistance that will inevitably be roused by any attempt to bring our navy up to the mark of the day. In the first place, there is the enormous mass of costly property to be sacrificed, pulled to pieces for the materials, or sold for an 'old song.' Anybody who has seen an old ship broken up will be ready to shed tears at the thought of such solid constructions and such excellent material being thrown away. The worship of work and of material is natural to all of us; but man is a still finer piece of workmanship and a still more costly material, and we cannot afford to pile sailors in tall ships where they are as devoted to destruction as the captives said to be crammed into huge figures of wicker-work by our British forefathers and burnt in honor of their gods. If it is hardly reasonable to expect that anybody who has had a share in the creation of one of our magnificent three-deckers should ever consent to its destruction, or even its disuse, it is fortunate that the stern sentence may have to be pronounced by others. This obstruction may be got over. Another remains, which, we confess, gives us greater anxiety. The officers of her Majesty's naval service are a very gallant body of men, and they are prepared to brave the foe and the fury of the elements; but they will not easily be persuaded to live below the water-line, and to be supplied with air by a steam-engine. It is said that these vessels are much more comfortable and agreeable than could be anticipated, that there is no feeling of insecurity, and that the temperature is well kept down; but, when we see the obstinate unpopularity of our iron-clads, we can scarcely hope to see the day when the flag-ship of the Mediterranean fleet will only rise thirty-six inches out of the water. We wait for war to convert old sailors to such a novelty as this. But how many ships and how many noble crews, that no money can replace, may be sent to the bottom before admirals can be brought to reason! It is the public, not the service, that will lead the way; and now, if ever, is the time to inquire into the changes of the art of naval warfare, naval gunnery, and naval construction, as they affect the ships and vessels now composing her Majesty's navy."

CHAPTER IV.

COPENHAGEN — THE KING'S VISIT — THE ROYAL DINNER — HOSPITALITIES — THE STONEWALL — THORVALDSEN — THE MUSEUMS.

ON Monday, July 16th, the Miantonomoh and the Augusta left the Nore for the Baltic, expecting to await Mr. Fox at Stettin, in Prussia.

The English pilot who accompanied the monitor from the Thames was somewhat suspicious of the strange craft, and had his doubts of her ability to stand a heavy sea. He afterward said that, in the first gale she encountered, when he saw a "green sea, eighteen feet deep of solid water, roll over her bow," he gave himself up for lost, believing that the monitor was going down head-foremost. But, the tops of the turrets keeping clear of the terrific waves, he gathered courage to look around, and, seeing an American sailor quietly sewing a patch upon his trousers, apparently unconscious of the coming on board of the water, which all his own experience had taught him was fatal to a ship, he regained his equanimity. In subsequent gales he became charmed with the steadiness of the vessel, and he left her with regret.

Mr. Fox arrived at Cologne on the 20th, and, hearing

that the cholera was prevailing at Berlin and Stettin, telegraphed to Mr. Yeaman, the United States minister to Denmark, to stop the ships at Copenhagen, as they passed through the straits. The squadron came to anchor at Copenhagen, Saturday, July 21st, and Mr. Fox joined it on the following Tuesday, with the expectation of sailing for Cronstadt the next day. But, hearing still more alarming accounts of the prevalence of cholera at the latter place, he determined to await the receipt of accurate information from the Honorable Cassius M. Clay, our minister at St. Petersburg, to whom he telegraphed.

Messrs. E. H. Green, of Boston, and J. F. Loubat, of New York, joined the squadron at Copenhagen, as secretaries to the mission, the former going on board of the Augusta, the latter of the Miantonomoh.

The arrival of the American ships caused much excitement in the city, and anchor had scarcely been dropped when curious crowds in small boats surrounded the monitor.

The Americans were not less attracted by the scene around them. The harbor of Copenhagen is a narrow arm of the sea, lying between the city proper, on the island of Seeland, and Christianshavn, on the small island of Amager, opposite. It is safe, deep, and capacious, having ample room for four hundred vessels. The city has an animated, busy appearance; but, being situated on low, flat ground, it has not the commanding look that its massive buildings and fortifications ought to give it. It is protected by the strong fortress of Frederickshavn, and has batteries, also, on the land side, but the latter are wholly inadequate for the requirements of modern defence. Although one of the oldest towns in Northern Europe, dating from the eleventh century, it has an entirely modern appearance, most of its buildings being comparatively new. It has frequently been besieged, and has suffered immense losses from both war and fire. In 1728 more than sixteen hundred houses were burned; and, in 1795, fifty streets and nearly a thousand buildings, including the famous palace, were destroyed. In 1807, when the English, under Admiral Gambier and Lord Cathcart, bombarded the city mercilessly for three days, over three hundred buildings were laid in ruins, and two thousand more were rendered uninhabitable. But Copenhagen has recovered from all its losses, and it is growing rapidly in size and population. It has now about one hundred and seventy-five thousand inhabitants.

Mr. Fox paid his respects to the American minister, the Honorable George H. Yeaman, at once, on his arrival, and spent Tuesday and Wednesday in visiting the city and in making the customary official calls. On Thursday, July 26th, he visited the Navy-Yard, officially. The Danish authorities received him cordially, showed him through the Government works, and gave him all the information in their power concerning their Department of Marine.

July 27th.—In the morning, Mr. Fox, Commanders Murray and Beaumont, and Messrs. Green and Loubat, were formally presented to the king, at the royal palace in the city, by the United States minister, Mr. Yeaman. His Majesty made numerous inquiries in regard to the

monitor, and, in response to an invitation from Mr. Fox, appointed the afternoon of the same day to visit her.

Christian IX., King of Denmark, mounted the throne in 1863, on the death of King Frederick VII., by virtue of the Treaty of London of May 8, 1852, and of the Danish law of succession of July 31, 1853. He is the son of the late Frederick William Paul Leopold, Duke of Sleswig-Holstein-Sonderburg-Glücksburg, and of Louise Caroline, Princess of Hesse, and was born April 8, 1818. He married, May 26, 1842, Louise Wilhelmine Frederica Caroline Augusta Julia, the daughter of William, Landgrave of Hesse-Cassel, and has the following children:

Frederick, Prince Royal, born June 3, 1843; married July 28, 1869, Louisa, daughter of Charles XV., King of Sweden and Norway.

Alexandra, born December 1, 1844; married, March 10, 1863, Albert Edward, Prince of Wales.

William, born December 24, 1845; married, October 27, 1867, Olga, daughter of the Grand-duke Constantine of Russia. He accepted, on the 6th of June, 1863, the crown of Greece, with the title of George I.

Dagmar, born November 26, 1847; married, November 9, 1866, Alexander, hereditary Grand-duke of Russia. She is now known as the Grand-duchess Marie Feodorovna.

Thyra, born September 29, 1853.

Waldemar, born October 27, 1858.

In the afternoon the King and the royal family visited the Miantonomoh. Suitable preparations had been made, and Mr. Yeaman, the United States minister, and the principal officers of the Augusta, had come on board of the monitor to aid in his Majesty's reception. At half-past one o'clock the thundering of the guns of the shore-batteries announced that the royal party was on its way. The marine guard of the Miantonomoh and the crew were at once drawn up in line on the port side of the deck, and the officers of both ships, in full uniform, took a position on the starboard side, near the gangway.

The royal party came alongside in a pretty little steamer, flying the royal banner, and managed by an officer of naval engineers. Admiral Irminger, aide to the King, was the first to step on board. He was received at the gangway by Mr. Fox and Commanders Murray and Beaumont. The King then followed, the officers receiving him with naval courtesy, and the marines presenting arms. At the same moment the royal standard was hoisted at the fore of the Augusta, and a salute of twenty-one guns was fired. His Majesty gracefully acknowledged the honor by standing uncovered.

Christian IX. is a tall, well-formed man, with dark hair, whiskers, and mustache. He wore on this occasion the full uniform of a general, with the Grand Cross of the Dannebrog, and several other decorations, upon his breast. The Queen was dressed simply but elegantly, and was exceedingly affable in her manners.

The Crown Prince wore a military uniform, with several decorations. The Princess Dagmar, in a blue-and-white striped silk and pink hat, the Princess Thyra and Prince Waldemar, in plain costume, and the King's brother, Prince John, in military uniform, constituted the royal family. Accompanying them, besides Admiral

Irminger, were Madame de Bille, Mistress of Robes to the Queen, Madlle. Rosenorn, Lady of Honor, several other ladies near the Queen's person, and a number of naval officers and officers of the King's household.

Next to the King, the Princess Dagmar, then the betrothed of the Cezarevitch of Russia, attracted the most attention. She is possessed of more than ordinary personal beauty. She has an oval face, regular in outline, a brilliant complexion, glossy brown hair, and bright, intelligent eyes. She conversed with freedom, speaking English fluently and correctly, as did all the party, and displayed a thorough knowledge of the general topics discussed.

The royal visitors were shown at once about the ship, each one being accompanied by an officer, who explained every thing. All parts of the monitor were thoroughly inspected, some of the ladies venturing even into the fire-rooms and the men's quarters. Many inquiries were made concerning the machinery for moving the heavy turrets and the guns, and the details of the voyage across the Atlantic were listened to with rapt attention. All expressed their gratification at the visit, and appeared to be much pleased with the ship and with every thing they saw.

On leaving, the officers and men joined in giving the royal party three hearty cheers. The Augusta again fired a royal salute, and the visit was ended.

July 28*th*.—Baron Nicholas de Nicolaÿ, the Russian minister at the court of Denmark, accompanied by Baron Wrangel, Secretary of Legation, and the consul-general of Russia, and their ladies, visited the Miantonomoh. As the representative of the country to which the American mission was credited, he was received with all the honors.

Mr. Fox heard of the successful laying of the Atlantic cable, through Mr. O. B. Suhr, of Copenhagen. As may be expected, the news was received with delight by all the Americans.

July 29th.—On Sunday, by royal invitation, the mission dined with the King and his family, at Bernstorff. The party consisted of the United States minister, Mr. Yeaman, Mr. Fox, Commanders Murray and Beaumont, Messrs. Green and Loubat, and a number of distinguished Danish officials.

Bernstorff, the royal summer residence, occupies a beautiful site in the environs of Copenhagen, about five miles from the city. Passing along the sea-shore road, or Strandvei, toward the north, one reaches, after a pleasant drive, the Charlottenlund, a park of about eighty acres of wood and garden, surrounding a country-house, belonging to the crown, and usually occupied by some member of the royal family. This is a place of great resort on Sundays and feast-days, when tens of thousands of the citizens of Copenhagen fill its pleasant walks and arbors, and amuse themselves with music, dancing, and harmless recreations, until late at night. Across this park the carriage-road, continued through a fine avenue of limes, leads to Bernstorff, a manor-house, built about a century ago by Count A. P. Bernstorff, then a noted man in Denmark. It now belongs to the crown, and is occu-

THE ROYAL DINNER.

pied generally by the King during the summer months, when Copenhagen, notwithstanding its high latitude, is hot and oppressive.

The gentlemen were received most cordially at Bernstorff. At dinner, the company, twenty-five in number, were seated in the following order:

GRAND-MARSHAL D'OXHOLM.

AIDE-DE-CAMP OF THE KING.	PRINCE WALDEMAR.
OFFICER OF THE DAY.	MASTER OF THE HORSE.
MR. YEAMAN.	PRINCESS THYRA.
MDLLE. LAVALIER, Lady to Princess Dagmar.	M. ESTRUP, Minister of the Interior.
PRINCE JOHN.	PRINCESS DAGMAR.
THE QUEEN.	THE KING.
COUNT FRYS, Minister of Foreign Affairs.	MADAME DE BILLE, Mistress of the Robes.
LADY-IN-WAITING TO THE QUEEN.	CROWN-PRINCE.
MR. GREEN.	MR. FOX.
REAR-ADMIRAL IRMINGER.	VICE-ADMIRAL BILLE.
COMMANDER MURRAY.	COMMANDER BEAUMONT.
MR. LOUBAT.	EQUERRY OF THE CROWN-PRINCE.

The *menu*, which was written on plain paper, with a narrow, red border, and with the royal arms in gold at the top, was as follows:

DÎNER DU 29 JUILLET, 1868.

Oporto, Sherry.	Potage aux écrevisses.
	Croustades à la financière.
Ch. d'Yquem.	Carpes au bleu, deux sauces.
	Roast-beef aux macaronis.
Ch. Montrose.	Poulets farcis aux truffes.
	Choux fleurs, saumon fumé.
Oporto blanc.	Pâté de foies gras de Strasbourg.
Champagne.	Pâté de canetons sauvages, compôte, salade.
Madère.	Glace.
	Dessert.

The band played, during the dinner, the Danish national hymn, "King Christian IX.'s March," the "Star-spangled Banner," and selections from "Il Trovatore" and "La Traviata." By order of the King, the "Star-spangled Banner" was repeated.

After dinner a very agreeable afternoon was spent, the royal family entertaining their guests in the most affable and unconstrained manner. The gentlemen of the party will ever retain a vivid remembrance of their reception, and of the kind efforts of his Majesty of Denmark to honor them as the representatives of the American people.

July 30*th*.—All the foreign ambassadors at the court of Denmark visited the Miantonomoh this morning. They were received by Mr. Fox, Mr. Yeaman, and Commanders Murray and Beaumont, and honored with a salute of fifteen guns from the Augusta. They inspected the ship, and appeared to be much interested in her novelties.

At two o'clock P. M., Count Frys, the Danish Minister of Foreign Affairs, made a formal visit to the monitor, and was received with due honors by the same officials, the Augusta flying the Danish ensign at her fore, and again saluting.

This ended the official visits, but the unofficial ones still continued, crowds of people from the city and the surrounding country flocking on board all day long, as they had done almost every day since the ship's arrival. Two steamboats, the Fulton and the El Ole, ran every half-hour from the city, loaded with sight-seers—men, women, and children—who swarmed on the Miantonomoh's deck and roamed through her at will, feasting their eyes on her wonders. The visit of the Americans will never be forgotten by the worthy burghers of Copenhagen.

In the evening, Mr. Fox, the officers of the ship, and the other gentlemen on board, attended a reception at the residence of the United States minister. Nearly all the members of the diplomatic corps, the Danish Minister of Foreign Affairs, and many other prominent persons, were present. The evening was passed in a very agreeable manner, although the absence of Mrs. Yeaman, the hostess, from indisposition, was noted, and universally regretted.

July 31st.—On Tuesday Mr. Fox received dispatches from Mr. Clay, announcing that the cholera was abating at St. Petersburg, and, hearing from the Russian consul-general that it no longer existed at Helsingfors, he decided to sail for the latter port and to await there more accurate information. He telegraphed to Mr. Clay, offering to go alone to St. Petersburg, being doubtful of the propriety of taking the ships where there was any possibility of the crews contracting the dreaded disease. Mr. Clay answered: "Come with the ships, if it takes all summer." The Augusta put to sea, therefore, at half-past two o'clock.

While in Copenhagen, our civil war was brought very forcibly to mind by the discovery that a quantity of Confederate war-material was stored in one of the Danish magazines. It will be remembered that the iron-clad ram, the Stonewall, was built originally for the Danish Government; but, failing to pass the inspection of the officials at Copenhagen, they refused to accept her, on the ground that she did not fulfil the contract specifications. This was precisely what her builder wanted, for he sold her immediately to the Confederates at an advanced price. The stores above mentioned were sent here to complete her outfit, but the Danish authorities, suspecting something wrong, refused to let them go on board. After a long stay, her officers became convinced that they would not be allowed to fit out here, and left the port, leaving the material in store, where it remained intact until our ships arrived. On Commander Murray's requesting its delivery to him, as property belonging rightfully to the United States Government, the Danish authorities at once complied, and it was transferred to the Augusta. Among the articles were two complete suits of sails for the ship, spare yards and masts, wind-sails, awnings, and covers, sails for small boats, two hundred rounds of 300-pounder Armstrong shell, two hundred rounds of 60-pounder shell, and other material. The sails were evidently of French manufacture; the rest were probably English. The Danish authorities acted in the most frank and unreserved manner in the transaction, and merited our thanks for responding so promptly to Commander Murray's request.

The Americans found much to admire in Copenhagen, and were sorry that their visit was necessarily so short a one. The city possesses many attractions, some of which are unique. Among the places meriting especial attention is the Thorvaldsen Museum, containing that artist's finest works and the private collection of pictures, books, cameos, coins, and bronzes, which he bequeathed to the city on his death. The museum building, which is also a mausoleum, for it contains the mortal remains of the sculptor, is in the form of a quadrangle, and has two stories. The frescoes on the exterior represent the triumphant reception of Thorvaldsen on his return to his native country, in 1838. The lower story is devoted to the sculptures alone, the upper contains the cabinets and a few of the sculptures that could not find room below. Of all the works in this incomparable collection, the celebrated group of our Lord and the Twelve Apostles, the originals of which are in the cathedral, receives the most attention. They stand together in the Hall of Christ, producing a wonderful effect by the solemn beauty and earnest expression of their countenances.

This museum, which contains all of the master's greatest works, either the originals or copies, is the most popular of all the public collections in Copenhagen. In the court-yard, under a bed of roses and evergreen, the artist lies buried, surrounded by his own immortal creations.

The Museum of Northern Antiquities is the most remarkable collection of the kind in Europe. It was arranged by Mr. Thomson, its late director, a zealous and noted archæologist, in conformity to his theory of three successive stages of civilization—a stone, a bronze, and an iron age. By the liberality of the Danish Government, the finder of any antiquarian object made of the precious metals receives the full value of it by offering it to the museum. The collection is unrivalled, consequently, in gold and silver ornaments. Here may be seen specimens from the *kjökkenmöddinge* (shell-mounds) and the *kistfunden* (coast-finds), the rude stone axes and knives of the earliest savage tribes, and the beautifully-polished implements belonging to the later division of the stone age; the first weapons of the bronze age, and the exquisitely chased and ornamented objects characteristic of its later development, under Roman influence; and a magnificent collection illustrative of the iron age through every period. Among the most noticeable specimens of the later iron age, the time of the Vikings, are huge swords and battle-axes, some of them inlaid with silver, great shields, and splendid suits of armor and horse-trappings. An ancient breech-loading cannon, one of the oldest pieces of ordnance known, attracted the attention of our officers. It was found in the wreck of a man-of-war, near the island of Anholt, and is supposed to date from the latter half of the fourteenth century.

The Ethnographic Museum is another remarkable collection, being the most perfect and best arranged of its kind. Its object is to illustrate the civilization of the various nations outside of the Scandinavian countries anterior to the classic period, and the development founded on this, by comparison with savage tribes still existing. It includes the whole world in its range, and is invaluable to the student of ethnology.

Rosenborg Castle, once a royal residence, is now devoted to the very interesting chronological collection of the Danish kings. One or more rooms illustrate the reign of each sovereign, being decorated in the style of the period, filled with furniture taken from the royal residences, embellished with portraits of the members of the royal family and famous men of the time, and many interesting objects—garments, arms, jewelry, etc.—that have belonged to the king, the court, or celebrated contemporaries. As a well-arranged historical collection it is unsurpassed.

There are so many objects of interest in Copenhagen, that it is almost impossible even to name them all. The Royal Library, with its 550,000 volumes and 25,000 manuscripts; the University Library, with 200,000 volumes and 4,000 manuscripts; the Royal Collection of Coins and Medals; the Arsenal, with its magnificent display of arms of every period; the Zoological and Mineralogical Museums; and the several splendid collections of paintings and engravings, offer attractions to the traveller and student unexcelled, if equalled, in Europe.

The famous Round Tower is worthy of a special note. It was built by Christian IV. for an observatory, and was used for that purpose for about two hundred years. It consists of two hollow cylinders, between which a spiral road winds from the street to the top, with ascent sufficiently easy for a carriage to drive up. It is said that Catherine of Russia, when she visited Copenhagen in 1719, drove a coach and four to the top, her husband, Peter the Great, preceding her on horseback.

The Tivoli and the Alhambra are great gardens, where the people congregate on summer evenings to drink beer, to listen to music and singing, and to enjoy pantomimes and the varied amusements there offered them. The former employs three or four bands of music, one of which is conducted by one of the most famous leaders in Europe. The Alhambra has a ballet-troupe among other attractions, and usually draws crowded houses. Among the thousands who frequent these places, all are quiet, peaceable, and contented; and disturbances are seldom seen. Indeed, the Dane seeks amusement and pleasure in a rational way. He takes his family to the gardens, finds a quiet retreat where he can listen to the music, and smokes his pipe and quaffs his beer with an equanimity which our more mercurial people might envy.

CHAPTER V.

IN THE BALTIC—SWEABORG—HELSINGFORS—GULF OF FINLAND—CRONSTADT.

A UGUST 1st.—Wednesday was clear and pleasant, with a light easterly wind. The squadron kept an easterly course during the morning, along the south shore of Sweden. Many vessels were in sight. At noon the south point of the island of Oland was descried; and, in the afternoon, the island of Gottland came into view.

August 2d.—Thursday opened cloudy, with a stiff breeze from the northwest, a drizzling rain, and a rough sea. The ships kept a northeast course. In the afternoon the weather moderated and ended fine, with a light breeze from the southeast, and a nearly smooth sea. Dago Island in sight. After leaving Copenhagen it was noticed that the water of the Baltic grew brackish, and, on approaching the Gulf of Finland, its freshness increased. The English coal obtained in Copenhagen compared with the anthracite previously used as eight to twelve.

August 3d (*July* 22d).[1]—A light breeze from the south and east, with a smooth sea and occasional fog. While standing into the Gulf of Finland, Esthonia, a province of Russia, was in sight on the southeast. Ran at slow speed, on account of the fog. At noon Finland was seen, the ships being then distant from Helsingfors anchorage twenty-four miles. Whole distance run from Copenhagen to Helsingfors, five hundred and forty-three knots; time, seventy-two hours.

In the afternoon, light variable winds and showery weather. The fortress of Sweaborg, which guards the entrance to the harbor, soon came into sight. The approach to Helsingfors is very striking. The coast is rugged and broken, with bare granite rocks rising from the water, and numerous little islands covered with firs. One of the first objects seen is a large church, with a gilded spire, standing on a hill close to the sea.

The fortress, whose massive granite bastions and curtains present a frowning rampart seaward, is built on seven islands that stretch across the mouth of the harbor, making a secure haven within, which is large enough to accommodate seventy ships-of-the-line. It is considered to be so nearly impregnable that it has been called the Gibraltar of the North. It was built by the Swedes, between the years 1749 and 1758, under the superintend-

---

[1] The Cæsarian calendar being still in use in the Russian Empire, the double dates are given in the account of the mission in that country. It differs from the Gregorian calendar, which is now in use in all civilized countries, excepting Russia, in making the year three hundred and sixty-five and a quarter days, or eleven minutes too long. The error has now amounted to about twelve days, the Russians being that much behind our time.

ance of Count Ehrenswerd, who lies buried within its walls. Sweaborg was the last rampart of Sweden against Russia, the rallying-point of her army and her navy, whence she sustained her province of Finland. In the spring of 1808, it was surrendered by the Swedish Admiral Cronstadt, after a two months' siege, to an inferior Russian force, although he was well supplied with provisions and with munitions of war. The reason of this almost unexampled capitulation is unknown to this day. Admiral Cronstadt had the reputation of being a man of courage and an officer of skill and of experience, and no proof was ever obtained that he betrayed his trust for money; but the fact stands against him that he surrendered these immense works, defended by seven thousand five hundred men and two frigates, to a force numerically inferior. This act lost the whole of Finland to Sweden.

Admiral Cronstadt was on the point, it is said, of going to Stockholm to explain his conduct to the King; but, hearing that he could not do so without danger, he retired to Helsingfors, withdrew himself from all his former friends, and lived a life of complete isolation from the world until his death, which occurred a few years after.

The customary salutes were exchanged as the ships passed the fortress, and, at twenty minutes after three o'clock, anchor was dropped in the harbor of Helsingfors. The civil governor, Major-General Baron Walleen, of the suite of the Emperor,[1] Vice-Admiral Nordman, and Cap-

[1] The military household of the Emperor is composed of aides-de-camp, officers of the suite, and aides-de-camp-general. Aides-de-camp may be of any rank below that of major-general and of rear-admiral. Officers of these

tain Rondakoff, commandant of the port of Sweaborg, attended by their suites, all in full uniform, came at once on board the Miantonomoh, and welcomed, in the name of the Emperor, the mission to Russian waters. They announced that they were directed by his Imperial Majesty to offer to Mr. Fox the courtesies of the city. Their greeting met with a most cordial and hearty response from our officers, who rejoiced with their hosts that they had reached Russian territory in safety after so long a voyage.

Helsingfors presents a handsome appearance from the harbor, the houses being large and regularly built, and a fine granite quay extending along its entire water-front. The streets are wide, straight, and laid out at right angles. On the principal square are the Senate-House and the University, both imposing buildings, and a very handsome church. The Senate and the University were removed from Abo, the ancient capital of Finland, after the destruction of that town by fire in 1827. The University, now called the Alexander University, was founded by Queen Christina, of Sweden, in 1640. It is in a flourishing condition, has twenty-two professors, and generally four or five hundred students. Helsingfors, since its removal thither, has increased much in importance and population. The town now numbers about twenty-five thousand inhabitants, exclusive of the garrison, which consists usually of half as many more.

August 4th (July 23d).—On Saturday Mr. Fox, his

ranks may be of the suite. None but lieutenant-generals, vice-admirals, and officers of higher grade, can be made aides-de-camp-general of the Emperor.

secretaries, and Commanders Murray and Beaumont, returned official calls in the city, and at noon attended, in company with the officers of the ships, an entertainment in honor of the mission. This banquet, which was given by the Civil Governor of Helsingfors, was held in the great mineral springs building. The military, naval, and civil dignitaries were present, as well as the members of the government institutions of Finland, in all, over one hundred and fifty persons. Among the guests were also three English officers of artillery, who happened to be in Helsingfors at the time. The hall was tastefully decorated with Russian and American flags, and with flowers and wreaths of leaves.

Baron Walleen, the Governor, made a short speech in French, at the close of the banquet, in which he expressed his gratification that Finland had had the honor of first welcoming the American envoy within the Russian Empire. Mr. Fox responded briefly, expressing his thanks for the hospitality which had been extended to him, and saying that his visit had a twofold object—to congratulate his Majesty the Emperor on his escape, and to thank the Russian people for the friendly disposition which they had always shown toward the United States, and particularly during the late struggle in our country. Mr. Fox ended by proposing a toast to the health of the Emperor, the Empress, and the Imperial Family. Baron Walleen then gave the health of the President of the United States, to which Mr. Fox responded fittingly, closing as follows: " The Emperor, the President, and the Imperial Family, having been toasted, I wish, gentlemen, to offer a sentiment to the Cezarevitch,[1] Alexander Alexandrovitch.[2] May he inherit the chivalric valor of Alexander Nevsky, the good fortune of Alexander I., and the heart of Alexander II." Admiral Nordman then toasted Commanders Murray and Beaumont, and all the officers of the squadron present, seizing the occasion to thank them and their comrades in America for the reception which they had given to the Russian fleets in New York, Boston, and San Francisco, in 1863. Admiral Nordman finished by amending his toast so as to include the whole American navy, which was drunk with all the honors. Commander Murray responded, after which toasts were given to the English officers present, and to the ladies of America. Admiral Nordman, who proposed the latter, specified particularly Mrs. Virginia Fox, the wife of the envoy of Congress.

Ole Bull, the celebrated violinist, who was present, delighted the company by playing a brilliant improvisation on Russian and American airs, interweaving the melodies with sparkling variations. The artist supplemented his performance, which was received with great applause, by a facetious speech, charging the Americans with ingratitude for not having visited the Norwegians, who were the first to discover America, even before Columbus.

[1] Since 1721, when Peter the Great took the title of Emperor, the Russian sovereigns have dropped the title of Czar, and the hereditary Grandduke, or heir to the Imperial throne, has been called Cezarevitch, instead of Czarevitch, as formerly. It is equivalent to "son of the Cæsar."

[2] It is customary in Russia to add to one's Christian name that of one's father, with an affix signifying "son of" or "daughter of;" as, Alexander Alexandrovitch, Alexander son of Alexander; Nicholas Nicholaevitch, Nicholas son of Nicholas; Marie Nicholaevna, Marie daughter of Nicholas.

During the speaking, Mr. Loubat, a part of the time, and Baron Walleen, Chamberlain to the Emperor and brother of the Governor, afterward, acted as interpreters.

In the afternoon the party called at Mr. Frenckel's, the United States consul, where they took coffee; and in the evening they were invited to a ball, in the same hall where the lunch had been given, which lasted until long after midnight. Notwithstanding its impromptu character, it proved to be a brilliant affair, and the evening passed in the most agreeable manner.

Further courtesies were planned, but, hearing that the cholera no longer prevailed at Cronstadt, Mr. Fox determined to proceed at once to that port. Leave was taken of the many friends made in Helsingfors with regret, and with numerous expressions of mutual regard.

August 5th (July 24th).—The Augusta and the Miantonomoh got under way, Sunday morning, at eight o'clock, amid the salutes of the batteries. The weather was thick, with light rain, the wind being from the southeast. After leaving the mouth of the harbor, the fog rose, and the Russian iron-clad fleet was descried, preparing to enter the pass, which is narrow and difficult of access. The squadron had been sent from Transund, to escort the Americans to Cronstadt, and expected to join them at Helsingfors.

As the Augusta neared the fleet, she hoisted the Russian naval ensign at the fore, and saluted it with twenty-one guns, which were answered, gun for gun, by the Sevastopol, the flag-ship of Rear-Admiral Likhatcheff, of the suite of his Imperial Majesty, and Commander-in-Chief of the Russian iron-clad fleet, with the American ensign at her fore.

The Russian rear-admiral then telegraphed (using the international code of signals) as follows: "Welcome. I will escort you to Cronstadt. Take the lead; your squadron between my lines."

Admiral Likhatcheff then sent on board of the Augusta, and afterward on board of the Miantonomoh, his fleet-captain and chief of staff, Captain Michael Novossilsky, to present his compliments to Commanders Murray and Beaumont, and to the Honorable Mr. Fox. Captain Novossilsky left on board of the Augusta, Lieutenant Kolontaeff, one of the aides-de-camp of Admiral Likhatcheff, and one of the pilot-officers of the iron-clad Sevastopol. These officers remained on the Augusta until she cast anchor in Cronstadt roads.

The Russian fleet then formed into two columns. The starboard line was led by Admiral Likhatcheff, with the flag-ship Sevastopol, which towed the monitor Lava. The Vladimir followed, towing the monitor Edinorog, and the Ne Trouno Menia brought up the rear. Rear-Admiral Boutakoff, of the suite of the Emperor, led the port column on the Khrabry. The Dmitry Donskoy followed, towing the monitor Perun; next came the Yakhont towing the monitor Streletz; and last, the Smertch. The American ships then took position in the centre, the Augusta leading, and in this form the combined squadrons steamed for Cronstadt.

The following diagram will show clearly the place in line of each of the ships:

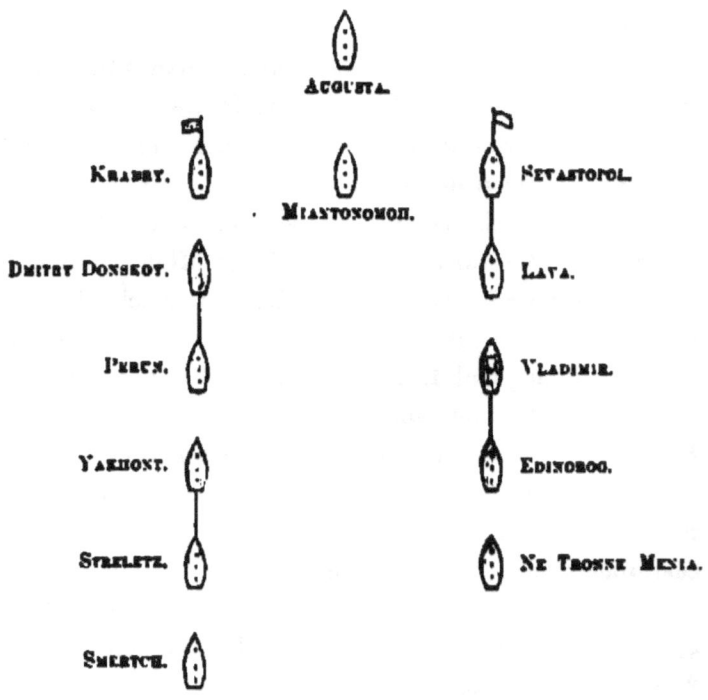

GENERAL DESCRIPTION OF THE RUSSIAN SHIPS.

Sevastopol, Captain Brummer, iron-clad frigate, carrying twenty-four steel eight-inch rifled guns, and five hundred officers and men.

Lava, Captain Wogak, single-turreted monitor, with two steel nine-inch rifled guns, and one hundred officers and men.

Vladimir, Captain Kondriavoy, paddle-frigate, old model, carrying four twenty-four pounders, and one hundred and fifty officers and men.

Edinorog (Unicorn), Captain Baron Klodt, single-turreted monitor, with two steel nine-inch rifled guns, and one hundred officers and men.

Ne Tronne Menia (Touch-me-not), Captain Selivanoff, iron-clad battery, carrying eighteen steel eight-inch rifled guns, and four hundred and fifty officers and men.

Krabry (the Bold), Captain Rehbinder, paddle-frigate, old model, with four twenty-four pounders, and two hundred officers and men.

Dmitry Donskoy (Dmitry of the Don), Captain Ankoudinoff, screw wooden frigate, carrying sixty sixty-eight pounders, and six hundred officers and men.

Perun[1] (God of Fire), Captain Karpoff, single-turreted monitor, with two smooth-bore fifteen-inch Rodman guns, and one hundred officers and men.

Yakhont (Jasper), Captain Kosuakoff, screw wooden clipper, carrying eight steel six-inch rifled guns, and two hundred officers and men.

Streletz (Archer), Captain Popoff, single-turreted monitor, with two steel nine-inch rifled guns, and one hundred officers and men.

Smertch (Water-spout), Captain Korniloff, iron-clad gunboat, on the Cole's system, with two turrets, carrying two steel eight-inch rifled guns, and one hundred and seventy-five officers and men.

[1] Perun was the chief divinity of the idolatrous Slavonians. When Vladimir embraced Christianity, near the close of the tenth century, he cast down the idol of Perun at Kiew, and dragged it at his horse's tail to the Borysthenes (Dnieper), into which he threw it.

The day closed fine, with a light westerly wind. At eight o'clock P. M. the combined squadrons, still keeping the same order, were off Hogland.

August 6th (July 25th).—Monday opened bright and clear. The weather was superb, and the blue waters of the Gulf of Finland rolled lazily in the sun, as the fleets moved into Cronstadt. The Augusta and the Miantonomoh, still forming the centre line, were a little in advance of the Russian ships. On approaching the forts of the great roadstead, the Augusta ran up to her mast-head the Russian ensign, and fired a national salute of twenty-one guns. A like number of guns were fired in answer from the commercial pier, and the American flag was hoisted upon the inner guard-ship. A second salute to the admiral's flag was then fired from the pier, to which the Sevastopol responded.

As the American steamer moved slowly into the lesser roadstead, many men-of-war's boats and yachts, belonging to the River Yacht Club of St. Petersburg, made the scene lively by beating about under sail in every direction. Early in the morning the public had been notified, by special bulletins issued by the Cronstadt *Messenger*, that the fleet would arrive at ten o'clock, and that at half-past nine the Oranienbaum steamboat, chartered by the city, would go out with passengers to meet the strangers. Accordingly, at the specified time, the Luna appeared in the roadstead, filled with people. As she approached the Augusta a band on board played "Hail Columbia," while her passengers and the crowd upon the wharves welcomed the American ship with loud and prolonged cheers, to which the officers and the crew of the Augusta responded heartily. The Luna then passed on and welcomed in like manner the Miantonomoh, which was coming into the lesser roadstead.

The piers of the commercial and of the middle port were crowded with spectators, and it seemed as if the cheering would never cease. The sight of the harbor at this time was imposing. The Russian squadron, and the massive fortifications in the background, small craft scudding in every direction, the shores and quays black with people, and in the foreground the Miantonomoh moving majestically along the lesser roadstead, in full view of all, presented a stirring picture.

At ten o'clock, when the ships came to anchor, Lieutenant Rikatcheff,[1] aide-de-camp of Admiral Novossilsky, aide-de-camp-general of the Emperor, governor-general of Cronstadt, and commander-in-chief of the port of Cronstadt, came on board to congratulate Mr. Fox and Commanders Murray and Beaumont, in the name of his chief, on their safe arrival, and to offer his services.

Soon after, Rear-Admiral Lessovsky, of his Imperial Majesty's suite, came to congratulate the American envoy, in the name of the Emperor, on his arrival in Russia. He informed Mr. Fox that, by imperial command, the mission and the officers and crews of the squadron were to be received as the guests of the government, and that he was charged specially with this duty, assisted by the

---

[1] Lieutenant Rikatcheff is editor-in-chief of the Cronstadt *Messenger*, the semi-official gazette of the Russian Navy.

following officers: Rear-Admiral Gorkovenko, of the suite of his Imperial Majesty; Captain Fedorovsky, aide-de-camp of the Emperor; Lieutenant-Captain Koltovskoy; Lieutenant Rikatcheff, Lieutenant Isenbeck, Lieutenant Lehman, Lieutenant Kupfer, Ensign Paltoff, and Mr. Moukhortoff, Chamberlain to the Emperor. Each of these gentlemen spoke English.

Following Admiral Lessovsky's boat came another, flying the Russian commercial flag, bringing the mayor, Mr. Stephanoff, and a deputation of the municipal government, to offer the hospitalities of the city. The mayor made an appropriate address, and presented his hearty congratulations.

As soon as these gentlemen had taken their departure, Mr. Fox and Commanders Murray and Beaumont went ashore, in company with Admiral Lessovsky, to pay their respects to the military governor of Cronstadt, his Imperial Majesty's aide-de-camp-general, Admiral Novossilsky.

During their absence, Rear-Admirals Likhatcheff and Boutakoff, of the iron-clad fleet, all their captains, and their staffs, called on the Miantonomoh to pay their respects to Mr. Fox. They were received by Mr. Loubat, and shown through the monitor by Lieutenant-Commander Cornwell. On leaving, Admiral Likhatcheff left his chief of staff, Captain Novossilsky, on board the Miantonomoh, to offer the services of the squadron to the American commanders, and to impart to them the hygienic regulations in use on the Russian vessels to guard against a recurrence of the cholera, which had then nearly disappeared. As Admiral Likhatcheff left the monitor, the Augusta saluted him with nine guns, the Sevastopol replying.

On his return from the visit to Admiral Novossilsky, at one o'clock P. M., Mr. Fox and his secretaries, Messrs. Green and Loubat, accompanied by Admiral Lessovsky, went up to St. Petersburg on the steamer Nova, a vessel belonging to the Navy Department. As Admiral Lessovsky left the Miantonomoh, a salute of nine guns was fired by the Augusta, the Sevastopol returning the compliment; and, as Mr. Fox set foot on the Nova, she ran up the American colors, when the Augusta saluted him with seventeen guns, as Assistant Secretary of the Navy, and displayed the American flag on her top-gallant mast.

On arriving at St. Petersburg, Mr. Fox paid his respects to Mr. Clay, the minister of the United States, and furnished him with a written report of his arrival, and with copies of all documents addressed to Mr. Fox by the State and Navy Departments; also with a copy of the Resolution of Congress, and of the speech which he proposed to make when presenting the Resolution to the Emperor.

Mr. Fox and his secretaries also took possession of the apartments assigned them at the Hôtel de France. After dining with Mr. Clay, the evening was spent in driving about the city.

August 7th (July 26th).—On Tuesday Mr. Fox made the customary official calls in St. Petersburg, in company with the United States minister.

On the morning of the same day Mr. Hübner, the chief astronomer of the naval observatory at Cronstadt, visited both of the American ships, and presented to their commanders documents written in English, giving in full the rules for finding the mean time at Cronstadt, and showing the differences of time between the meridians of Greenwich, of New York, and of Cronstadt.

At ten o'clock, Admiral Novossilsky, accompanied by his chief-of-staff, Rear-Admiral Izilmentieff, by Captain Bajenoff, and the aide-de-camp of the staff, came to return the official visits made by the commanders the day before. The Augusta saluted him with seventeen guns, and hoisted the Russian flag, and the screw-corvette Griden returned the compliment with the same number of guns and the American flag. After inspecting the Augusta, the admiral visited the Miantonomoh, and examined her thoroughly. The turret machinery was put in motion in the presence of his Excellency, and he was shown the play of the fifteen-inch guns, and the action of the ventilators for supplying air to the cabins and state-rooms of the almost submarine ship. The admiral freely expressed his admiration of the monitor, and of the manner in which she had demonstrated her sea-going ability by crossing the Atlantic.

After the admiral's departure, came two other boats, bringing deputations from the Naval Club of Cronstadt and from the Naval Library. These gentlemen presented to Commanders Murray and Beaumont, and to all the other officers of the ships, cards of membership of the two associations.

At noon arrived in the eastern roadstead the steam-yacht Neva, displaying the flag of the River Yacht Club of St. Petersburg, and accompanied by the whole fleet of little yachts under sail. On reaching the ships a deputation of the members of the club came on board from the Neva to congratulate the Americans on their safe arrival. They were courteously received and thanked by the officers, who were much moved by the attentions showered upon them from every side.

At one o'clock Commanders Murray and Beaumont, accompanied by Mr. Wilkins, the United States vice-consul, made official calls on Vice-Admiral Choulepnikoff, commandant of the fortress of Cronstadt, and on the other authorities of the port.

At two o'clock the steamer Ijora called for the American officers, who, to the number of thirty, accepted an invitation to go ashore. On nearing the haven these gentlemen, under escort of a lieutenant of the Imperial Navy, were transferred to the steam-barge Koldounchik, which landed them at the middle port, whence they walked by the Gospodskaia Street to the building of the Naval Club and Naval Library. They were cordially received by the committee of members appointed for their reception, and invited into the library, where finely-bound copies of the catalogue were presented to each officer. They were shown, also, the charts presented, in 1863, by the city of New York and the State of Rhode Island, to Admiral Lessovsky, who had placed them for preservation in the museum of the library.

After the officers had finished their inspection of the

building, they were invited into the great hall of the Naval Club, where they sat down to lunch, the band meanwhile playing "Hail Columbia." This little breakfast, which was invested with no official character, passed off most agreeably, and will long be remembered by those who received the hospitalities of the club. The occasion was marked throughout by a warmth of feeling and a delicacy of attention on the part of their hosts which put the Americans at once at their ease, and caused them to forget that they were in a foreign land.

The commanding officers of the two ships and some of the authorities of Cronstadt were invited to dine with Admiral Novossilsky, at five o'clock in the evening.

CHAPTER VI.

PETERHOF—THE IMPERIAL AUDIENCE—THE RESOLUTION OF CONGRESS—AT THE FORTS—THE NAVAL BANQUET.

*A*UGUST 8*th* (*July* 27*th*).—At ten o'clock A. M., the Honorable Mr. Fox, accompanied by General Clay, Commanders Murray and Beaumont, Mr. Green, Mr. Loubat, and Mr. John Van Buren, of New York, left in the train for Peterhof, to present to his Majesty the Emperor the Resolution of Congress, of which he was the bearer. The party were received on their arrival by the officials of the court at the railway-station, where carriages were in waiting, a state-coach, drawn by four horses, being provided for Mr. Fox, and driven at once to the palace of Peterhof, where apartments were assigned to them.

This imperial residence was built originally by Peter the Great, and, although many alterations and additions have been made since his time, the general character of the structure is preserved very nearly as he left it. It stands on a plateau sixty feet in height, and is reached by a broad flight of marble steps in front. It is painted of a dull yellow color, and has few claims to architectural pretension. The grounds around it are, however, very beautiful, being laid out in terraces, adorned with fountains and water-falls, from the palace to the sea-shore. The water-works are little, if any, inferior to those at Versailles—the great fountain called "Samson" being especially remarkable. The interior of Peterhof is rich in tapestries, *tazzas* of porcelain, malachite, and marble, and other priceless articles of virtu.

Among other noted buildings in the park are Marly and Monplaisir. The former was a favorite residence of Peter the Great, who loved to watch his fleet moored in the waters beyond; and in the latter he breathed his last. The room in which he died is still shown, the furniture being preserved in the same condition in which he left it.

The Emperor has a private house and grounds, adjoining the lower garden of the old palace, called Alexandria, where he resides when at Peterhof. The building, which is in the style of Louis XV., occupies a most charming site. There are several other cottages in the grounds, among them the house of the late Emperor Nicholas, from the roof of which he was wont to watch the allied fleets when in front of Cronstadt.

There are also, among the older buildings, the cottage of the Empress Catherine—remarkable for its plainness without and its beauty within—the "Hermitage," and a thatched structure called the "Straw Palace."

At two o'clock P. M. the mission had the honor of being received by his Imperial Majesty the Emperor. His Excellency Prince Gortchakoff, Chancellor of the Empire and Minister of Foreign Affairs, stood at the Emperor's right during the audience. Mr. Fox was presented by the United States minister, Mr. Clay, without the customary intermediation of the master of ceremonies.

Mr. Fox read the following address in the English language:

SIRE: The Resolution which I have the honor of presenting to your Imperial Majesty is the voice of a people whose millions of lips speak from a single heart.

The many ties which have long bound together the great Empire of the East, and the great Republic of the West, have been multiplied and strengthened by the unwavering fidelity of the Imperial Government to our own, throughout its recent period of convulsion.

The words of sympathy and friendship then addressed to the Government at Washington, by command of your Imperial Majesty, are fixed in the eternal remembrance of a grateful country. As one of the wide family of nations, we yield our willing homage to that act of humanity which is especially referred to in the Resolution of Congress. The peaceful edict of an enlightened sovereign has consummated a triumph over an inherited barbarism, which our Western Republic has only reached through long years of bloodshed.

It is, therefore, with profound emotion that I offer to your Imperial Majesty, to the emancipated subjects, and to all the people of this vast realm, our heart-felt congratulations upon the providential escape from danger, which led to this spontaneous expression of regret for the attempt, and thankfulness for its merciful arrest and failure.

The story of the peril from which a kind Providence has delivered your Imperial Majesty brings with it the remembrance of the mighty sorrow which so lately filled every loyal heart in our own land at the sudden loss of our chief, our guide, our father.

We thank God that a grief like this was spared to our friends and allies—the Russian people.

May the Father of all nations and all rulers protect, prolong, and bless the life which He has so signally preserved, for the service of the people to which it belongs, for the good of mankind, and for the glory of His holy name!

G. V. Fox,
Assistant Secretary of the Navy.

At the close, Mr. Fox handed to his Imperial Majesty the joint Resolution of Congress, congratulating him on his escape from threatened assassination.

The Emperor replied to Mr. Fox's address, his words being translated by Prince Gortchakoff into English, substantially as follows:

His Majesty said that he rejoiced at the friendly relations existing between Russia and the United States, and he was pleased to see that those relations were so well appreciated in America. He was convinced that the national fraternity would be perpetual, and he, for his part, should contribute all his efforts to sustain it, and to strengthen the bonds. He was deeply sensible of the proofs of the personal sympathy and affection of the American people, conveyed in the resolution of Congress, and he was grateful for them. He desired to thank those who had come so great a distance to bear these proofs to him, and he assured them of a warm welcome to the soil of Russia.

His Majesty closed by remarking that the cordial reception which had been given to his squadron in the United States would never be effaced from his memory.

Alexander II., Emperor of Russia, succeeded to the throne March 2 (February 18), 1855, on the death of his father, the late Emperor Nicholas I.

Nicholas I., Paulovitch, born July 6 (June 25), 1796, married, July 13 (1), 1817, Alexandra Fedorovna,[1] previously Frederica Louisa Charlotte Wilhelmine, daughter of Frederick William III., King of Prussia. Of this union were born the following children:

1. Alexander Nicholaevitch (the present Emperor), born April 29 (17), 1818.
2. Marie Nicholaevna, born August 18 (6), 1819; married, July 14 (2), 1839, Maximilian Joseph Eugene Augustus Napoleon, Duke of Leuchtenberg, and Prince of Eichstaedt. He died November 1 (October 20), 1852, and she married, November 16 (4), 1856, Gregory, Count Strogonoff.[2]

[1] Foreign princesses, about to marry into the imperial family of Russia, adopt the Greek faith and with it a change of name.
[2] The Strogonoffs, ancestors of Count Strogonoff, were wealthy landholders of the province of Nijny-Novgorod, in the sixteenth century. Yermak, a Cossack chieftain, had given them much trouble by ravaging their estates.

3. Olga Nicholaevna, born September 11 (August 30), 1822; married, July 13 (1), 1846, Charles Frederick Alexander, Prince Royal, now King of Württemberg.

4. Constantine Nicholaevitch, born September 21 (9), 1827; married, September 11 (August 30), 1848, Alexandra Josefovna, previously Alexandra Frederica Henrietta Pauline Marianne Elizabeth, daughter of Joseph, Duke of Saxe-Altenburg. He is grand-admiral and aide-de-camp-general, president of the Council of the Empire, chief of the corps of naval cadets, of the 29th equipage of the fleet, chief of the regiment of hussars of the late Grand-duke Michael Paulovitch, proprietor of the Austrian infantry regiment No. 18, and chief of the 2d regiment of Prussian Hussars of the Rhine, No. 9.

5. Nicholas Nicholaevitch, born August 8 (July 27), 1831; married February 6 (January 25), 1856, Alexandra Petrovna, previously Alexandra Frederica Wilhelmine, daughter of Peter, Prince of Oldenburg. He is general of engineers and aide-de-camp-general, inspector-general of the corps of engineers, of the troops of the Guard, and of all the cavalry, commander-in-chief of the troops of the military circumscription of St. Petersburg, president of the supreme committee of organization and of instruction of the troops, chief of a regiment of grenadiers, of the regiment of Astrakhan Dragoons, of the regiment of Alexander Hussars, and of the first battalion of sappers of the Caucasus, proprietor of the Austrian regiment of

---

About 1580 they bought him off, and hired him to go into Asia and conquer territory for them. He crossed the Ural and subjugated Siberia, which has ever since been a part of the Russian dominions.

hussars No. 2, and chief of the Prussian regiment of cuirassiers No. 5, West Prussia.

6. Michael Nicholaevitch, born October 25 (13), 1832; married, August 28 (16), 1857, Olga Fedorovna, previously Cecilia Augusta, daughter of Leopold, Grand-duke of Baden. He is a general of artillery, grand-master of the artillery, aide-de-camp-general, Governor-General of the Caucasus, chief of a regiment of lancers, of a regiment of dragoons, chief of the regiment of grenadiers, formerly of Taurida, also of the regiment of hussars of White Russia, of a regiment of chasseurs, of the grenadiers of the Caucasus, and of the Black Sea infantry regiment No. 149, proprietor of the Austrian infantry regiment No. 26, and chief of the first regiment of Prussian Hussars of Silesia No. 4.

Alexander Nicholaevitch (the Emperor), married, when Cezarevitch, April 28 (16), 1841, Marie Alexandrovna, previously Maximilienne Wilhelmine Augusta Sophia Marie, daughter of Louis II., Grand-duke of Hesse. She was born August 8 (July 27), 1824. Of this union were born the following children:

1. Nicholas Alexandrovitch, Cezarevitch, born September 20 (8), 1843; died April 24 (12), 1865.

2. Alexander Alexandrovitch, Cezarevitch (since 1865), born March 10 (February 26), 1845; married, November 9 (October 28), 1866, Marie Fedorovna, previously Marie Sophia Frederica Dagmar, daughter of Christian IX., King of Denmark. They have two children: Nicholas Alexandrovitch, born May 18 (6), 1868, who is chief of

the regiment of infantry of Moscow No. 65; and George Alexandrovitch, born May 9 (April 27), 1871, who is chief of the regiment of infantry of Irkutsk No. 93. The Cezarevitch is aide-de-camp-general and lieutenant-general in the suite of the Emperor, chief of the regiment of Cossacks of the Guard, and of the regiment No. 3 of Smolensk, Ataman of all the Cossacks, colonel-proprietor of the Austrian regiment of infantry No. 61, chief of the regiment of dragoons of Perosiasslaff No. 18, of the battalion of Finland tirailleurs No. 9, of the regiment of Astrakhan Grenadiers No. 12, of the regiment of Prussian Lancers of West Prussia No. 1, and second chief of the regiment of the Emperor's Grenadiers of Eriwan.

3. Vladimir Alexandrovitch, born April 22 (10), 1847. He is colonel and aide-de-camp of the Emperor, chief of the regiment of dragoons of New Russia, of the infantry regiment of Dorpat, of the infantry regiment of Samour No. 83, and of the regiment of Prussian Hussars of Thuringia No. 12.

4. Alexis Alexandrovitch, born January 14 (2), 1850. He is captain and aide-de-camp of the Emperor, chief of the regiment of infantry of Ekatherinenburg, of the first company of the equipage of the Finland fleet, and a lieutenant in the navy. He visited the United States in 1871.[1]

5. Marie Alexandrovna, born October 17 (5), 1853.

6. Sergius Alexandrovitch, born May 11 (April 29), 1857. He is chief of the second battalion of Chasseurs of the Guard, and of the infantry regiment of Tobolsk.

[1] Appendix E.

7. Paul Alexandrovitch, born October 3 (Sept. 21), 1860. He is chief of the infantry regiment of Kura, and of the hussar regiment of the Guard (Hussars of Grodno).

Immediately after the reception of Mr. Fox, Mr. Clay had the honor to present to his Imperial Majesty the following gentlemen: Commanders Murray and Beaumont, and Messrs. Green, Loubat, and Van Buren.

The Emperor then addressed a few words to Mr. Fox, and asked several questions of the others, after which the mission retired.

After the audience, Mr. Fox sent a telegram by the Atlantic cable, which had just been laid, to the Honorable Mr. Seward, Secretary of State of the United States, announcing the delivery of the Resolution of Congress. It read as follows:

"William H. Seward, Secretary State, America. Resolution of Congress presented personally to Emperor of Russia at one to-day.   Fox.

"ST. PETERSBURG, *Wednesday, August,* 8, 1866."

This was the first message ever sent from Russia to America by the Atlantic cable.

Mr. Fox having expressed a desire to visit Mr. Komissaroff-Kostromsky, who resided at Peterhof, Mr. Abaza accompanied him and the other gentlemen to his house.

Mr. Fox addressed the savior of the Emperor as follows:

"I have come to express to you my personal respect,

and to congratulate you, in the name of the people of the United States, in having been chosen by Divine Providence to save a life dear not only to Russia, but to the civilized world."

Mr. Abaza translated these words to Komissaroff, who shook hands with Mr. Fox and the gentlemen with him, and expressed his profound gratitude for the honor they had done him.

The party lunched with the Minister of the Court, and, after visiting the grounds and several of the palaces at Peterhof, returned to St. Petersburg at five o'clock P. M.

Meantime, the other officers of the United States vessels had not been forgotten. At half-past ten of the same day that Mr. Fox and the gentlemen accompanying him were presented to the Emperor, Rear-Admiral Lessovsky, with several other members of the Committee of Reception, called for them on the steamer Onega. An hour after they were landed at Peterhof, where they found court-carriages [1] awaiting them. In these they rode through the shady avenues of the park, visited the fountains, the pond of Marly, the isles of Czaritzine (of the Czarina) and of Olgine (of Olga), and the other chief objects of interest in that paradise of nature and of art. They were shown also through the private residence of the Emperor, which is rich in articles of virtu and in pictures.

After visiting the palace of Peterhof, the company returned, at half-past three o'clock, to Monplaisir, in the

[1] Open carriages of a style resembling the hunting equipages of the time of Louis XIV. They are used in Russia by the Imperial Court only.

lower park, where dinner had been prepared for them. After dinner, the baths, the fountains of the old park, and the imperial stables, were inspected, when the carriages were again brought into requisition, and all returned to Monplaisir, where a band of musicians was placed, and a numerous and distinguished company had gathered to see the guests of the Emperor. As usual, the music began with "Hail Columbia" and "Yankee Doodle," which were received enthusiastically by the assemblage.

Two episodes connected with the visit of our officers to Peterhof are worth relating. While passing through the lower garden, near the imperial baths, they met by chance General Todtleben, the hero of Sevastopol. On his being pointed out to them, the Americans expressed a desire to be presented to him. To this the general gladly assented, and the entire party, with feelings of peculiar admiration and regard, shook hands with the world-renowned engineer, who so long and so ably held in check the combined allied forces in that never-to-be-forgotten siege. In parting, they gave him three lusty cheers, which awoke the echoes of Peterhof. The other episode occurred on the island of Czaritzine. An oak-tree was pointed out that grew from an acorn taken from the tree that shades the tomb of Washington. Our officers surrounded the young tree with a feeling akin to religious sentiment. Each reverently plucked a leaf from its branches to carry home with him, to testify how profound is the homage paid in Russia to the memory of the great founder of our republic.

The remainder of the day was spent on the island of Yelaguine, where a grand display of fireworks took place in honor of the Empress, it being the anniversary of her birthday. Night had already fallen when the Onega entered the Little Nevka, and stopped alongside the steam-yacht Neva, belonging to the Minister of the Navy. The banks of the river were lined with spectators. Bonfires blazed, and the stream was literally covered with thousands of row-boats, carrying lanterns and torches. Music resounded everywhere, and on all sides the Onega was greeted with cheers and with our national air. Our officers were received on the yacht Neva by Aide-de-Camp General Crabbe, who invited them to witness the fireworks from his boat. Whichever way they moved, wherever they were seen, they were received with enthusiastic shouts, which proved how heart-felt and sympathetic were the feelings of the masses. Deeply impressed, they responded freely with cheers to the acclamations of the people.

At eleven o'clock the fireworks came to an end, and the party, gratified with the experiences of the day, departed for the Hôtel de France, where apartments had been prepared for them.

August 9th (July 28th).—On Friday morning, Mr. Fox, his secretaries, Commanders Murray and Beaumont, General Clay, and Mr. Jeremiah Curtin, Secretary of the U. S. Legation at St. Petersburg, proceeded to Cronstadt to join the squadron, and assist at the reception of his Majesty, who had signified his desire to visit the ships.

At eleven o'clock, the imperial yacht Alexandria, bearing the "swallow-tailed" flag of the Emperor, was seen approaching the roadstead from the direction of Oranienbaum. As she came within close signal-distance, the Augusta saluted with twenty-one guns, which was answered by the Russian corvette Griden.

The Emperor went first on board the Miantonomoh, accompanied by his Imperial Highness the Cezarevitch, Grand-duke Alexander Alexandrovitch, and by their Imperial Highnesses the Grand-dukes Vladimir Alexandrovitch and Nicholas Nicholaevitch, the elder—brother of the Emperor. With the imperial party were the most distinguished officials. After examining the monitor critically, the Emperor, accompanied by his imperial and official associates, proceeded to the Augusta, where he was received by Mr. Fox, General Clay, Commanders Murray and Beaumont, and all the other officers, with the naval honors usual on such occasions. From the deck of the vessel his Majesty witnessed an imperial salute, fired by the fifteen-inch guns of the Miantonomoh—the first and only salute ever given by this class of guns, whose huge mouths are, by orders of the Navy Department, closed except for war purposes. After a short stay on board the Augusta, the Emperor took his departure. As he left, the yards of the Augusta were manned, an imperial salute was fired, and the officers and crews of the squadron cheered.

Before leaving the Augusta, the Emperor invited General Clay, Mr. Fox, Commander Murray, Commander Beaumont, and Mr. Van Buren, to accompany him to visit the Russian fleet, and witness target-firing from one of the forts. They first boarded the monitor Perun, Captain Karpoff. The Americans were much gratified at the appearance of the ship and her accessories, and at the alacrity with which she was cleared for action when the drums beat to quarters. Thence the party went on the imperial yacht Alexandria to the greater roadstead, where the Russian squadron lay at anchor, and visited the great iron-clad battery, Ne Tronne Menia, which also cleared for action and fired her guns. The artillery practice showed the perfection of drill and discipline, and the Emperor was so pleased with the result that he expressed his satisfaction to Rear-Admiral Likhatcheff and to the captains of the Ne Tronne Menia and the Perun, and ordered a gratuity of money to be distributed among the crews.

The Americans had the honor of lunching with the Emperor on board his yacht. During the repast, his Majesty offered the following sentiment: "I drink to the prosperity of your country, and that the fraternal feelings which now exist may continue forever."

At two o'clock the Alexandria touched at the landing of Fort Paul, when the Emperor, his suite, and his guests, entered the fortress, and took a position on the upper parapet. The signal was given for the gun-practice to begin, by lowering the Emperor's flag on the yacht. Fort Paul immediately hoisted the red flag, and fired the first shotted gun at the target, when Fort Alexander also opened fire. The practice lasted about twenty minutes, and the two targets were riddled with numerous holes. The

Emperor expressed much pleasure with the way in which the artillery was handled, and with the efficiency of the steel guns. The experiments were made under very favorable circumstances, the day being fine and clear, and the sea calm.

After the close of the single-gun practice, the steamer Yermoloff towed out from the port a large floating target to a distance of about three hundred yards, and retired out of range by paying out the cable. Fort Paul then opened fire on this new mark in general discharges. The port-holes were closed, then, on a given signal, the towing was stopped, the ports thrown open, and the guns sighted and fired. After each discharge the steamer towed the target into a new position, so as to represent the movements of a ship.

At four o'clock the firing ceased, and the imperial party again took passage on the Alexandria. When off Fort Mentchikoff, the square imperial standard was hoisted on the yacht. When this flag is raised, a salute is fired from every gun in sight, both on land and sea. Accordingly, the forts and all the ships opened their batteries at the signal, a truly imperial close to the festivities of the day. The Alexandria then returned to Peterhof, whence Mr. Fox and party were sent in a steam-yacht to Cronstadt.

At five o'clock of the same day a grand dinner was given to the mission and to the American officers by the members of the Cronstadt Naval Club.

The cards of invitation read as follows:

"NAVAL CLUB, CRONSTADT.

"SIR: On the occasion of the arrival of the United States squadron in these waters, the members of the Cronstadt Naval Club, wishing to express the sentiments of friendship which they bear toward the citizens of the United States, as well as to show their appreciation of the warmth and heartiness of the reception accorded to the Russian fleets in the cities of New York, Washington, Boston, and San Francisco, have the honor to invite you, in the name of the whole Russian fleet, to a dinner, arranged to take place at five o'clock on Thursday next, July 28th (August 9th) at the Naval Club House.

"For the Directors: A. ASLANBEGOFF."

The two steamers Ijora and Koldounchik were put at the service of the American guests, and, on their arrival at the pier, carriages were ready to convey them to the banquet-hall. A great crowd had assembled in front of the Naval Club House to see the visitors as they entered. As the carriages drove up, they were received with cheers and greeted with the inspiriting strains of "Hail Columbia" from the splendid naval band stationed at the entrance. A committee of naval officers, with whom the Americans had already become acquainted at the breakfast at the club on the 7th, received them at the door, and conducted them, arm-in-arm, to the private dining-room, where were tables elegantly laid with an appetizing "zakuska," [1] and provided with both Russian

[1] In Russia various relishes or *hors-d'œuvres* and several kinds of drinks are served to guests before dinner. This is called "zakuska," and consists

and American drinks. After partaking of the refreshments, hosts and guests adjourned to the grand saloon of the club, where the dinner was served.

On entering the hall, the sight was magnificent. The walls, hung with pictures, flags, and banners, with garlands and wreaths of evergreens; pedestals and niches filled with busts, and with pots of shrubs and rare exotics; the long ranges of tables gleaming with silver and glass, and decorated with flowers; the splendid chandeliers and the hundreds of wax-tapers shedding a brilliant yet soft light over all, gave the scene an air of enchantment, which was heightened by the music of the bands.

One of the most prominent and most tasteful of the decorations was a shield on one of the walls, bearing upon a ground of red cloth the portraits of Washington, Lincoln, and Johnson, encircled with wreaths of flowers and of leaves. The portrait of his Majesty the Emperor, alike adorned with drapery and with garlands, occupied the opposite wall. The Russian and the American ensigns, intertwined and wreathed, were displayed everywhere. The state staircase was brilliantly ornamented with lamps, candelabra, and pots of flowers. Opposite the entrance, amid shrubs and exotics, were placed upon pedestals the busts of Peter the Great and of Alexander II. Two splendid bands occupied the galleries opposite each other, one the orchestra of Ladoff, from St. Petersburg, the other the port band of Cronstadt. The musicians were crowded close to the front by the ladies, who filled

usually of caviar, smoked salmon, herring, olives, pickles, etc., with such drinks as anisette, kümmel, and other cordials.

all the space behind them, anxious to witness the brilliant scene below. The bands played alternately, giving the national airs of the two countries and the most popular selections from the operas. The "Komissaroff March" was also performed during the evening.

The tables were splendidly served. Beside each plate was a bill of fare, printed on heavy card-board, fourteen by nine inches in size, ornamented with beautiful and artistic designs. At the top was a vignette representing the port of Cronstadt, with one of the forts on the right, shipping on the left, and the Miantonomoh passing in the foreground. In a circle above was "1866," and beneath, "Miantonomoh's Arrival at Cronstadt." Surrounding the vignette was a chain-cable, which hung below it, supporting a shield on which was the bill of fare. On each side of the vignette was the coil of a hempen cable, in which were the names of distinguished men of each country. In the left coil were "862," the year of the foundation of the Russian Empire, and the names of "Vladimir Ravnoapostolnoy,[1] Dmitry Donskoy,[2] Peter the Great, Alexander II.;" in the right, "1492," the date of America's discovery, and "Columbus, Washington, Fulton, Lincoln." On the sides, beneath the coils, was a sailor of each nation, standing on a ship's yard, each holding the flag of his country, the two ensigns being crossed beneath the

---

[1] Vladimir the Apostle, the ruler of all Russia from A. D. 980 to 1015, when he died. In 988 he married the sister of the Emperor of Constantinople, and was baptized in the Greek Church on his wedding-day. The following year he ordered the introduction of Christianity into his dominions.

[2] Dmitry IV., who defeated the Mongols, in 1380, at the battle of Kulikoff, on the banks of the Don (hence his surname Donskoy, of the Don).

vignette. On loops of ribbon were the names, glorious in naval history, of Gangudd, Tchesma, Revel, Navarino, Sinope, Sevastopol, Lake Erie, Plattsburg Bay, New Orleans, Charleston, Mobile, Fort Fisher.

Gangudd, or Gangout (Hangoud, Hango Udde, Hango Head), is a promontory on the north coast of the Gulf of Finland, near its entrance. Peter the Great, acting as *schaubenacht* (commodore) of the fleet commanded by Admiral Apraxine, attacked, with a number of galleys, a Swedish fleet stronger than his own, July 28, 1714, and defeated it. The Swedes, under the command of Rear-Admiral Ehrenschield, lost nine hundred and thirty-six men in the engagement, five hundred and seventy-seven of whom were made prisoners, among the latter being the commander himself. The Russians captured one frigate of twenty guns, six galleys of fourteen guns each, and three smaller vessels of four guns each. For this gallant action, Peter the Great was advanced by the Senate to the rank of rear-admiral.

Tchesma, or Tchesme, is a village of Anatolia, Asia Minor, opposite the island of Scio, and about forty miles west-southwest of Smyrna. In 1770, a Russian squadron, under the orders of the celebrated Count Alexis Orloff and of Admiral Spiridioff, attacked, with fire-ships, and totally destroyed, the Turkish fleet, which had sought refuge in the bay. Rear-Admiral Greig, the grandfather of Aide-de-camp-General Greig, greatly distinguished himself in this action.

Revel, a seaport-town of Esthonia, in a large bay on the south side of the Gulf of Finland, was captured by the Russians, under Peter the Great, from the Swedes, in 1710. In the reign of Catherine II., a fleet commanded by the Crown-Prince of Sweden attacked the Russian fleet in the bay, and was totally defeated. A fine painting of this brilliant action hangs in the Navy Club at Cronstadt.

Navarino, Sinope, and Sevastopol, names glorious in Russian annals, are too well known to need description.

The *menu* was as follows, being printed in both Russian and English:

>Sterlet-soup (Tcha).
>Printanier.
>Koulebiaka.
>Bouchées à la Reine.
>Rissolles.
>Timballes à la chasseur.
>Roast-beef.
>Gatchina trout, with fresh butter.
>Chicken, minced à la d'Orléans.
>Snipe, stuffed with truffles.
>Punch, à la Victoria.
>Cauliflower.
>Artichokes à la Lyonnaise.
>Peas à l'Anglaise.
>Young capons.
>Grouse.
>Quail, wood-hen.
>Salad.
>Fruit-cake à la Portugaise.
>Ices.
>Fruits, bonbons.
>Tea, coffee.

Beneath the shield, on which was the bill of fare, was a scroll containing the programme of the music played by the two bands during the evening. It was as follows:

I.	March (Op. Life for the Czar)	Glinka.
1.	Komissaroff March	Schubert.
II.	Overture (Op. Martha)	Flotoff.
2.	Potpourri, Italian Opera	Metadorff.
III.	Dagmar Waltz	Ladoff.
3.	Potpourri, Ballet, Daughter of Pharaoh	Punny.
IV.	Potpourri, Op. Masquerade	Verdi.
4.	Potpourri, Ballet, Kaniok Gorbounok	Punny.
V.	Bohemian Songs	Ladoff.
5.	Polka	Strauss.
VI.	Kamarenskaya	Glinka.
6.	Potpourri, Russian Song	Derfelt.
VII.	Yankee Doodle	
7.	Galop	Schulhoff.

Besides Mr. Fox and his secretaries, Messrs. Green and Lonbat, there were present at this dinner the United States minister, Mr. Clay, the Secretary of Legation, Mr. Curtin, Commanders Murray and Beaumont, and all the officers of the Miantonomoh and Augusta who could be spared from duty.

Among the distinguished Russian naval officers present were Vice-Admiral Crabbe, aide-de-camp-general of the Emperor and Minister of the Navy; Admiral Novossilsky, aide-de-camp-general of the Emperor, Governor-General of Cronstadt, and commandant-in-chief of the port of Cronstadt; Rear-Admiral Lessovsky, of the suite of the Emperor, vice-commandant of the port of Cronstadt, and commandant of the Russian fleet in America in 1863; Lieutenant-General Greig, Assistant Minister of Finances; Rear-Admiral Popoff, of the suite of the Emperor; Rear-Admiral Galitzine, of the suite of the Emperor; Vice-Admiral Choulepnikoff, commandant of the fortress of Cronstadt; Vice-Admiral Zelenoy, chief of the Hydrographical Bureau and president of the Scientific Committee of the Navy Department; Major-General Zelenoy, commander of the school of pilots; Major-General Tiesenhausen, of the engineers, under whose directions the new docks of Cronstadt are building; Captain Vsevolojsky, port-captain of Cronstadt; Colonel Pestitch, commandant of the naval artillery of Cronstadt; and many others.

Four of these gentlemen, Admirals Crabbe, Novosilsky, Lessovsky, and Popoff, are well known to Americans, a part through their intimate relations with the mission while in Russia, and the two latter through their memorable visits to this country.

Admiral Crabbe won distinction first in the Black Sea. When lieutenant in command of a gunboat during a landing made by the Russian fleet on the coast of Circassia (Tcherkessia), he attacked the enemy in flank and routed him, which greatly facilitated operations in that quarter. On account of this important service, General Raevsky, the commander-in-chief of the west coast of Circassia, put him on his staff. After distinguishing himself further in several engagements with the same foe, Lieutenant Crabbe was sent to the Baltic, where Prince Mentchikoff appointed him his aide-de-camp. In this position Captain Crabbe served through the Crimean War, and for his gallantry was named aide-de-camp to the Emperor. He soon became admiral and director of the inspection-bureau of the department of the navy, and afterward, through the regular grades, aide-de-camp-general to the Emperor and Minister of the Navy.

Admiral Crabbe succeeded to the charge of the navy at a difficult period in Russian history. After the Crimean War great reforms became necessary. A fleet of steamers was about organizing when the Polish insurrection broke out, and diplomatic troubles arose with England and France which threatened Russia with a new foreign war. There were no iron-clads in the navy, the imperial dock-yards were not prepared to build vessels of the new models, and private resources were limited. But the times were urgent, and a navy had to be constructed on a wholly new plan. Admiral Crabbe proved to be equal to the difficult task. In 1862, '63, and '64, under the auspices of the Grand-duke Constantine, he created an iron-clad fleet, consisting of two frigates, the Sevastopol and the Petropaulovsk; three batteries, the Perventez, the Ne Tronne Menia, and the Kremlin; ten single-turreted monitors and a double-turreted gunboat, the Smertch; and, in the mean time, immense works were executed in the imperial navy-yards. Private enterprise received a great impetus, and Admiral Crabbe, animated by the patriotic desire of freeing Russia from foreign vassalage, encouraged and aided Russian naval contractors. With the resources of the navy department at his disposal, he caused to be built the works of Mr. Abukhoff, where steel rifled guns of twelve-inch calibre are now made. Since his administration the rule has been adopted that all ships and machinery shall be made in the imperial navy-yards, or, if given to private enterprise, that the contractor shall employ none but Russian workmen, and use none but Russian material.

Admiral Novossilsky came into prominence in the war with Turkey in 1828, by aiding in the gallant defence of the brig Mercur (Mercury), of which he was second in command, in the Black Sea. One morning, on the rising of a dense fog, the Russians were surprised at finding their vessel between two Turkish men-of-war. The commander, Captain Kazarsky, was equal to the situation. He determined to die rather than surrender his ship, and it was agreed by the officers that, if it became necessary, the last survivor should blow up the magazine with his pistol. Inspired by their heroism, the crew fought desperately, and the brig was extricated from her perilous position. In remembrance of their bravery, the Emperor authorized each of the officers to emblazon a pistol in his coat-of-arms. Admiral Novossilsky is now the sole survivor of the gallant band.

In the battle of Sinope, Admiral Novossilsky was rear-admiral and second in command of the Russian fleet. On account of that ever-memorable action, he was promoted to vice-admiral, and made a Commander of the Order of St. George, one of the highest honors in Russia, being given only for the most distinguished military service. During the siege of Sevastopol he commanded Bastion No. 4, called by the French the Bastion of Death (*Bastion de la Mort*).

Admiral Lessovsky, now (1873) vice-admiral and aide-de-camp-general, is a sailor of whom Russia may well be proud. The true type of a naval officer of our times, he knows but one motto—"Duty and honor." After graduation at the Naval Academy at St. Petersburg, he was ordered to the Black Sea, where he soon became conspicuous. In 1853 Captain Lessovsky was sent on a special mission to Japan in the frigate Aurora. Having fulfilled his duties, he was preparing to leave when an earthquake occurred, followed by a typhoon which blew his ship ashore in the Bay of Simoda. Through his indefatigable exertions and presence of mind, his crew were all saved. Unwilling to remain inactive in Japan, when the war with the allied powers was raging, he built a cutter with the aid of his men alone, and put to sea in her. He navigated the little craft safely through the enemy's cruisers to the Amoor River, the entrance of which was intrusted to him to defend. With limited resources at command, he erected fortifications so strong that the enemy's vessels were kept in check during the entire war.

At the close of the conflict, Captain Lessovsky was made captain of the port of Cronstadt. In 1863, as rear-admiral, he commanded the fleet which visited this country, and did so much to strengthen the bonds between the two nations. On his return, he was promoted to the suite of the Emperor. In 1865, the Mediterranean fleet under his command performed the sad duty of carrying home to Russia, on the Alexander Nevsky, the mortal remains of the ever-to-be-regretted Cezarevitch Nicholas Alexandrovitch. In 1866 Admiral Lessovsky was made assistant to Admiral Novossilsky, governor-general and commander-in-chief of the port of Cronstadt. The following year he succeeded to this important position. He soon became vice-admiral and aide-de-camp-general to the Emperor, and in 1872 was made assistant-minister of the Navy.

Rear-Admiral Popoff distinguished himself greatly in the Black Sea, in 1854-'55. When the allied fleets came in sight of Sevastopol, he went out from under the forts on the steamer Tamane, and spent a night in the midst of the enemy's ships. He was discovered and pursued, but succeeded in escaping to Odessa, where he carried the first news of the landing of the allies in the Crimea. While the Russian fleet was blockaded in Sevastopol, he made frequent sorties, and burned several vessels near Constantinople and in sight of Varna. During the siege he had charge of the difficult duty of supplying the ports and batteries with material. At the close of the war he was made aide-de-camp of the Emperor. He was twice in command of the Russian fleet in the Pacific, in 1858 and in 1863, in both of which years he visited San Francisco, and left such everlasting souvenirs. At present there is constructing at Cronstadt, from the plans and entirely new ideas of Aide-de-Camp-General and Vice-Admiral Popoff, the most powerful armored vessel in the world, a double-turreted monitor, to which the Emperor has given the illustrious name of Peter the Great; and in the Black Sea are building two iron-clads of peculiar form, on new principles of his invention.

Besides those connected with the navy, there were present many noted officials belonging to other departments of the Government. Among them were Prince Gagarine, privy-councillor and president of the Council of Ministers; Lieutenant-General Count Schuvaloff, aide-de-camp-general of the Emperor, and chief of the third section (gendarmerie) of the privy cabinet of the Emperor; Lieutenant-General Todtleben, aide-de-camp-general of the Emperor, and director-general of engineers; Lieutenant-General Zelenoy, aide-de-camp-general of the Emperor, Minister of the Demesnes; Count Tolstoy, privy-councillor, Minister of Public Instruction; Mr. de Reutern, privy-councillor, Minister of Finances; and Mr. Tatarinoff, privy-councillor, and Comptroller-General of the Empire. Prince Gortchakoff was prevented from attending, by illness.

The city of Cronstadt was represented by the mayor, Mr. Stephanoff; Messrs. Koudriavtzoff and Nikitine, members of the municipality; the honorary citizen, Mr. Baikoff; and the distinguished merchants, Messrs. Blinoff, Vassilieff, Mouracheff, Ossetroff, and Taicssoff. There were in all about four hundred and fifty guests.

The dinner passed off in the most brilliant manner. After the several courses, sentiments were offered and responses made by a number of the principal gentlemen, which were received with enthusiasm. Admiral Lessovsky acted as interpreter, translating into Russian the English speeches, and the Russian into English. The first toast was to the Emperor, after which Mr. Fox made a brief but telling speech, which elicited great applause. He spoke of the friendliness existing between Russia and America, which dated from the armed neutrality of Catherine II., and of the indebtedness of our country to Alexander II., who, in the darkest hour of our trials, when the other sovereigns of Europe stood aloof, sent us words of sympathy, which had united the two nations in friendship forever.

Toasts followed to the Grand-duke Constantine; to "Our Teachers, the Americans;" to the Russian Navy; to Commanders Murray, Beaumont, and the officers of their ships; to General Todtleben, by Commodore Murray; and by the gallant general himself, to "The Defenders of Sevastopol and the Conquerors of Sinope."

After the toasts were ended, many of the older officers retired, when the room was cleared. The scene then became very lively. All the American guests were treated to a peculiarly Russian custom—a tossing in the air at the hands of their hosts. The sensation is any thing but an agreeable one, but, as it is considered a mark of honor of the highest character, it was submitted to with a good grace by all who were subjected to it.

This dinner, the first of the many given to the mission, was heartily enjoyed by all the Americans. The kindly and cordial reception by the gentlemen of the Imperial Navy, the magnificence of the entertainment, the warmth and sincerity that characterized the speeches, left an impression that time cannot efface. Unfortunately, no report was made, at the time, of the speeches and toasts, and the description of the dinner is necessarily a brief one.

The Russian navy has made a great advance of late years, both in the character of its shipping and of its *personnel*. It now (1873) comprises among its vessels three iron-clad frigates, five turreted frigates, three iron-clad batteries, ten single-turreted monitors, three iron-clad gunboats, and probably the most powerful ship afloat, the double-turreted monitor, Peter the Great. These vessels are armed with fifteen-inch and twenty-inch Rodman smooth-bore guns, and with cast-steel rifles of eight-inch, nine-inch, and twelve-inch calibre. There are also two large steam sloops-of-war, the Alexander Nevsky, and the General Admiral, half wood and half iron-clad, built from plans of Admiral Popoff, each carrying eight rifled guns of the largest calibre, which are intended to be used as fast cruisers, in case of war, to destroy an enemy's shipping. The officers and crews on all the ships are picked men. The former are thoroughly instructed in naval science, and are animated by an *esprit de corps* which would make them dangerous adversaries to contend with. The sailors are well drilled, as all can testify who saw how easily the ships of Admirals Lessovsky and Popoff were worked and manœuvred when in this country.

CHAPTER VII.

CRONSTADT—THE ARSENAL—THE STEAMSHIP-WORKS—THE MUNICIPAL BANQUET.

AUGUST 10th (*July* 29th).—This morning Mr. Fox, accompanied by his secretaries, Messrs. Green and Loubat, visited the Vladimir and the Dmitry Donskoy, to return the calls of Admirals Likhatcheff and Butakoff. He was received on each vessel with a salute of seventeen guns, the American ensign being hoisted to the fore. The Augusta acknowledged the compliment with a similar salute, and the Russian ensign at the fore.

At half-past twelve o'clock a deputation of Russian officers met the officers of the American squadron at the Petrovsky landing, and escorted them to the arsenal, where they were received by Colonel Pestitch, commandant of artillery at Cronstadt. He showed them much politeness, and called their attention to the various objects of interest preserved in this great collection of arms and trophies. Our officers were particularly struck by the many captured battle-flags, the glorious records of Russia's naval prowess, and by the collection of models of Russian men-of-war. The latter, which occupy a special chamber, constitute an almost complete history of Russian naval architecture. A plan of Cronstadt, its environs and fortifications, executed in relief with the most minute care and artistic finish, was examined also with great interest.

From the arsenal the party went to the summer-house of the Navy Club, where a lunch awaited them. Here they were joined by deputations from the Club of the Nobility and from the Merchants' Mutual Aid Society, who had come with invitations to banquets at their respective clubs. After lunch, they visited the steamship workshops, then in full operation, where they were most cordially received by the director, Lieutenant-Colonel Sokaloff, who showed them through the establishment. The works are remarkable for their extent, for their admirable mechanical appliances, and for the order and system everywhere displayed. They would be a credit to any country.

Colonel Sokaloff having put a steamer at the disposal of the party, the landing-place of the new docks was next visited. After examining the works there, remarkable for their gigantic dimensions, they returned to the steamboat-shops, and went thence to the Naval Observatory, where they arrived about four o'clock. The hour intervening between this and the time of the municipal dinner, to which they were invited at five o'clock, was spent in examining the observatory, and in resting after their long walk.

At five o'clock, carriages called for the officers at the observatory, and conveyed them to the City Hall, where the banquet given in their honor by the civil authorities of Cronstadt was to take place. The municipality of the city is entirely distinct from the government officials, being elected by the people, as in the United States.

The invitations to this dinner were as follows:

"SIR: The Mayor of Cronstadt, in the name of the municipal corporation, requests the favor of your company to dinner, on Friday next, July 29th (August 10th), at the Town Hall, five P. M.

"*July 26, 1866.*"

Gospodskaïa Street, in which is situated the Town Hall, was literally obstructed by crowds of people, who had flocked in from all directions to see the strangers, and it was with no little difficulty that the carriages made their way to the entrance. Our officers were welcomed at the door with "Hail Columbia" from a military band, and with loud and repeated cheers from the multitude.

The steps and the great staircase were covered with rich carpets, and the halls were decorated with flowers and garlands, and hung with the Russian and American colors. On the walls of the reception-hall were the portraits of Alexander II., of Washington, Lincoln, and Johnson, and of Komissaroff-Kostromsky, all wreathed with flowers and greens.

At the entrance of Mr. Fox and the American officers, they were received with a cordial welcome by the officers of the feast. The presence of Komissaroff-Kostromsky, the savior of the Emperor's life, was particularly gratifying to them, and those who had not yet been presented to him sought an introduction. The young man appeared to be much affected by the attentions showered upon him.

At half-past five the invited guests marched, to the sound of music, to the grand dining-room, each American walking arm-in-arm with one of the managers of the banquet. The dinner was admirably served, and the floral decorations and ornaments were unexcelled. The place of each guest had been marked in advance, the seats being so distributed as to place next to each American a Russian who could speak English. Beside each plate was the card of the dinner and the programme of the music to be played.

The bill of fare was a fine work of art, printed in gold on sheets of glazed Bristol board, twelve by nine inches in size. At the top, between the Russian mercantile and the American flags, were two clasped hands, surrounded by a wreath of oak-leaves. Directly beneath were "1866" and "Dinner, July 29." On the sides were broadsides of men-of-war, with anchors, cables, and other naval paraphernalia; and, on the bottom, the arms of the city of Cronstadt, with Mercury, the protector of commerce, and Neptune, the ruler of the seas, on each side, as supporters.

The arms of Cronstadt are worthy of a passing note. They are *azure* and *gules per pale;* in the first, a light-house, *argent;* in the second, a kettle, *sable*, on an island, *vert*. It is said that Peter the Great, at the time of the founding of Cronstadt, picked up a broken iron kettle on the island, where it had been left, probably, by fishermen; and, in commemoration of the circumstance, gave it to the new city for its arms.

The *menu* of the dinner, which was furnished by the celebrated *restaurateur* of St. Petersburg, Dusaux, was as follows:

Soups.
- Fresh-cabbage soup.
- Crawfish-soup.
- Printanier.
- Turtle-soup (à la Française).

Pies.
- Bouchées à la Reine.
- Rissoll.
- Timballes à la Monglas.
- Fish-pies.

Filets de bœuf and veal, with vegetables.
Sterlets à la Russe and river-trout.
Woodcock with truffles.
Punch à la Romaine.
Vegetables: peas, cauliflowers, and beans.
Roasts: Bohemian pheasants, great snipe, chicken, grouse, partridges.
Salad.
Fruit pudding à la Nelson.
Ices of different descriptions.
Fruits.
Confectionery.
Coffee.
Yellow tea.

During the dinner delightful music was furnished by two bands, the orchestra led by Ladoff, of St. Petersburg, and the port band of Cronstadt. Besides the national airs of Russia and of America, and selections from Italian operas, were performed the "Columbia Quadrilles," composed for the occasion by the chief-of-orchestra Reinboldt.

About one hundred and fifty guests sat down at the

tables. Among the distinguished persons present, in addition to the city officials and their American guests, were Mr. Lilienfeld, president of the regency of the district of Peterhof; Mr. Atriganieff, marshal of the nobles of the district of Peterhof; Admiral Novossilsky, the military governor of Cronstadt; Rear-Admirals Lessovsky and Popoff; the chief of staff of the commander-in-chief of the port of Cronstadt; and all the authorities of Cronstadt, both of land and sea.

When the champagne was brought on, the Mayor of Cronstadt, Mr. Philip Stephanoff, gave the first toast to the health of the Emperor, accompanying it with the following words:

"This day is to us a fête-day. We see among us guests who are dear to us, who have come from across the ocean with congratulations for the happy safety of the precious life of the Emperor, the liberator; and I propose to them to give with us a toast to the 'Health and long life of our Sovereign.'" (Hurrah!)

This toast, which was given in the Russian language, was translated into English by Admiral Lessovsky, who also translated the English toasts and speeches into Russian.

The mayor's loyal sentiment was received with loud and enthusiastic cheers, which were mingled with the solemn strains of the Russian national hymn.

Mayor Stephanoff then gave the "Health of the President of the United States," which was greeted with acclamations no less enthusiastic and prolonged.

When the cheering had subsided, Mr. Fox responded as follows:

"Gentlemen, I desire to propose to you the health of an exalted person, whose preëminent virtues have awakened our profound admiration; an admiration not dependent on political creeds, nor international relations, but founded on the principles of our mutual Christian faith, and, like them, imperishable—her Imperial Majesty the Empress."

This sentiment created the liveliest satisfaction, exhibited by repeated bravos.

At their termination Mr. Baikoff gave the "Health of the Cezarevitch and of all the Imperial Family," which elicited another outburst of cheers.

The mayor then gave the "Health of the Hon. G. V. Fox, the Envoy of the American Congress," which was received with the most enthusiastic applause.

Mr. Nikitine then arose to speak:

"We, the citizens of Cronstadt," he said, "seize this opportunity to offer to the honorable representative of a great and glorious nation, Mr. Fox, our sincere and cordial congratulations for the sympathy and friendship shown by the American for the Russian people, on the occasion of the 4th of April, so feelingly expressed in the Resolution of the Congress of the United States of America. This sympathy is precious to Russians. The citizens of America, in the persons of their representatives here with us to-day, share in the joy of our entire people for the safety of the life of our beloved sovereign; and it is therefore, gentlemen, that I propose a toast to the guests of to-day's banquet, to the 'Citizens of the great American Republic.'" (Hurrah!)

After the cheering had subsided, Mr. Baikoff gave the "Health of General Clay, Minister Plenipotentiary of the United States of America to the Court of Russia."

Mr. Clay responded:

"As representing the Republic of the United States of America, I am, of course, a republican; and it would be difficult to find on either side of the ocean a more fervent republican than I am; but, after living in a country which possesses a monarchical form of government, I am convinced that monarchy may be the best form of government, when at its head is found a man the best and most virtuous of earth. My honorable friend, Mr. Fox, a sincere democrat also, will not fail to be alike convinced when he has lived some time longer in Russia; and this is why I think it my duty to propose a toast to the whole of Russia: 'To the Russian Government, to the Russian Navy, to the Russian Army, and to all the Citizens of Russia!'"

Loud and prolonged applause followed this speech, after which the mayor gave the "Health of Commanders Murray and Beaumont, and of the Officers of the American Squadron," which was duly acknowledged by Commander Murray.

Toasts to the "Health of the Commander-in-Chief of the Port of Cronstadt," and to "The Mayor of the City," followed; the first by the mayor, the second by Admiral Novossilsky. All the toasts were received with applause.

Mr. Nikitine then proposed the health of a person

dear to all Russians—of "Komissaroff-Kostromsky." Russians and Americans arose and touched glasses with him. The cheers within the hall were echoed by the crowd in the street until it seemed as if the hurrahs would never cease. Komissaroff was visibly affected by the enthusiasm with which his name was received.

Mr. Nikitine then spoke as follows:

"Among the reforms of the present reign, one of the greatest is that of local self-government, which summons our country to an independent intellectual activity; and I therefore propose a toast to the 'Success of Provincial Administration in Russia,' and I join with it the names of the honorable gentlemen of the Assembly of Peterhof now present with us, Messrs. Lilienfeld and Atriganieff." (Cheers.)

Mr. Lilienfeld responded by a long and eloquent speech, showing the great importance of Cronstadt, which, surrounded with fortresses of granite, and defended by impenetrable monitors, is the bulwark of the empire. He closed with the wish that nothing in Russia might prove an obstacle to the great and benevolent reforms which open for her a new era, an era of equitable and independent justice, an era of social and national development.

Prolonged hurrahs followed Mr. Lilienfeld's remarks, after which Mr. Mouracheff proposed a toast to the "Indissoluble Friendship of Russia and the United States of America." (Loud cheers.)

Mr. Curtin, the secretary of the American Legation,

then spoke in the Russian language, which he had learned to use with fluency during his residence in St. Petersburg. He said:

"When Peter the Great had opened a window looking toward Europe, he founded Cronstadt, and created there a military fleet to be the guardian of that window. The fleet of the Baltic has fulfilled sacredly the duty which the great reformer of Russia bequeathed to it. For more than a century have Cronstadt and her fleet jealously guarded their sacred post, and none of the many enemies that have attacked Russia have been able to close that window, and I am fully persuaded that no one in the future will be able to close it. I therefore beg leave, gentlemen, to propose a toast to the 'City and Fortress of Cronstadt, to the Russian sailors in general, and to all the present inhabitants of Cronstadt.'"

Mr. Curtin's speech in the Russian tongue, and his happy allusion to a verse of Pushkin's, one of Russia's most popular poets, that Peter the Great had opened a window into Europe, created a tremendous burst of applause, loud and prolonged.

A toast given by Mayor Stephanoff, to Admiral Lessovsky and the Russian officers and sailors who were with him in the United States, was also greeted with cheers.

Other toasts given toward the end of the dinner were to the prosperity of commerce between Russia and the United States; to Mr. de Stoeckl, the Russian minister at Washington, by the Hon. Mr. Fox; to the people, to the army and the navy of the United States; to the statesmen and public men of Russia; and, lastly, to the

American and the Russian ladies, by Commander Beaumont.

After dinner the guests retired to the reception-rooms, and enjoyed an animated conversation while they took their tea and coffee. In one of the rooms punch was preparing in the Russian style. It is made of rum, sugar, fruits, etc., set on fire, and, after burning for some time, is quenched with champagne. The Americans, attracted by the blue flames, gathered around the table on which stood the silver bowl. This was the signal for more speeches, all of which were greeted with the heartiest applause.

When all the ceremonies were concluded, a large number of ladies, belonging to the families of the gentlemen present, came into the hall. On their appearance, one of our officers proposed the health of the Russian ladies, accompanying the toast with a few words in praise of the beauty and courtesy of the fair citizens of Cronstadt. In response to this act of gallantry, a Russian gentleman made a speech, in which he complimented the loveliness and the attractions of the American ladies, and the cordiality with which they received the Russians when in the United States.

At ten o'clock in the evening the guests separated. The people still pressed in a solid mass about the building, and it was with the greatest difficulty that our officers could reach their carriages. At last all were safely seated, and the carriages rolled away, amid a tempest of hurrahs such as only Russian throats can give.

Thus ended the reception in Cronstadt.

CHAPTER VIII.

ST. PETERSBURG—ST. ISAAC'S—THE FÊTE OF THE RIVER YACHT CLUB—CZARSKOË-SELO.

AUGUST 11*th* (*July* 30*th*).—On Saturday Mr. Fox left officially for St. Petersburg. He was accompanied by his secretaries, by Commanders Murray and Beaumont, and by about twenty-five other officers. All the officers of the squadron were invited by the Emperor, but, as it was impossible for all to accept at once, they were obliged to alternate. Under the escort of Admiral Lessovsky and others of the Russian members of the committee of reception, the party took passage on the Onega. The little steamer flew the American flag at the fore, and all of the many boats that met her were similarly decked. Although the day was cloudy and threatened rain, most of them were filled with people, who greeted the Onega with cheers and wavings of hats and handkerchiefs, while the bands played "Hail Columbia."

All the Americans were furnished with guide-books to Russia, in the English language, and also with manuals of Russian conversation, during the passage, by the committee of reception.

The Onega steamed into the Neva, and landed at the English quay, where a multitude of people was assembled to see the visitors. Mr. Fox was greeted with loud and enthusiastic cheers as he crossed the gang-plank, and it was with some difficulty that a passage was made for him to his carriage. Admiral Lessovsky took a seat beside Mr. Fox in the first barouche, and the rest of the party followed, Russians and Americans mingled, in other open carriages.

St. Isaac's Cathedral was visited first. This noble structure, probably the finest church in Northern Europe, stands in the great square called Isaac's Place, which extends to the banks of the Neva. It occupies the site of a church originally built by Peter the Great, and dedicated to St. Isaac of Dalmatia, because the city of St. Petersburg was founded on the day sacred to him. Like nearly all of the Greek churches, it is in the form of a Greek cross, with four equal sides, and is surmounted with a cupola of copper overlaid with gold, supported by pillars of polished granite. Each of the four grand entrances is reached by three flights of granite steps, each entire flight chiselled from a single block. The four porticos have monolithic granite columns, sixty feet in height, with Corinthian capitals in bronze.

The magnificent proportions of this cathedral, the grand simplicity of its architecture, and its imposing situation, strike the visitor with awe as he approaches it from the side of the square facing the river. On the left is the Admiralty, its side six hundred and fifty feet in length, its front extending half a mile to the square of the Winter Palace; on the right, the Senate-House and the Holy Synod; and in its front is the colossal equestrian statue of Peter the Great.

The interior of St. Isaac's is as remarkable for its magnificence of decoration as is the exterior for its grandeur and sublimity. Polished variegated marbles of every hue, all from the Russian dominions, splendid columns of malachite and of lapis-lazuli, gilded bronze-work, and pictures and mosaics by Russian artists, present a *coup d'œil* almost impossible to describe. The inmost shrine, presented by Mr. Demidoff,[1] is valued at a million rubles. The Royal Door of the *ikonastas*, or screen, is of bronze, and is twenty-three feet in height by fifteen in breadth. To one accustomed to our plainer edifices of worship, St. Isaac's appears to have an exuberance of decoration, but the grand ceremonial of the Greek Church demands corresponding surroundings.

Mr. Phonin, the inspector, and Mr. Seraphimoff, the pastor of the cathedral, received Mr. Fox and those accompanying him, and conducted them through all parts of the building, finishing by taking them to the lantern on the great dome, whence they had a view of the whole city. Beneath them flowed the Neva and the Little Neva, with their islands of palaces and splendid bridges, their steamers and sailing-craft; and beyond, to the east, the Great Nevka, whose course could be seen almost to the Gulf of Finland. From this point, St. Petersburg ap-

---

[1] Prince of San Donato, in Tuscany.

pears to be, what it really is, a city built amid the waters. As far as the eye can reach, palaces and public buildings, churches and schools, factories and private dwellings, face the rivers and line the canals. Down at one's feet lies the great Admiralty, with the Winter Palace beside it, and the three principal streets of the city diverging from it like the sticks of a fan. These thoroughfares, the Nevsky Prospect, or Neva Perspective, the Gorokhovaïa-Ulitza, or Peas Street, and the Voskresensky Prospect, or Assumption Perspective, intersect the three divisions of the south part of the city made by the canals, and determine the courses of most of the other streets.

St. Petersburg is a city of magnificent distances. Every thing is on a large scale. It has broad streets, noble squares, long perspectives, and grand monuments of art. Its only drawback is, that it is built on a dead level, with no elevation to relieve the monotony or to give it picturesqueness. The splendor of its structures is thus, in a measure, hidden. But a more intimate acquaintance with its architectural wonders convinces one that it is little behind the more ancient capitals of Europe in beauty or in interesting associations.

Before leaving St. Isaac's, Mr. Phonin, the inspector, presented to Mr. Fox a plan and description of the cathedral. It is a comparatively new building, even where every thing is of the present, having been begun in 1819, by Alexander I., and consecrated in 1858, by Alexander II. Its foundation alone, of piles driven into the swampy soil, is said to have cost over a million dollars. It was built by M. Montferrand, a French architect, who erected also the great Alexander column. If he had never accomplished any other works, these two ought to immortalize his name.

The equestrian statue of Peter the Great is one of the most noted monuments of Europe. The Emperor is reining in his horse on the brink of a precipice, a serpent, writhing under his charger's feet, being emblematic of the difficulties which beset the founder of Russia's greatness in the beginning. The block of granite which forms the pedestal weighs fifteen hundred tons, and was brought from Lakhta, in Finland, four miles from the city. The transportation of this immense monolith to its present site was effected by Count Marino Carburis, a Greek engineer in the Russian service, to whom Catherine II. intrusted the work. The stone, a detached mass of granite, lay embedded fifteen feet deep in a swamp. How to raise it from its position and convey it to St. Petersburg was a problem which daunted the ablest engineers. But Carburis invented a machine which overcame the mechanical difficulties, and under his superintendence it was safely shipped to the banks of the Neva and moved thence by land to its appointed site, where it was erected September 30, 1769. This was considered so wonderful an engineering feat, that the apparatus with which it was effected was placed, at the request of the French Government, in the *Conservatoire des Arts et Métiers*, at Paris.

On each of the two sides are the following simple but noble inscriptions, in Russian and in Latin:

Петру Первому, Екатерина Вторая.
Petro Primo, Catharina Secunda.
MDCCLXXXII.

The bronze statue, which is seventeen and a half feet in height, was the work of the celebrated French sculptor, Étienne Maurice Falconet, who executed it in St. Petersburg, in 1776, by order of Catherine II. It is considered his greatest work. The horse, which is rearing, is supported by the hinder legs and tail, the latter being ingeniously connected with a coil of the serpent, which is fastened firmly to the rock.

From St. Isaac's Place the party were driven to the Hôtel de France, where they took possession of the rooms provided for them by the Emperor's orders. They found every thing needful put at their disposal, free of expense —carriages to visit any part of the city, and steam-yachts to return to the ships, or to go to Cronstadt.

At two o'clock a lunch was given to Mr. Fox and suite at the residence of Mr. Clay, the American minister. A large number of government officials and most of the foreign diplomats were present.

The evening was spent with the River Yacht Club of St. Petersburg, whose members gave a special and superb festival in honor of the visitors. The squadron of rowboats belonging to the club went, under the commodore's flag, to meet the Americans near the landing-place of Kamenoy (Stone) Island. Boats were in waiting here for the guests, who, as they took their places, were saluted with oars by the club, a band meanwhile playing the American national airs. Mr. Fox's barge, in which were also Mr. Clay, Mr. Van Buren and his daughter and niece, and Commanders Murray and Beaumont, took the lead, with the commodore's boat, and the little squadron floated gayly down the river, pausing now and then to acknowledge the demonstrations of the people who lined the banks.

When the fleet came in sight of the Club-House, the American flag was hoisted upon the flag-staff, and the yachts, all displaying our colors, fired a salute of twenty-one guns. A military band played "Hail Columbia," and, as the party ascended the landing-steps, an orchestral band took up the same air.

As soon as Mr. Fox and the gentlemen with him had received the greetings of the club, the commodore, Mr. Poznansky, invited him to assist in the launching of a little yacht. Miss Van Buren kindly consented to perform the christening ceremony. As Mr. Fox knocked away the blocks from under the boat, the lady broke a bottle of wine over the bow, and named it the "G. V. Fox."

The evening passed quickly in dancing, promenading, and in social converse. As soon as the darkness set in, fireworks, signals, and blue-lights, were displayed on the river, giving a beautiful and weird appearance to the scene. After the first division of dances, the guests were invited to tea, which was served upon a terrace overlooking the river, whose banks and the boats upon it were hung with countless lanterns. A choir of musicians, stationed at the landing, sung at the same time a number of Russian national songs. At the close of the second part of the programme there was a serenade from illuminated gondolas on the river, the singers chanting the wild songs of the Volga.

After the last division of the dances, supper was served in a beautiful pavilion erected for the occasion, at which were drunk the customary toasts to the President of the United States and to the Emperor of Russia, the latter being given by Mr. Fox. Each of these healths was received with the same enthusiasm which it had inspired everywhere before, and was accompanied with the usual music. During the supper the choir of singers alternated with the band, and another grand illumination took place.

After the ceremony of leave-taking was over and the guests were ready to depart, the band, with the Russian and American flags flying, took its position in front of Mr. Fox's carriage, and the members of the club, forming on each side, escorted the party as far as the first bridge, the road being illuminated by lines of sailors burning blue-lights.

Our officers pronounced this one of the most beautiful entertainments of the kind they ever witnessed. The weather was superb, and nothing occurred to mar the harmony of the arrangements from the beginning to the end. The River Yacht Club of St. Petersburg will never be forgotten by those who enjoyed its hospitalities at this unique *fête*.

August 13*th* (1*st*).—The morning opened rainy, but the sun broke through the clouds early, and the weather became fine. At ten o'clock Mr. Fox, Commanders Murray and Beaumont, Messrs. Green and Loubat, the Russian officers of reception, and other gentlemen, twenty-two in number, started for Czarskoë-Selo, to visit the palace and the arsenal there. On arriving at the railway station, they were met by the directors of the road, who put at their service a special train, made up of the Emperor's carriages. The fifteen miles between St. Petersburg and Czarskoë-Selo were run in twenty minutes. In the imperial waiting-rooms of the station at the latter place they were received by General Gogol, the governor of the palace, who had court carriages in readiness for the party. Rear-Admiral Gorkovenko, who was also present, kindly offered his services as *cicerone*.

Czarskoë-Selo, or the Czar's Village, of all the crown estates in the vicinity of St. Petersburg, has been, for more than a century, one of the most favored resorts of the imperial family. It was built in 1744, in the reign of the Empress Elizabeth, but it has been greatly improved and embellished by succeeding sovereigns, particularly by Catherine II., who expended vast sums on the adornment of the palaces and grounds. The latter, which receive the most careful attention, and are unexcelled in Europe for artificial beauty, are eighteen miles in circumference. The façade of the principal palace, which is seven hundred and eighty feet in length, has an imposing appearance. In the time of Catherine, the capitals of all the columns, the statues, vases, and other ornaments, were overlaid with gold-leaf; but it has now worn off, and no gilding is seen excepting on the dome of the chapel, which occupies a conspicuous position in front.

The interior of the palace is very beautiful, its rooms and halls being decorated with the most costly and tasteful designs, each being a contrast to the other. The Amber Room is the most celebrated, the walls of which are entirely panelled with that precious material, carved and moulded in artistic forms, bass-reliefs, monograms, coats-of-arms, and other appropriate devices. The amber for this room was presented by Frederick the Great to Catherine II., and his arms occupy conspicuous places in the ornamentation. Another room is incrusted with lapis-lazuli, with a floor of ebony inlaid with flowers of mother-of-pearl. Catherine's bedchamber has walls of porcelain with pillars of purple glass. The Chinese Room is ornamented with fantastic designs, and furnished in the style peculiar to the Flowery Kingdom. The ceilings of almost all the state-apartments are lavishly gilded, and the walls of the grand dining-room are covered with gold. The floors are no less beautiful, costly marbles, malachite, lapis-lazuli, and inlaid woods, meeting the eye in every direction.

At the palace, the party were joined by Madame Gogol, her three daughters, and her son, and by several other ladies, many of whom spoke English well. While enjoying a conversation with them on the Grecian Terrace, which overlooks the lake, the Americans had an opportunity of witnessing one of the most striking ceremonies of the Greek Church, the blessing of water. As the procession of long-robed priests passed by, bearing symbolical banners and emblems, and chanting the solemn service, all reverently removed their hats, and paid close attention to the ceremonial, which was to them both grand and novel. The ladies kindly explained to them the meaning of the rite, and of the symbols borne in the procession.

In the afternoon the party enjoyed a drive through the park, and had pointed out to them the various objects of interest: the Palace of Alexander I., the tower where the present Emperor resided with his tutor when heir-apparent, the Turkish kiosk, the marble bridge, the aërial garden, the miniature fleet in one of the lakes, constructed for the amusement of the Grand-duke Constantine when a boy, the Swiss *chalet*, and the many monuments, statues, and commemorative pillars, with which the grounds abound. The Gothic building called the Admiralty, with its miniature dock-yard, was also visited, where a large and fine collection of row-boats was seen. A crowd of people had collected here to see the strangers.

The party called next on Mr. Svertchkoff, celebrated as an animal-painter, who had a temporary studio in a pavilion near by. He showed them some of his works, among others his latest picture, representing a grand review of troops near Moscow by the Czar Alexis. Thence they went to the Dutch farm, also in the park, where a milk lunch was served, and afterward to the Arsenal to see the splendid collection of antique armor and arms. This building is a red-brick structure, in the Gothic style, and was erected by the late Emperor Nicholas for the reception of this museum. It contains a great collection of arms and armor, ancient and modern, of almost all nations. In the centre of the building is a large vaulted hall, where, standing on pedestals at the entrance of the different alcoves, are equestrian figures, fully armed and accoutred for the field. From the ceilings hang captured standards, and upon the walls, arranged in fanciful devices, are the implements of war of all ages and of all countries, Christian and pagan. Many are of great historic or of intrinsic value. Among the latter are numerous weapons studded with diamonds and other precious stones, that have been presented to the different Czars and Emperors by the sovereigns of Europe and of Asia.

At five o'clock the party sat down to dinner in the orange-house adjoining General Gogol's residence. The meal was enlivened with toasts and speeches, but all of a friendly and unofficial character. Admirals Lessovsky and Gorkovenko, and Miss Gogol, the daughter of the host, acted as interpreters and translated the several speeches into Russian or English, as the case demanded. Coffee and yellow tea were served in the garden, and the evening passed in delightful conversation, until the time for the departure for Pavlovsk was announced.

At eight o'clock a special train conveyed the whole company to Pavlovsk, about three miles distant. The directors of the Czarskoë-Selo Railway, which was the first railroad built in Russia, had offered a *fête* in the Vauxhall, at the railway-station, in honor of the mission. The gardens were thronged with the most refined people of St. Petersburg, with whom this is a favorite summer resort. There were said to be twelve thousand persons present. The Vauxhall was illuminated with gas-jets, and the fountains and water-works of the gardens were lit with different-colored electric lights. Opposite the great building an arch was erected, radiant with transparencies and Chinese lanterns. The whole scene was indescribably beautiful, and elicited frequent applause from the spectators.

When Mr. Fox, walking arm-in-arm with Admiral Lessovsky through the dense crowd in the garden, came in front of the orchestra, the band played "Hail Columbia." Every man in the audience removed his hat and remained standing until the close, when the most enthusiastic applause ensued, and the band was forced, at the demand of the people, to repeat the air. During the evening the "Miantonomoh Galop" was played, a new piece of music composed by Mr. Fürstnow, the leader of the orchestra, who presented Mr. Fox, to whom it was dedicated, with a copy.[1]

The following is the programme of the music:

CZARSKOË-SELO RAILWAY.

VAUXHALL AT PAVLOVSK. MONDAY, AUGUST $\frac{1}{13}$, 1866.

AN AMERICAN-RUSSIAN FEAST.

PROGRAMME OF THE MUSIC.

Part I.

1. Hail Columbia and the Russian National Hymn,
2. Overture to the opera "Life for the Czar," . . . *Glinka.*
3. Over Land and Sea, Waltz, ... *Jos. Gungl.*
4. Yankee Doodle, ...
5. Kamarinskaïa, Russian Dance, ... *Glinka.*

---

[1] Appendix C.

Part II.

6. Overture, "Jota Aragonesa," . . . . *Glinka.*
7. Prayer, Solo for Violoncello, with Harp, . . *Warlamoff.*
8. Miantonomoh Galop, dedicated to Captain G. V.
   Fox, ... *H. Fürstnow.*
9. Bouquet of Russian Melodies, ... *Schubert.*

Part III.

10. Overture, "Rousslan and Ludmilla," . . . *Glinka.*
11. Komissaroff Polka, ... *H. Fürstnow.*
12. Finale of the opera "Life for the Czar," . . *Glinka.*

A Military Band will play between the Parts.

GAS ILLUMINATION AND ELECTRIC LIGHTS.

After the music was ended the party were invited into the hall to a supper spread in the great railway-station, which was attended with the usual speeches, toasts, and manifestations of good feeling. In response to the loud calls of the crowd outside, Mr. Fox made a few appropriate remarks from one of the windows, concluding by giving a toast to the health of the Emperor. His words were received with deafening cheers, and Commanders Murray and Beanmont were then obliged to show themselves in a similar manner, in compliance with the popular wish.

At midnight the whistle of the coming train put an end to the festivities. While waiting in the station, which was carpeted and brilliantly lighted, a crowd of people, chiefly ladies, pressed around the car in which the Americans were seated. As the warning bell rang, the gentlemen cheered, and the ladies waved their handkerchiefs. Mr. Fox drew some flowers from a bouquet he held and presented them to a young lady near him, who was particularly demonstrative in her applause. She accepted them with blushes, and her companions pressed to the windows for similar souvenirs. The gentlemen hastily distributed their bouquets, and the train moved from the platform amid a tempest of hurrahs.

CHAPTER IX.

THE ADMIRALTY—IMPERIAL LIBRARY—WINTER PALACE AND HERMITAGE—DINNER TO THE CREWS.

AUGUST 14*th* (2*d*).—Tuesday opened bright and clear. At ten o'clock Mr. Fox and party went, in company with Admiral Lessovsky and a number of other Russian officers, to visit the Admiralty. This great building, which is nearly half a mile in length on the front facing Admiralty Place, and six hundred and fifty feet on the two sides or wings which extend to the river, occupies three sides of a hollow square. Its dome and spire are visible even at Cronstadt, and from its galleries the whole city may be seen. It is devoted principally to the civil departments of the navy, to the school for naval cadets, and to the naval museum. The open place around the Admiralty, on which stand the principal public buildings of the city, is about a mile in circumference. On one side of it is the equestrian statue of Peter the Great, and on the other, the northeast side, fronting the Winter Palace, is the splendid column of Alexander I. This is the largest monolith in the world. It is a granite shaft, eighty feet in height by fifteen feet in diameter, upon a pedestal ornamented with bronze bass-reliefs, and with a bronze capital, cast from metal obtained from captured Turkish cannon. The whole is surmounted by a statue of Victory, upholding the Cross. Although the column is of native Finland granite, the severe cold of this almost arctic climate makes every winter cracks and cleavages which have to be carefully repaired with cement.

To naval men the collection in the museum is of great interest. It occupies two large halls, and consists chiefly of models of all the vessels that have ever been connected with the Russian navy, from the earliest attempts at shipbuilding under the Czar Alexis and the Emperor Peter the Great, down to the latest iron-clads of Alexander II. Arranged in chronological order, this superb collection presents an epitome of Russian naval history from the first victory of Peter the Great down to Navarino and Sinope. The models of the monitors, which type of vessel Russia adopted as soon as their efficiency had been proved in our Civil War, attracted the particular attention of our officers. The museum contains, also, many naval curiosities and ethnographical and mineralogical specimens.

The mission visited next the Imperial Public Library, on the Nevsky Prospect. This magnificent collection is one of the finest in Europe, containing eight hundred thousand volumes of printed books and over twenty-five thousand manuscripts, in all languages, ancient and modern. Of the printed books, ninety thousand are in the Russian language, and more than thirty thousand, in all languages except the Russian, relate to Russia. Among the manuscripts are many of great value. The oldest extant manuscript in the Russian language, a book containing the evangelists, is preserved here. It is written in the Slavonian character, and bears the date of 1056. In early Hebrew manuscripts the library is richer than any other in Europe, and its Oriental collection is very extensive. It contains also a vast number of literary curiosities, such as autographs and portraits of celebrities, specimens of writing-materials of all ages, and a series of prints produced by all known processes, from the earliest invention down to the present time.

The party was received by Mr. John Delianoff, the director of the library, who politely showed the different rooms, and pointed out all the objects worthy of special attention. Several volumes and splendidly-bound catalogues were presented to Mr. Fox on his departure.

In the afternoon, the Winter Palace, the Hermitage, and the Museum of Agricultural Management, were visited. The Winter Palace, the residence of the Emperor and of the imperial court during the winter season, stands on the left bank of the Neva, facing the river, between the Admiralty and the Hermitage. It is an immense structure of four stories in height, with a frontage of four hundred and fifty feet. The principal entrance is from the river by a stately flight of marble steps. The chief state apartments are the Throne-room of Peter I., the Hall of St. George, the White Hall, the Alexander Hall, and the Gallery of the Field-Marshals. The Hall of St. George is a magnificent apartment, one hundred and forty by sixty feet in size. The Field-Marshals' Hall contains portraits of the Russian field-marshals and generals who distinguished themselves in the War of 1812-'14. In the Alexander Hall and in other rooms are many battle-pictures of both the Russian army and navy.

The crown jewels are kept in a room of the Winter Palace. Among the treasures to be seen here, is the great Orloff diamond, of one hundred and ninety-four and three-fourths carats, so called from Count Orloff, who presented it to Catherine II. It is set in the top of the imperial sceptre. With the exception of two slight flaws, it is a perfect stone, and it is the largest of all the crown diamonds of Europe. The imperial crown and the coronet of the Empress are resplendent with jewels, the most of them of immense value. Many of the gems in this collection are of great interest, besides their intrinsic worth, from historical associations.

The drawing-room of the Empress in the Winter Palace is a gorgeous apartment, the walls and ceiling of which are gilded. When lighted at night by hundreds of wax-tapers, the effect is very striking. In direct contrast to this elegant saloon is the small, plainly-furnished room in which the great Emperor Nicholas died. His military cloak is folded on the narrow iron camp-bedstead on which he expired, and his helmet and sword lie where he put them last. On the wall hangs the portrait of his favorite daughter, the Grand-duchess Olga, who was esteemed in her day the most beautiful woman in Europe. She is a lady of great and varied accomplishments and honors the throne of Württemberg, which she graces. She married, July 13, 1846, the Crown-Prince of Württemberg, who now reigns under the title of Charles I.

The Hermitage is an immense building adjoining the Winter Palace, with which it is connected by several galleries. It is in the Greek style, and forms a parallelogram of five hundred and fifteen feet by nearly four hundred. It was built by Catherine II. for a picture-gallery and museum. The collection, begun by her, has been added to by all the succeeding sovereigns, until it has assumed colossal proportions. The galleries contain about seventeen hundred pictures, representing all the celebrated schools. It is particularly rich in Flemish and Spanish canvases, having many examples of Rubens, Murillo, Velasquez, Vandyck, Rembrandt, Wouvermans, and other masters.

The numismatic collection is one of the finest in Europe, containing over two hundred thousand specimens, many of great rarity and value. The collection of gems is unrivalled, combining with several other cabinets the celebrated one of the Duke of Orleans.

The Gallery of Peter the Great is devoted to objects of art and industry illustrative of the life of that Emperor. Here are preserved the tools with which he worked, his mathematical instruments, his books, his canes, and articles of wearing-apparel. His effigy is placed in the centre of the room, which belongs properly to the Winter Palace, but is entered from the Hermitage. Many other costly and curious objects, connected with different Russian sovereigns, are shown in this apartment.

To describe even a moiety of the treasures in this great museum would require a volume. In many departments it is unique. Among the most interesting collections are the antiquities from the Cimmerian Bosphorus, and the Siberian and Scythian ornaments. Many of the latter are exquisite in design, and show evidences of the influence of Greek art. The museum is rich also in weapons and utensils of the bronze age.

The Agricultural Museum, in a building near the Winter Palace, was visited last. The various products and the diffcrent agricultural implements of the provinces are to be seen here, and all the processes connected with the cultivation of the soil in the empire may be studied in detail in its rooms.

In the evening Mr. Fox and several of the gentlomen connected with the mission accepted private hospitalities.

The record of the day would not be complete without an account of the banquet given by the port of Cronstadt to the crews of the Miantonomoh and the Augusta. A canvas shed, one hundred and twenty feet long, was erected in one of the principal alleys of the public garden. The interior was decorated with the flags of the two nations, and festooned with evergreens. On the front waved the Russian and American ensigns, their staves crossing each other; and in the rear was a large shield emblazoned with the arms of the United States, and bearing the motto " *E Pluribus Unum*." Tables and benches stretched the entire length of this improvised dining-room.

At ten o'clock, the Russian officers who had charge of the dinner, in company with Mr. Wilkins, our vice-consul at Cronstadt, went off to the ships in the Ijora and brought ashore one hundred and sixty men and marines, eighty from each vessel. From the landing-place they marched, four abreast, to the garden, where a body of Russian tars made them welcome. A number of the latter belonged to the crew of the Svietlana, and had picked up some English when in America with Admiral Lessovsky in 1863. Before sitting down at the tables, the whole body, Russians and Americans, were conducted to a place surrounded by trees, where they were formed into a picturesque group and photographed. The Mayor of Cronstadt, Vice-Consul Wilkins, the Russian and American officers accompanying the crews, and the two flags crossed, made an effective centre, while the seamen, arranged on the sides, bore also the flags of their respective countries at the wings.

The tables were served simply but abundantly, beer and hydromel being furnished for drink instead of strong liquors, which are interdicted in our navy. The men appeared to enjoy themselves greatly, and, despite the difference in language, hosts and guests were soon on the very best of terms. Two bands of music played alternately during the feast, which lasted until five o'clock in the afternoon. The festivities were kept up until late in the night, when the sailors were returned to their ships, well pleased with the hospitality they had received.

On this day, Mr. Fox received, through Prince Gortchakoff, the following address from the citizens of Chouïa, a town of about eight thousand inhabitants, in the government of Vladimir:

"*To his Excellency, the Vice-Chancellor,* PRINCE GORTCHAKOFF:

"We respectfully pray you to communicate the following to Mr. G. V. Fox, Assistant Secretary of the Navy of the United States:

"In the resolution of the American Congress, and in your mission, we recognize an important event, demonstrating the fraternal friendship of two great nations.

"The congratulations and the sympathy of our transatlantic brethren touch deeply our hearts, which are filled to overflowing with love for the liberator and regenerator of Russia, preserved by Divine Providence for the grand future of our dear country.

"Estimating highly the friendship of the sons of America, and comprehending the full importance of this friendship, at the present time, we, citizens of the town of Chouïa, hasten to express to you, the honorable representative of a great people, the sentiments of our sincere gratitude. We beg you to transmit to your people the expression of our sentiments, with our heart-felt wishes for the prosperity and the happiness of their great nation.

"We sympathize deeply with their affliction caused by the loss of the illustrious Lincoln, whose tragic death affected us most painfully.

(Signed)   "NICHOLAS KALLOUJSKY, *President,*"
                    and seventy-six other signatures.

This address was sent by telegraph. Mr. Fox replied as follows:

"*To* MR. NICHOLAS KALLOUJSKY, *Mayor of the City of Chouïa:*

"I have received your friendly telegram, which has been transmitted to me by his Excellency the Vice-Chancellor.

The fraternal love which exists between Russia and the United States is the result of the noble aspirations which carry forward the two nations in the path of civilization. The life of him who leads the way at the head of the Russian people, the life of the Emperor-Liberator, who has given a new existence to his subjects, could not be endangered without stirring the feelings of the people of the United States, who, though afflicted sorely by their own misfortune, unanimously gave thanks to God that Russia had been spared from a similar grief.

"G. V. Fox."

About the same time, Mr. Fox received also an address from Ufa, the capital of the government of Orenburg, on the Asiatic frontier. Orenburg is the home of the nomadic race called Bashkirs, a Tartar or Mongolian tribe subdued by Ivan the Terrible. They are Mohammedans in religion. They live mostly by pasturage, and are peaceable subjects of Russia. Ufa, the capital, is situated at the junction of the Ufa and Bielaya Rivers, tributaries of the Volga. Its inhabitants are chiefly Russian.

Their address was as follows:

"From distant Ufa, from the Bashkirian centre, we send friendly greeting to dear guests, who have sailed through the ocean for the sake of bringing to us Russians the congratulations of the American people on the occasion of the happy preservation of our Emperor-Liberator. The great American Union could in no way show more clearly her friendly feelings toward Russia and Russians, who love and honor their Emperor above all else on the earth. The brotherly address of the Americans can never be rooted out of the hearts of Russians, not even in the most distant provinces of our vast country. In our land, rich by nature, and peopled by various races, we are, to use the language of the magnificently-speaking Captain Fox, endeavoring to carry the light of civilization and of Christian instruction to the heathen. We supplicate the Almighty to help us, under the shadow of the blessing-bringing administration of our Father Gosudar, to push forward the great project of melting together the men of other races with us Russians, and into one only belief in God, and love and boundless devotion to the reigning Gosudar and his imperial descendants.

"We conclude with the earnest wish that the universal national fellow-feeling, now uniting two mighty nations, may be strengthened in those nations' future generations, and may assist them to obtain the full deliverance, proclaimed by Providence, of all subjected nations from the chains of ignorance and of false beliefs."

(Signed)   "K. BECH,   } *Elders.*"
                     "N. BASILIEFF,

and by more than fifty of the principal inhabitants.

This address, coming from the distant Ural country, on the borders of Asia, shows how deeply the whole of Russia was affected by the American mission. It was answered by Mr. Fox in suitable terms.

CHAPTER X.

THE NEVSKY PROSPECT—ALEXANDER NEVSKY—STEEL-GUN FOUNDERY — EXCHANGE AND ACADEMY OF SCIENCES— THE MERCHANTS' DINNER.

AUGUST 15*th* (3*d*).—Wednesday morning was bright and warm. At ten o'clock the mission started to visit the Monastery of St. Alexander Nevsky, one of the most celebrated religious establishments in Russia, situated on the banks of the Neva, at the end of the Nevsky Prospect.

The party drove through this splendid street, which is probably in every respect the finest in Europe. It is one hundred and thirty feet in width and four miles long. The buildings on it are not contiguous, but are erected on large plots, so that there are not more than fifty in a mile's distance. The cathedral of Our Lady of Kazan, with its blue domes decked with stars, is one of its most conspicuous features. It is named in honor of a picture of the Virgin, which was found miraculously preserved after a fire in the city of Kazan on the Volga, but it was built in commemoration of the defeat of Napoleon. In its front are statues of Kutusoff-Smolensky and of Barclay de Tolly, by the Russian sculptor, Boris Orloffsky.

Its magnificent ikonastas is made of silver plundered from Moscow by the French, and recaptured by the Cossacks during the terrible retreat. An inscription upon it records that it was the zealous offering of the Don Cossacks after the campaign of 1812. The tomb of Kutusoff stands on the floor of the church, on the spot where he knelt to pray when about to leave to meet the enemy. This church is visited by the imperial family on occasions of special thanksgiving. It was here that Alexander II. came, first alone and afterward in state, to render thanks for his preservation from the bullet of Karakozoff.

There is another beautiful church on the Nevsky Prospect, with similar blue domes and golden stars, and also a Roman Catholic and an Armenian church, a Dutch church, and a Protestant German church, all costly buildings. Here too is the palace of the Grand-duke Michael, the Hôtel de l'État Major, or military headquarters, an imposing building, the great Bazaar, or Gastinnoy Dvor, with its ten thousand merchants, the Institute of St. Catherine, and other noble structures.

The monastery of St. Alexander Nevsky is at the extreme end of the street, near the limits of the city. It covers several acres of ground and encloses within its walls, besides the convent proper, a cathedral, chapels, monks' cells, and beautiful gardens and lawns.

Alexander Nevsky is the seat of a metropolitan, and is one of the three chief monasteries of the empire, being inferior only to those at Moscow and Kiew. It was founded by Peter the Great, in honor of the canonized Grand-duke Alexander, who defeated the Swedes in a great battle on its site in 1241, and acquired thereby the surname of Nevsky (of the Neva). The cathedral, which was built by Catherine I., is one of the largest and finest churches in the city and contains a vast amount of treasure. The shrine of the saint is of solid silver, weighing over three thousand pounds. The whole interior of the church is richly ornamented with Italian marbles, and with pearls and precious stones. The monastery has a magnificent collection of jewelled mitres, croziers, and crosses, pontifical robes of gold brocade, and the various utensils and dresses belonging to the splendid ceremonials of the Greek Church. The crown of Alexander Nevsky and the bed on which Peter the Great died are among the relics preserved here.

The monastery proper contains about sixty monks, whose chief duty is to superintend an academy connected with it for the education of ecclesiastics. The Americans were very graciously received by them, and politely shown all the objects of beauty and of interest in the buildings and gardens.

Mr. Fox and party, attended by the Russian officers, went thence in open carriages eleven miles up the Neva, to the steel-gun foundery of Mr. Aboukhoff, which is under the direction of Admiral Crabbe, the Minister of Marine. It is a singular fact that the process of casting steel in such enormous quantities was discovered almost simultaneously in Russia by Aboukhoff and by Krupp in Prussia; and it is only at this foundery and at Krupp's, at Essen, that the process is carried on after methods known only to the inventors. The works of Mr. Aboukhoff are very extensive, although not yet completed, and are capable of furnishing cannon unsurpassed by any similar establishment in the world. The steel is of great tenacity, and the guns made from it will stand very heavy charges of powder.

Admiral Crabbe met the party and showed them through the works, explaining every thing of interest. The method of fusing the steel in crucibles was exhibited, and a gun cast in their presence. These crucibles can stand a heat of 2,800 degrees centigrade.

The huge steam-hammers in this foundery are noteworthy, particularly the largest, which is named "Grandfather." It weighs forty tons, and its anvil, which is in four parts, about four hundred tons. To fix this giant hammer, and to consolidate its foundations, was one of the most difficult problems of modern science. An excavation of eighty feet in depth had to be made before the bed of solid granite was reached. On this the foundations were laid, and now its strokes thunder on the great anvil with impunity.

When the Americans were about to leave, the assembled workmen gave them three hearty cheers. After a drive through the beautiful park of Count Apraxine, the party stopped at the country-house of Mr. Poutiloff, one of the proprietors of the steel-foundery, where they sat down to a lunch, which was enjoyed by all after their long drive.

In the afternoon the return to St. Petersburg was

made by steamer, and the Exchange and the Museum of the Academy of Sciences were visited. Both of these buildings are on Vassilievsky[1] Island, on the point formed by the Neva and the Little Neva, directly opposite the Winter Palace and the Admiralty, with which the island is connected by the Palace Bridge.

The Exchange is a massive building, originally erected in 1784, but entirely rebuilt in the beginning of the present century. In the open space in front of it stand two columns, over a hundred feet in height, each surmounted by figures holding hollow globes, in which fires are sometimes built. The great hall, which is lighted from the roof, is of imposing dimensions.

The Academy of Sciences was founded in 1724, by Peter the Great. Its museums[2] are very extensive, embracing collections illustrative of ethnography, anatomy, zoology, mineralogy, botany, etc. Its library contains one hundred and fifty thousand books and manuscripts, among the latter being the papers of Kepler. The cabinets of medals and coins are also very valuable and instructive. In the Asiatic Museum are over twenty thousand specimens from the East alone. The Ethnographic Museum is devoted to the costumes and implements of all the races inhabiting the Russian Empire. In the Zoological collection are shown the remains of mammoths

[1] Basil's Island, so called from the name of its occupant in the time of Peter the Great.

[2] When these museums were opened, it was suggested that an entrance-fee should be charged, as is done in similar institutions in some European cities. But Peter the Great, with that far-sightedness which marked his whole career, replied that he would rather pay the people for visiting them.

that have been frozen in the ice of Siberia since the early geological periods. The flesh of these antediluvians is so well preserved that the wolves and bears feed upon it when accident reveals any of their enormous bodies, which are larger than elephants.

At five o'clock, Mr. Fox was entertained at a grand dinner, given in his honor, by the Merchants' Association of St. Petersburg, at their Club-House on the Nevsky Prospect. Among the invited were General Clay and Mr. Curtin, Messrs. Green and Loubat, Commanders Murray and Beaumont, and all the other officers of the squadron who could be spared from duty. The rooms were elaborately decorated with flags and banners, with the American and Russian coats-of-arms, and with portraits of the great men of the two countries wreathed with flowers and evergreens. Hundreds of laurel, orange, and lemon trees, and other rare shrubs and flowers, were distributed along the walls and on the staircases with charming effect, giving the dining-hall the appearance of an illuminated garden.

The wide street in front of the Club-House was filled with a multitude of people, who welcomed the Americans with shouts as they drove up to the entrance. The guests were received by the officers of the club, and, after the customary "zakuska," were conducted arm-in-arm to the dining-room, where nearly four hundred persons sat down at the tables. The various ranks and positions, public and private, were represented at this feast, which was the first of a general character given to our officers in St. Petersburg.

The bill of fare was printed in gold on glazed Bristol-board, in English on one side and in Russian on the other. It read as follows:

MERCHANTS' CLUB, ST. PETERSBURG.
BILL OF FARE.
(August 3d, 1866.)

1. Turtle-soup.
    Purée à la chasseur.
2. Petits Pâtés.
3. Snipe, with jelly. Strasbourg pâtés.
4. Sterlet à la Russe.
5. Capons, with truffles. Sauce suprême.
6. Roman punch.
7. Pheasants, partridges, chickens.
8. Artichokes, with peas.
9. Gâteau à l'Américaine.
10. Ices.
11. Fruits and confectionery

A similar card, also printed in both English and Russian, contained the list of regular toasts:

TOASTS.

1. The President and People of the United States.
2. His Majesty the Emperor of Russia.
3. Her Majesty the Empress of Russia, the Grand-duke Héritier, and the Imperial Family.
4. The Honorable Mr. Fox, Assistant Secretary of the American Navy.
5. General Clay, Minister of the United States.
6. The Merchants of Russia.
7. The Merchants of the United States.
8. The American Navy.
9. The Russian Navy.

Wines of the choicest vintages, and the music of an orchestra, added zest to the feast. The tables, spread with a superb service of silver and crystal, and adorned with bronzes and porcelain vases, mingled with choice flowers, presented a luxurious and inviting sight in the soft light of the hundreds of wax-tapers and candelabras. A notable feature of the table decoration was ripe pineapples growing in boxes. These, as well as the most of the exotic plants, were sent by Mr. Outine, one of the directors of the club, from his hot-houses at his splendid country-seat of Kamenoy-Ostrov. This gentleman also contributed his silver, bronzes, and porcelain for the occasion, and gave his personal attention to the decorations of the rooms.

The toasts began, according to the Russian custom, with the second service. Mr. Vargounine, a director of the club, gave the first toast, prefacing it by a few remarks in the Russian language, which were translated into English by Admiral Lessovsky.

"The Hon. G. V. Fox," he said, "has honored us by accepting the unanimous invitation of the Russian Corporation of Merchants of St. Petersburg to the dinner to-day. It is not the first time that our Society has expressed its sincere and heart-felt friendship for the citizens of the United States. I think that the respected General Clay has not forgotten the cordial reception which was given to him by the Society in February last, nor the speeches expressive of friendly attachment made on that day. But now we are still more closely bound to this great nation by the sympathy which it has shown to us for the sorrowful event of the 4th of April. The heart of every Russian beat with joy when it was known that our friends beyond the ocean were sending a deputation from Congress, with congratulations for the wonderful preservation, through Divine mercy, of our beloved and dear Emperor. This act clearly shows to us that we have sincere friends, who rejoice in every success of Russia, and who sympathize with us in every trial. Our friendship is not founded on selfish political considerations, nor on the possible benefits of commercial treaties. No; it is a bond of affection, and the feeling of conscious independence and power. And we think that the bonds uniting these two great powers are indissoluble, and that our sincere friendship will remain unchanged for ages; and we shall forever, as we do now, raise our glasses for the health of the President of the United States, and the whole American nation."

Mr. Vargounine was interrupted frequently by applause during the course of his remarks, and, at the close, the President's health was drunk, amid the greatest enthusiasm. It is worth noting here that at all Russian banquets it is customary to drink the toast to the Emperor before all others; and the giving the precedence to our President was an extraordinary compliment never before bestowed on a foreign ruler.

Mr. Fox replied by summing up compactly, in the following toast, the five great measures of reform which have made illustrious the reign of Alexander II.:

"To him whose intrepid heart, inspired by God, has abolished in Russia serfdom and corporal punishment, who has endowed the country with local self-government, trial by jury, and liberty of the press—the Emperor of Russia."

The sentiment was received with loud cheers.

After the toast to the Empress, the Cezarevitch, and the imperial family, had been drunk, Mr. Outine rose and announced, in a few graceful remarks, that the Russian Merchants' Club, in testimony of its deep sympathy with the mission confided to the Hon. Mr. Fox, and of its gratitude for the honor of his visit, had elected him an honorary member. He closed by proposing "The health of the new member."

Mr. Fox replied in fitting words, thanking the club for the compliment, and saying that he appreciated highly the honor conferred upon him.

Mr. Clay, in response to the toast to the American minister at the imperial court, spoke of the importance of industry and commerce in a state, pointing his remarks with illustrations drawn from the Civil War in the United States, where the artisans who made a part of the army repaired in a short time what the enemy had destroyed, thus aiding the triumph of the Union and bringing to a happy issue the bloody struggle. He closed by giving "The health of the Merchants of Russia."

Mr. Kokoreff, a distinguished and wealthy merchant of Moscow, responded:

"The arrival in Russia of our American guests has for us a deep significance. Under the influence of this great occasion we are unable to define even approximately its importance. Our valued guests have honored us with this visit not on account of political or of commercial interests, but from the disinterested, the pure and lofty desire of the American people to join in the general rejoicing of the people of Russia. Mr. Fox has expressed the feelings of his countrymen to our beloved imperial reformer. We most respectfully request the honored envoy of the United States, upon his return to his native land, to inform his people that they could not have chosen a better means of creating a brotherly feeling of love for Americans in every Russian mansion and in every Russian cabin throughout the empire than by such a manifestation of their joy for the preservation of the life of him who sheds light upon Russian life by his philanthropy, justice, enlightenment, and mercy. The citizens of America, understanding Russia and her history, know that the long life and health of Alexander II. is for us a pledge of glory, happiness, and strength. Profoundly grateful for such sympathy, I beg to propose a toast: "To all the members of Congress who voted to send to Russia the national American mission."

When the acclamations with which Mr. Kokoreff's speech was received had subsided, the merchants of the United States were honored with a toast.

Admiral Crabbe, the Minister of the Navy, made the next speech. He called the Americans the masters of the Russians in the art of navigation, and instanced the Russian monitors, which are constructed on American models. He proposed "The health of our masters, the Officers of the American Navy."

This complimentary toast brought Captain Murray to his feet.

"In bringing across the ocean," he said, "the sympathies of a great people, the vessels-of-war which I have the honor to represent have come freighted with a cargo more precious than the wealth of the Orient or the mines of California; but we were not the first to bear across the ocean wares as treasured. I shall never forget the thrill of joy that pervaded America when the Russian fleet, under Admiral Lessovsky, anchored in the harbor of New York and spread the glad tidings that one great nation sided with us in our troubles. It is always a pleasure to renew the remembrance of such national sympathy, and I am rejoiced that the duty of toasting the Russian Navy has devolved on me. It is always agreeable to drink to our friends, our sympathizers, our allies; but to one who is the recipient of so much kind attention, who has had bestowed upon him and upon the officers and crews of his command so much honor and such generous hospitality, the task becomes doubly agreeable. (Cheers.) The time of this company is too precious to waste in words which must fail to do justice to this gallant offspring of Peter the Great. Let me point to its record, which is illustrated by a Tchesma, a Navarino, and a Sinope, and is adorned by such names as its imperial chief, the Grand-duke Constantine, and the heroes that I now see around me. I propose 'The Russian Navy.'"

This speech, which was received with applause, was replied to briefly but happily by Admiral Lessovsky. He spoke of the warm reception he had received in the United States, and expressed his pleasure in having an opportunity of returning the kindness in his own country. The friendship between Russia and America could not but be permanent.

After the punch had passed around, a singing band of emancipated serfs, male and female, entertained the company with the Russian national hymn and "Hail Columbia," singing both in Russian. They were loudly applauded, and obliged to repeat the latter several times.

While the dinner was going on within, a great popular demonstration was taking place in the streets. The space in front of the Club-House and all the avenues of approach to it were densely crowded with people of all classes, who had gathered to do honor to the Americans. Travel was stopped and vehicles were compelled to turn into the adjacent streets. Loud calls were made for Mr. Fox and for others, and he and our officers were obliged to show themselves from time to time on the balcony, each appearance being greeted with extraordinary applause. It was a splendid popular reception, and proved how deeply the masses of the Russian people were moved by the unprecedented act of our Government in sending its sympathy and congratulations by a special envoy.

Besides the distinguished gentlemen already mentioned, there were present at this banquet Prince Michael Gortchakoff, the son of the vice-chancellor; Count Schouvaloff; Mr. Abaza, Secretary of the Department of Ceremonies of the Imperial Court; Komissaroff-Kostromsky, and many others.

The festivities were kept up until a very late hour, but Messrs. Fox, Green, and Loubat, and Commanders Murray and Beaumont, were obliged to leave comparatively early, in order to take the train for Krasnoë-Selo, where they had been invited by the Emperor, to attend the review of the Imperial Guard on the morrow.

The card of membership presented to Mr. Fox by the club is a beautiful specimen of art, printed in gold and colors. At the top, on the right, are the arms of St. Petersburg; on the left is the *caduceus*, the rod of Mercury, the god of merchants, the two being connected by a running border. On the back is the following, in English: "Ticket of Membership for Mr. G. V. Fox, Assistant Secretary of the United States Navy, Honorary Member of the Mercantile Association of St. Petersburg, Russia."

CHAPTER XI.

KRASNOË - SELO — MANŒUVRES — HONORARY CITIZENSHIP — CATHEDRAL OF PETER AND PAUL — MINING INSTITUTE.

AUGUST 16*th* (4*th*).—Krasnoö-Selo, or the Red Village, the great parade-ground of the Imperial Guard, is distant about eighteen miles from St. Petersburg, on the line of the Peterhof Railway. The Guards are encamped here during the summer months, remaining under canvas until some time in August, when they are reviewed by the Emperor, and engage in a sham battle.

Mr. Fox and the gentlemen accompanying him were furnished with apartments in the Ambassadors' House, a building belonging to the Government.

At nine o'clock in the morning, the weather being exceptionally fine, the party started in carriages for the field. On reaching the ground, Mr. Fox met and conversed with the Emperor. His Majesty was exceedingly courteous, and showed our representative remarkable attentions.

The sham battle began at noon. The following programme of the manœuvres distributed on the field shows the number of troops engaged, and their respective movements. The original is in French.

PROGRAMME OF THE MANŒUVRES.

The Corps d'Armée of the South, coming from Louga, advances in two échelons toward St. Petersburg.

At the beginning of the manœuvres, the first échelon, following the march of the enemy, takes possession of Krasnoë-Selo.

The second échelon halts at Sivoritzy.

The Corps d'Armée of the North, which is not so strong as that of the South, falls back in presence of the enemy, from Krasnoë-Selo upon St. Petersburg, by the highway, and takes position at Ligovo (on the line of the railway), to await the arrival of the detachment concentrated at Strelna.

Having received news that the enemy has taken possession with a part of his force of Krasnoë-Selo, the two columns of the Army of the North attack the enemy vigorously, with the object of destroying his army in detail.

DISTRIBUTION OF THE TROOPS.

CORPS D'ARMÉE OF THE SOUTH.

Chief of the Second Division of Infantry of the Guard, Aide-de-camp General, BARON BISTROM.

FIRST ÉCHELON.

Aide-de-camp General, Baron Bistrom.

	Battalions.	Squadrons.	Pieces.
The Second Division of Infantry of the Guard......	13	..	..
The regiment composed of the Battalion of Instruction, and of the battalion of the military schools.	2		..
The Second Brigade of the Artillery of the Guard on foot...		..	12
The Battery of Instruction on foot...............		..	4
The regiments of the Second Division of the Cavalry of the Guard...............................		16	
The regiment composed of the Squadron of Instruction and of those of the School of the Ensign-bearers of the Guard........................		3	..

PROGRAMME OF MANŒUVRES.

	Battalions.	Squadrons.	Pieces.
Two squadrons of the regiment of the Cossacks of the Ataman, his Imperial Highness the Hereditary Grand-duke........................		2	..
The Battery No. 2, of the Horse Artillery of the Guard......................................	..	..	8
The Battery of Cossacks........................	..	..	8
The Horse Battery of Instruction................	..	..	4
Total............................	15	21	86

SECOND ÉCHELON.

Chief ad interim of the Twenty-fourth Division of Infantry, Major-General Den.

The regiment composed of the battalion of the Finland Tirailleurs of the Guard, and of the companies of Tirailleurs of the Infantry Regiments Nos. 93 and 88....................	3	..	..
The Infantry Regiment No. 94..................	3	..	..
" " " No. 95..................	3	..	..
The twenty-fourth Brigade of Artillery on foot.....	..	..	12
Total............................	9	..	12
General total.....................	24	21	48

CORPS D'ARMÉE OF THE NORTH.
Aide-de-camp General, Prince Galitzine.

DETACHMENT OF LIGOVO.
Lieutenant-General Drenteln.

The First Division of Infantry of the Guard........	13	..	..
The Battalion of Sappers of the Guard.............	1	..	..
The First Brigade of Artillery of the Guard on foot.	..	..	12
One squadron of the regiment of the Cossacks of the Guard.................................	..	1	..
Total............................	14	1	12

DETACHMENT OF STRELNA.
Lieutenant-General Soukodolsky.

	Battal-ions.	Squad-rons.	Pieces.
The battalions of Sappers No. 7, of the Grenadiers and of the Reserve....................	3		
The regiment composed of the companies of Tirailleurs of the Infantry Regiments Nos. 85, 86, and 87................................	3	..	..
The 23d Brigade of Artillery...................	..	..	12
The Battery of the Michael School of Artillery.....	..	..	4
The regiments of the First Division of Cavalry of the Guard......................................		16	..
One squadron of the regiment of Cossacks of the Guard......................................		1	..
The Battery of Position of the Horse Artillery of the Guard......................................			8
The Rifled Battery No. 1 of the Horse Artillery of the Guard..................................	..	..	8
Total............................	6	17	32
General Total....................	20	18	44

PRESUMED COURSE OF THE MANŒUVRES.

First day (August 2d). Krasnoë-Selo is attacked by the two columns of the Corps d'Armée of the North; a battle takes place near Krasnoë-Selo; the first échelon of the Corps d'Armée of the South retires behind the Poudoste River.

Second day (August 3d). The Corps d'Armée of the North continues its march; battle is given on the banks of the Poudoste River. The first échelon of the Corps d'Armée of the South falls back upon the second, and retires from Sivoritzy to Gatschino (it is understood that the troops stationed at Sivoritzy are unable to take part in the battle fought the second day of the manœuvres).

Third day (August 4th). The whole Corps d'Armée of the South energetically takes the offensive.

It was the manœuvres of the last day that the mission witnessed. The battle was a very brilliant spectacle, the grand cavalry charges being especially noticeable.

About thirty-five thousand men were engaged in the operations, all of them belonging to the Imperial Guard, which forms an army by itself, entirely distinct from the line, embracing in its ranks every branch of the service. All commissioned officers of the Imperial Guard, and all officers of the Navy, have the right of going to court in Russia; but, in the line regiments, none but officers of and above the rank of major have this privilege.

After dining with a number of the principal officers in a pavilion near their quarters, the Americans returned to St. Petersburg about four o'clock in the afternoon.

August 17*th* (5*th*).—At nine o'clock a deputation of the Mayor and Corporation of St. Petersburg called on Mr. Fox to inform him that, by permission of the Emperor, he had been elected an honorary citizen of the city.

In announcing this great honor, the dean of the corporation of hereditary nobles, Mr. Zablotzky-Dessiatovsky, spoke as follows:

"Through her deans, the city of St. Petersburg bids you welcome to the capital of Russia. We are convinced that the American people, who have themselves so recently suffered the affliction of a great loss in the person of their chief, will appreciate better than others the feeling of joy which filled the hearts of Russians when Providence averted from them a horrible danger.

"Your presence here is another manifestation of the interest taken by the American people in the preservation of a life so precious to Russians, of the life of him who, by great reforms, has given to Russia new vigor in civilization.

"Once more we wish you heartily welcome, and in your person we thank the great American people for its sentiments toward the Emperor and the Russian people.

"In memory of our gratitude, the city of St. Petersburg begs you, the Envoy Extraordinary, to accept the title of honorary citizen of St. Petersburg."

Mr. Fox replied as follows:

"Gentlemen, representatives of the city of St. Petersburg, my arrival here with the Resolution of the Congress of the United States of America is for every Russian heart a proof that the danger which menaced the life of his Imperial Majesty, and consequently the civilization and progress of the Russian nation, has deeply moved the American people. The cordiality with which the Russians have received us, the amicable sentiments we have exchanged with them, are the sincere expressions of our mutual feelings.

"I receive with the deepest gratitude the rare gift which the capital confers upon me, with the authorization of the Emperor, the title of honorary citizen of St. Petersburg. This honor is not addressed to me, but to the entire people of the United States."

The diploma of citizenship presented to Mr. Fox is engrossed on heavy Bristol-board, within an exquisitely executed border in the Byzantine style. In the centre of the top of this border are the arms of the city of St. Petersburg, with the Slavonic letter "A," the initial of the Emperor's name, on each side. On the right corner at the top is the Slavonic shield of the middle ages. Next below it, on the side, is the cross; under it, in a medal, the bust of Alexander II., with the inscription "Liberator;" and, still farther down, the allegorical attributes of the arts and sciences. On the left corner, at the top, is the cap of Monomachus, worn by the Russian Czars until the time of Peter I. Next below it, on the side, is the cross; under it, in a medal, the bust of Peter the Great, with the inscription "Reformer;" and, beneath it, the allegorical attributes of commerce. At the bottom, in the centre of the border, is the seal of the city of St. Petersburg, with an engraving of St. Isaac's cathedral on the left, and of the Exchange on the right.

The inscription, which is in Russian, is translated as follows:

"The Commonalty of the City of St. Petersburg, with the permission of his most gracious Imperial Majesty, has nominated Mr. G. V. Fox, Ambassador of the Congress, and Assistant Secretary of the Navy, of the United States of North America, and Member of the Cabinet of Washington, an honorary citizen of the City of St. Petersburg, as a sign of special respect for him, as the Representative of the People of North America, through whom they expressed their most sincere sympathy toward Russia and her Emperor, and in remembrance of the feelings with which this declaration was received by the City of St. Petersburg.

"ST. PETERSBURG, *on the 3d of August*, 1866.

"The Mayor of St. Petersburg: POGREBOFF.
"Seniors: ZABLOTZKY-DESSIATOVSKY, NICOLAI BYKOV, AVERIN.
"Secretary of the City: TREVILLE."

The diploma is contained in a splendid case of Siberian malachite, with ornaments of gilt bronze. In the centre of the lid are engraved the arms of the city of St. Petersburg.

Honorary citizenship is one of the greatest distinctions that can be conferred in Russia. It is very rarely bestowed, as no city nor municipality has the right to give it without unanimity, and the permission and authorization of the Emperor. The compliment to Mr. Fox, and through him to the people of the United States, whom he represented, was, therefore, a notable one.

During the remainder of the morning, Mr. Fox and party visited the Navy-yard and the Sailors' House of Correction; and, in the afternoon, the museum of the Mining Institute, and the fortress and cathedral of St. Peter and St. Paul.

The fortress, on the little island at the junction of the Neva and the Little Neva, was begun by Peter the Great in 1703. The corner-stone of its cathedral was laid in 1714, but the building has undergone various changes. The present spire, which is one of the most beautiful in the city, was erected in 1772. It is the tallest in Russia, with the exception of the one at Revel, the cross on its summit being three hundred and eighty-seven feet above the ground. Under its floor repose the bodies of all the Emperors of Russia, excepting Peter II., who is buried in Moscow.

The walls of the cathedral are hung with trophies captured from the many nations with which Russia has warred. Flags, standards, and pennons, float above the tombs; and shields, lances, swords, and the keys of fortresses, are disposed among them in many effective forms.

The Imperial Mint stands within the walls of the fortress, the gloomy casemates of which are used as a state-prison.

Not far from the fortress stands the cottage built by Peter the Great, in 1703, the first building erected on the banks of the Neva at the time of the founding of the city. Like all the other relics of the author of Russia's greatness, it is religiously preserved, the entire house being covered with a casing to protect it from the elements. It contains but two rooms and a kitchen. In one of them, now used as a chapel, is the miraculous picture of the Saviour, which accompanied Peter in almost all of his campaigns. It was to this chapel that Komissaroff was going when he was turned back providentially in time to save the Emperor's life.

One of the most interesting of the relics in the house is the boat called in Russia *Dedouchka Russkago Flota* (Dear Grandfather of the Russian Fleet), from which Peter the Great conceived the idea of forming a navy. The remains of the sails, and every thing connected with the little vessel, are preserved with the greatest care.

The Mining Institute is a Government school for the education of mining-engineers. Its pupils, about two hundred and fifty in number, dress in uniform, and are subject to military rules. Its mineralogical collection is one of the most valuable in the world, the specimens of the more costly productions of Nature being unequalled. In the garden of the school is a model of a mine, and of the machinery used in working it. Visitors are led by guides, with lighted tapers, through its devious underground passages, and shown the different metalliferous deposits, and the methods of extracting the ores. The school-building is a large and imposing structure, near the western end of Vassilievsky Island.

CHAPTER XII.

DINNER OF THE GOOD-BIRTH SOCIETY — POEM OF OLIVER WENDELL HOLMES.

IN the afternoon of the same day, at five o'clock, Mr. Fox and party went to dine with the Gentlemen's Club, or Good-birth Society (Blagorodnöe Sobranie), of St. Petersburg, at their beautiful summer pavilion on the estate of the Countess Strogonoff.

The cards of invitation, printed in Russian, read as follows:

GOOD-BIRTH SOCIETY

OF ST. PETERSBURG.

(Villa of the Countess Strogonoff.)

DINNER GIVEN IN HONOR OF THE AMBASSADOR OF THE UNITED STATES OF NORTH AMERICA.

AUGUST 5, 1866, 5 o'CLOCK.

Director, G. ZOUBINSKY.

When the carriages drove up to the gates of the villa, the Americans were agreeably surprised to find the entire-club, numbering three hundred gentlemen, in waiting to receive them. A great crowd of spectators also had gathered along the river-bank, anxious to welcome the strangers.

As Mr. Fox stepped from his carriage, a band of music, concealed behind a neighboring trellis, played "Hail Columbia," and Mr. Zoubinsky, the director of the society, bade him welcome, at the same time offering bread and salt, according to the Russian custom. The assembled members followed with a friendly hurrah, which was echoed by the spectators at the gates, and the guests passed into the gardens of the park.

After partaking of the usual "zakuska," which was spread in the dancing-pavilion, guests and hosts passed through the garden and into another tent, where dinner awaited them. Both the garden and the gallery of the house were adorned with costly plants. The interior of the dining-pavilion resembled a garden, so filled was it with shrubs and flowers. From above hung garlands and wreaths, entwined with the national colors of the two countries. On the right side, in a niche among the mass of verdure, was a large bust of the Emperor, and on the left were portraits of Washington, Lincoln, and Johnson. In two galleries, opposite each other, and almost hidden in greens and flowers, were stationed the bands, one military and one orchestral. Lamps and lustres, tastefully distributed among the decorations, shed a soft light throughout the tent.

The tables were arranged in the shape of the letter E, the Americans being placed at the principal one, directly opposite the bust of the Emperor. Care was taken that each should have next to him a Russian who could speak English. The dinner was thus made exceedingly agreeable, and more like a party of friends than a formal reception of strangers.

The *menu*, neatly printed in black, on glazed board, in both Russian and English, was as follows:

August 5, 1866.

DINNER

OF THE ST. PETERSBURG SOCIETY OF NOBLES.

Soup.
Pastry.
Chine of beef, with truffles and vegetables.
Steamed sterlet, with champagne.
Creamed partridges, with truffles.
Young peas and artichokes and white mushrooms.
Imperial punch.
Roasts: snipe, partridges, sea-snipe, etc., with Italian salad.
Iced Madelen of fresh fruit, peaches, apricots, and pineapples.
Fruit.
Coffee and tea.

Soon after the dinner began, Mr. Domontovitch spoke as follows, in the Russian language:

"Much-esteemed Mr. Fox and gentlemen Americans: This year our country has experienced an extraordinary national acknowledgment of sympathy and friendship. At the command of your great country of the two oceans, you, her plenipotentiary, have made a long voyage across the sea to lay her congratulations before our Emperor, and to express the heart-felt good wishes of her people.

"We were impatient to see you, of whom we always thought well. Dear guests, although you are far away from your own land, you are in a land near neighbor to yours in sentiment. You have brought the sympathizing congratulations of your mighty nation to our adored Emperor (Gosudar), nay, to the whole Russian people, but now preserved from a sore affliction by the mercy of Divine Providence. Your coming, your heart-felt address on your arrival, your salutes at Cronstadt, every thing so handsomely done, has won our love. In houses, in markets, in streets, everywhere, meet and follow you the cheers and greetings of Russians. And we, who are but a small part of the Russian race, we too give you our friendly greeting.

"It would take long to explain how this friendly alliance began, that has grown up and become so strong between the American and the Russian nations, almost unconsciously to both. Nobody will deny that here is the mutual sympathy of exalted souls, that here is the foundation of a lasting attachment. Under its influence, dear guests, we not only esteem you, we love you. Your sorrows and your joys never passed by us uncared for. The melancholy death of your illustrious President, we in Russia have not forgotten it, was heard of by us with real sympathy. We remember, too, with what enthusiasm we Russians watched your efforts to destroy the remnant of barbarism on your own soil, your enormous sacrifices to effect this, and the exploits of your heroes who, for this end, laid down their lives at Charleston, Mobile, New Orleans, and so many other places. We account it our distinguished good-fortune to be able to tell personally, in living, heart-felt speech, the representatives of your mighty nation our admiration of her heroic efforts, and to congratulate her on the glorious deeds which she achieved.

"From our deepest Russian soul we thank you, much-esteemed and dear guests, for this solemn national visit to our land, and for this your congratulation of the Russian people and of our adored Emperor, who has received the sympathy of both hemispheres. From a sincere heart we wish to you and to your country all prosperity and happiness, as to the best friends of our native land. The brotherly welcome that we now give you is echoed on the banks of the Volga and Ural, and we trust that it is answered on the Mississippi and Missouri. May it be well with the United States and with Russia, may both countries stand at the head of the world, and may this American-Russian friendship flourish and grow stronger, both in our day and in the days of our most distant posterity!"

After this speech, Mr. Zoubinsky gave the first regular toast: "To the health of the President of the United States of America, and to the good-fortune and grandeur of the American nation. God grant that this disinterested, warm, and ancient friendship of America and Russia may have no end!"

This toast was received with cheers, and the following telegram was at once dispatched to President Johnson, at Washington:

"The gentlemen of the St. Petersburg Good-birth Society, at an entertainment in honor of Mr. Fox, Envoy of the American Congress, are drinking the health of your Excellency, and to the happiness of the great American people. May the friendship of America and Russia endure forever!"

Mr. Fox responded as follows:

"The words of the speaker have not been translated for me, but it is impossible that I should not comprehend their signification, interpreting them by the hearty welcome that everywhere greets the mention of my country, its people, and the President. In answer to that speech, I have something agreeable to offer; but, first, let me say that though our language, laws, customs, and religious forms, separate us, to-night our hearts respond in harmony to one sentiment—mutual regard for the first and best of men, the Emperor Alexander II."

When the enthusiastic cheering that followed these words had subsided, Mr. Fox continued: "I allude to some verses, written especially for an occasion of this kind, by one of America's most fascinating poets, Oliver Wendell Holmes, who was kind enough to send me the lines before I left England on my way to Russia."

Mr. Fox then read the following poem in English:

POEM.

Though watery deserts hold apart
The worlds of East and West,
Still beats the self-same human heart
In each proud nation's breast.

Our floating turret tempts the main,
  And dares the howling blast,
To clasp more close the golden chain
  That long has bound them fast.

In vain the gales of ocean sweep,
  In vain the billows roar,
That chafe the wild and stormy steep
  Of storied Elsinore!

She comes! she comes! her banner dips
  In Neva's flashing tide,
With greeting on her cannon's lips,
  The storm-god's iron bride.

Peace garlands with the olive-bough
  Her thunder-bearing tower,
And plants before her cleaving prow
  The sea-foam's milk-white flower.

No prairies heaped their garnered store
  To fill her sunless hold;
Nor rich Nevada's gleaming ore
  Its hidden caves enfold.

But lightly as the sea-bird swings
  She floats the depth above,
A breath of flame to lend her wings,
  Her freight a people's love.

When darkness hid the stormy skies
  In war's long winter night,
One ray still cheered our straining eyes,
  The far-off Northern light.

And now the friendly rays return,
  From lights that glow afar,
Those clustered lamps of heaven that burn
  Around the Western star.

A nation's love in tears and smiles
  We bear across the sea;
O Neva of the hundred isles,
  We moor our hearts in thee!

Three cheers were given immediately for the American poet, Oliver Wendell Holmes.

Mr. Maikoff followed Mr. Fox with a Russian version of the poem, which he had translated for the occasion. The rapture of the listeners appeared to be boundless, and so pronounced were the *encores* that he was obliged to read it a second time, after which the company testified their gratitude in the Russian fashion—they tossed him in the air.

Toasts followed to the Empress, the Hereditary Grandduke, his newly-affianced bride, the Princess Dagmar, and to all of the reigning house.

Mr. Zoubinsky next toasted Mr. Fox, and read an address, asking him to accept, as the representative of the American people, the honorary membership of the Society.

To which Mr. Fox replied:

"Gentlemen, although it is probable that, after going back to America, I may never return and renew my acquaintance with the members of this Society, nevertheless I shall preserve a warm interest in the happiness and prosperity of the club, and remember with satisfaction the day spent here in your hospitable rooms."

Mr. Clay, in answer to a toast to himself, gave one to the Russian aristocracy (*dvorianstvo*), eulogizing them for so willingly sacrificing their individual interests to secure the success of the Emperor's projected system of equality.

After this came a toast to the prosperity and grandeur of Russia, with which Mr. Zoubinsky coupled the prosperity of the United States. Others followed to the officers of the American squadron, to the Russian Navy, to the Russian ladies, to the family of Mr. Fox, to Kommisaroff-Kostromsky, who was present, and to other guests.

The company arose from dinner at half-past eight and adjourned to the gardens, where a brilliant illumination met their eyes. The principal building of the club and the pavilion were aglow with fires, the terraces and the trees blazed with innumerable lights of many colors, and all the main alleys of the gardens were hung with lanterns and transparencies. The grounds of the villa were filled with people from the neighboring country residences, and, as the crowd moved to and fro through the illuminated paths, the scene was enchanting.

Unfortunately, the wind rose and a little rain fell about nine o'clock, and the guests were obliged to seek the pavilions; but it was soon over, the skies cleared again, and the scene without became as brilliant as before.

Dancing began in the pavilion at an early hour, and soon became animated, the ladies, who had joined the party after the dinner, doing all in their power to render the *fête* a success. The crowd upon the floor was great, but it only added to the gayety. Such of the ladies as could speak English chatted merrily with the Americans, and challenged them to the dance, so that the entertainment assumed the character of a meeting of intimate friends.

At half-past eleven Mr. Fox bade his kind hosts farewell. Almost everybody present accompanied him to his carriage, the military band meanwhile playing our national air. In the court-yard blazed great vases of colored fires, and Bengal lights lit his road from the park to the Strogonoff bridge.

A number of the Americans remained later, and the *fête* did not close until long after midnight.

The Russian Society in Warsaw sent to the Gentlemen's Club a telegram, giving a friendly salutation to the mission, to which Mr. Fox responded appropriately.

The card of honorary membership of the Gentlemen's Club, presented to Mr. Fox, reads as follows:

"*To the Envoy of the American Congress, Assistant Secretary of the Navy of the North American States, Member of the Washington Cabinet,* Mr. Fox:

"The St. Petersburg Good-birth Society (Gentlemen's Club) receiving this 5th of August, 1866, their friends, gentlemen of the United States of America, and anxious to preserve the remembrance of this fortunate day, ask you, Mr. Fox, as the representative of your nation, to accept the position of an Honorary Member of our Society.

"*Director,* G. ZOUBINSKY."

CHAPTER XIII.

RECEPTIONS ON THE MIANTONOMOH—PRESENTATIONS AT COURT—RACES AT CZARSKOË-SELO—DINNER OF MERCHANTS' SOCIETY OF MUTUAL ASSISTANCE.

A UGUST 18*th* (6*th*).—Saturday opened with a heavy rain. Arrangements had been made, the day before, to receive the diplomatic corps and some ladies of the court on board the Miantonomoh, and Mr. Fox went to Cronstadt for that purpose. About three o'clock the diplomats, accompanied by General Clay, came down from Peterhof in the Admiralty yacht. Mr. Fox, Commanders Murray and Beaumont, and the officers of the squadron, received them with the honors due to their rank, and offered them every facility to examine the monitor.

At the head of the diplomatic corps was the ambassador of France, Baron de Talleyrand, of the family of the famous Talleyrand. There came also the minister of Italy, the minister of Sweden, the minister of Portugal, Mr. de Muruaga, *chargé d'affaires* of Spain (the ambassador being absent), the two secretaries of the Prussian legation (the minister also being absent), and a number of other secretaries and *attachés*.

Mr. Fox, Mr. Clay, and Commanders Murray and Beaumont, were obliged to excuse themselves after greeting the distinguished visitors, as they had an engagement to attend the annual dinner of the Preobrajensky Regiment, at Krasnoö-Selo, at which the Emperor was expected to be present. The diplomats were left, therefore, in charge of Mr. Loubat, who explained to them the method of working the turrets and the gun-machinery, and showed them every thing of interest in the ship.

The Preobrajensky (Transfiguration) Regiment is one of the two oldest military organizations in Russia—it and the Semenovsky Regiment having been founded by Peter the Great, who served in the former through all the grades from private to colonel. With these two regiments the Czar destroyed the turbulent guards called Streltzi (archers, from *strela*, an arrow), formed by Ivan the Terrible in the latter part of the sixteenth century. Peter the Great was aided in this by a part of the Streltzi, which, under command of Colonel Sokoleff, remained faithful, and turned their weapons against their insurgent brethren.

The Preobrajensky Regiment always observes its anniversary by a grand dinner, which is usually attended by the Emperor. Unfortunately, Mr. Fox and party arrived in the city too late to take the train for Krasnoö-Selo, and missed this interesting festival, much to their regret.

After the departure from the Miantonomoh of the diplomatic body, the weather having become pleasanter, some ladies of the court, accompanied by Rear-Admiral Prince Galitzine and others, came from Peterhof in a yacht belonging to the Navy Department. Their visit was made as agreeable as possible, the gentlemen on board doing their utmost to entertain them, and extending to the party all the pleasant courtesies which naval officers are so familiar with. They appeared to enjoy the occasion, notwithstanding the unpropitious skies.

Among the visitors was the charming young Countess Apraxine, the daughter of Count Ivan Apraxine, grand-equerry of the Emperor, who attracted particular attention. She was most becomingly dressed in what one may call, very properly, the American costume, inasmuch as it represented the flag of our country. The bodice was blue, spangled with stars, and the skirt of alternate stripes of red and white. A sailor's hat, prettily trimmed with ribbons, and with the name "Miantonomoh" across the front, completed her costume, which attracted admiring eyes wherever she went.

Admiral Galitzine invited Mr. Loubat to go back to St. Petersburg with him on his yacht. The party, after leaving the Miantonomoh, went on board of the Gornostay, a gunboat about to sail for the Amoor River. She was commanded by Lieutenant Lütke, aide-de-camp of the Grand-duke Constantine, and son of Admiral Lütke, who had charge of the Grand-duke's education. After a short visit on the vessel, where they were received most courteously, the party returned to the city.

August 19*th* (7*th*).—At ten o'clock in the morning, the mission went by rail to Peterhof, to be presented to her Imperial Majesty the Empress. The presentation took place in the palace at half-past twelve, through Mr. Clay, the American minister. The party thus honored consisted of Mr. Fox, Messrs. Green and Loubat, and Commanders Murray and Beaumont, all of whom had been presented to the Emperor on the day of the presentation to his Imperial Majesty of the Resolution of Congress.

The Empress received the gentlemen most graciously, addressing a few words to each in English.

At the same time, Lieutenant-Commanders Cornwell and Pritchett, Messrs. Post, Adams, Lattimer, and Sawyer, of the American squadron, and Dr. Thomas D. Evans, of Paris, who had just been appointed by General Clay temporary *attaché* of the United States Legation, were formally presented to his Imperial Majesty the Emperor; and immediately afterward the same gentlemen had the honor of a presentation to the Empress.

From the palace of Peterhof, Mr. Fox, Commanders Murray and Beaumont, and Messrs. Green and Loubat, accompanied by Mr. Clay, went to Znamensky, the palace of the Grand-duke Nicholas, brother of the Emperor, where they were presented to his wife, the Grand-duchess Alexandra Petrovna.

The palace is beautifully situated on a high embankment on the road leading from the private grounds at Peterhof.

The party went thence to the country palace of the Grand-duchess Marie Nicholaevna, sister of the Emperor,

where they had the honor of presentation to her Imperial Highness, and to the Princess Eugénie of Leuchtenberg.

The Princess Eugénie is the third child and second daughter of the Grand-duchess Marie by her first marriage. She married, January 7, 1868, Alexander Frederick Constantine, Prince of Oldenburg.

Mr. Fox and the gentlemen accompanying him had the honor of lunching with their Imperial Highnesses the Grand-duchess Marie and her daughter, after which they returned to St. Petersburg.

In the afternoon, some of the American officers attended the races at Czarskoë-Selo. The Emperor and several of the imperial family were present, and the tribunes and the galleries were filled by the *élite* of St. Petersburg society. Our officers were assigned a stand on the right of that of the Emperor. The race was conducted in the English manner, the jockeys were all English, and the English language was heard on all sides. The return from the races to the Vauxhall, at the railway-station, was a brilliant and exciting spectacle. The road was filled with splendid equipages carrying fair ladies and dazzling uniforms, many of the teams being harnessed three abreast in the Russian style, and all driving at the top of their speed.

At six o'clock of the same day Mr. Fox, Messrs. Green and Loubat, Commanders Murray and Beaumont, General Clay, Mr. Curtin, and a number of officers of the ships, dined with the Russian Merchants' Society for Mutual Assistance, at their summer-house, near the Strogonoff bridge, on one of the islands in the Neva.

The dinner-tables were set in a great tent used ordinarily by the club for a dancing-hall. Large as it was, it could scarcely contain the members and the guests, who numbered more than four hundred. It was decorated with garlands and wreaths of oak-leaves, and with the national colors of the two countries. At one end was hung the portrait of the Emperor, surrounded with wreaths of flowers.

Unfortunately, the rain, which had fallen at intervals all day, increased in the evening, and interfered seriously with the illumination of the grounds. The fireworks, which had been prepared for the occasion, had to be postponed, disappointing a large number of spectators who had gathered to witness them.

The bill of fare of this dinner was as follows:

THE RUSSIAN MERCHANTS' SOCIETY FOR MUTUAL ASSISTANCE.

Dinner of August 7, 1866.

Potage à l'Américaine.
Potage à la Royale.
   Petits pâtés.
Salade de Terchis et queues d'écrevisses.
   Sauce Ravigote.
Filet de bœuf à la Monitor.
   Sauce Montpensier et truffes.
Filets de volailles et de gélinottes.
Chouxfleurs et artichaux.
Punch Victoria.
   Rôts.
Poulets, gélinottes, et brianaux.
   Salade.
Plombière aux fruits.
   Dessert.

During the dinner the orchestra played the following music:

PROGRAMME.

1. Le 19 février, marche dédiée à S. M. l'Empereur . . *Reinbold.*
2. Bouquet de mélodies Américaines . . . . *Reinbold.*
3. Ouverture de Sémiramis . . . . *Rossini.*
4. Le Vol de la Colombe (valse) . . . . . *Farbach.*
5. "Columbia," quadrille sur des motifs Américains . . *Reinbold.*
6. La Belle Amazone, pièce de caractère . . . . *Laschhorn.*
7. Le Réveil du Lion, caprice héroïque . - . . *Kontski.*

As soon as the champagne was brought on, Mr. Lapotnikoff proposed a toast "to the health of the President of the United States, to the health of all the Members of Congress, and to the prosperity and progress of the American nation."

Mr. Fox replied to this toast by giving one to the health of the Emperor, adding: "I see before me the portrait of a great sovereign. That portrait is decorated with flowers, emblems of peace and kindly feeling, and significant, I trust, of the future relations of Russia and America."

The usual toasts to the Empress, the hereditary Grandduke, and to all the imperial family, were received, like the others, with hearty Russian cheers. Mr. Lapotnikoff then proposed the health of Mr. Fox, for which the latter returned his thanks and said: "We are the guests of a society whose designation is 'mutual assistance.' May these words be prophetic of the future moral relations of Russia and America! The significant sympathies which Russia offered to the United States during our struggle for the Union will always be remembered and reciprocated."

General Clay made a speech, in response to a personal toast, in which he remarked that "many foreigners look at the friendship of Russia and America as artificial and chimerical. Let them look at the Russian and the American monitors at Cronstadt, and they will be convinced that that friendship is neither artificial nor chimerical." In conclusion, Mr. Clay proposed the health of his friend General Khrouleff, to which that gentleman replied with kind expressions for the future of the United States, and with wishes for continual friendship between the two nations.

Mr. Kokoreff, of Moscow, then arose and said:

"At the dinner given by the Merchants' Club of St. Petersburg to our dear transatlantic guests, we raised our glasses in honor of the authors of the national mission to Russia — the members of the American Congress. Moved by the succession of great festivals, we have not yet mentioned the origin of this mission. It is impossible not to be touched by this event. Men separated from us by wide oceans have felt the need of coming to us to express their joy at the preservation of the priceless life of our Emperor. Whence comes this mutual brotherly feeling, this expanding friendship, which has proved so strong?

"The monitor, invented for the destruction of mankind, has been charged by the American Congress with the duty of conveying those who express the holy feeling of brotherly love. In vain, for ten days and nights, did the waters sweep the deck of this iron ark which carried the ambassador. The ceaseless fury of the waves could not prevent the transmission to Russia of the feelings of joy and friendship for the Emperor and for his people. The cause which produced those feelings arose simultaneously in both countries: it was the desire of giving to each the right of free labor.

"In what did the Americans and the Russians resemble each other at this time? The former did not regret the blood of noble sons shed to obtain this right; and, in Russia, the nobility, who owned the serfs, did not regret the sacrifice of material interests which enabled them to fulfil the act of humanity and the wish of the Emperor. This sacrifice of interests proves the great and unmistakable prerogative of Russia before all other nations. And the citizens of the United States could not acknowledge (let us say it with pride) the men who were averse to those feelings.

"The estimation of these deeds, in America and in Russia, though different in their results, yet equal in their motives, is the task of history. It is our duty to honor the cause of the brotherly union of the Americans and the Russians.

"I offer, therefore, a united toast to 'the health and long life of all those who, in America as well as in Russia, have sacrificed their interests for the abolition of slavery and of serfdom.'"

Soon after the dinner the dances began, and they were kept up until two o'clock in the morning. It was estimated that more than two thousand persons were present at this *fête*.

Mr. Fox and party having been invited by the Emperor to attend a military review on the morrow, he, together with Commanders Murray and Beaumont and Messrs. Green and Loubat, left the scene of festivity, in company with General Clay and Admiral Lessovsky, at nine o'clock, and took the train for Krasnoë-Selo. They reached their destination in a heavy rain, and were assigned rooms in the Ambassadors' House, as before.

On this day Commander Murray received news of his promotion to the rank of captain, and received the congratulations of his friends, both Russians and Americans.

CHAPTER XIV.

REVIEW AT KRASNOË-SELO — MR. GROMOFF'S FÊTE — NAVAL REVIEW — THE IMPERIAL DINNER — BALL AT THE ENGLISH PALACE.

*A*UGUST 20*th* (8*th*).—Monday morning gave little promise of a successful review, the clouds still hanging low and the rain falling. But, about eleven o'clock, the rain ceased, and the party drove out in carriages to the field. Positions were assigned them on the mound, on the edge of the field, which overlooks the whole plain. The Imperial Guard was drawn up in front on the three sides of a hollow square.

The Russian Imperial Guard, although belonging to the regular army, forms an organization of its own. Since the reconstruction of the army, it alone has preserved the name of corps, the line in time of peace being divided into divisions. It forms a part of the troops of the military circumscription of St. Petersburg, and its officers have peculiar privileges, as stated before. It comprises twelve regiments of infantry, four battalions of chasseurs, twelve regiments of cavalry, and nine batteries of artillery, numbering in all over forty thousand men. The cavalry of the Guard forms two divisions. The first division comprises four regiments of cuirassiers, two regiments of Cossacks, a half-squadron of gendarmes, and a squadron of the body-guard, the latter composed entirely of noble Circassians, or Tcherkess.[1] The second division has two regiments of dragoons, two of lancers, and two of hussars.

At this review, after which the Guard leaves its summer camp and goes into its regular quarters, the Emperor distributes decorations, and promotes meritorious officers. His Majesty, attended by a brilliant staff, rides around the inside of the square. As he passes each regiment he salutes it with the words: "*Zdorovo rebiata*"—Good-day, children—the flag meanwhile being dipped, and the band playing the national hymn. The soldiers reply in unison: "*Zdravia gelaem vasche Imperatorskoë Velichestvo*"—Good health to your Imperial Majesty.

After this ceremony, on the present occasion, the Empress, accompanied by her ladies in waiting, rode around the field in a carriage, escorted by the Emperor and his staff. The imperial progress was attended by the music of the bands, and by the cheers of the soldiery.

The Empress and her ladies then left the carriages, and came to the pavilion on the mound, and the Emperor and his staff, still on horseback, took a position in front. All the troops then marched by, with bands playing and

---

[1] Circassia is properly Tcherkesala, or Tcherkeskala, a name given to the country by the Tartars. The Circassians call themselves Adighe, "the noble."

colors flying, the regiments cheering as they passed. The Cossacks of the Guard went by on the charge, the bands playing "Yankee Doodle."

When the review was ended, the Emperor came to the pavilion, and lunch was served. Mr. Fox was invited to a seat at his Majesty's table. Besides the Emperor and the Empress, there were present at the same table, the Grand-duke Nicholas Nicholaevitch, the Grand-duchess Alexandra Josefovna, wife of the Grand-duke Constantine Nicolaevitch, and the British ambassador, Sir Andrew Buchanan.

Mr. Fox and party returned to St. Petersburg at four o'clock, and dined at six o'clock with Mr. Winans, of Baltimore, the well-known contractor, who has had much to do with the construction of Russian railways.

At nine o'clock all attended a *fête* given in honor of the mission, by Mr. Gromoff, one of Russia's wealthiest merchants, at his country residence at the islands, in the suburbs of St. Petersburg. This entertainment, which cost more than forty thousand rubles, was equal to any which the Americans attended. Mr. Gromoff's spacious and beautiful villa is noted for the elegance of its surroundings. Its hot-houses have a well-deserved celebrity in St. Petersburg. But the principal charm of this place is its magnificent park, whose extent, natural beauty, and artistic development, render it a most agreeable and attractive summer resort.

On the night of the reception of our mission, the lawn before the house was set with a great number of lanterns, of all colors, arranged so as to form many beautiful and appropriate designs. In the centre appeared the legend, "Russia-America—1863-1866," the dates of the reciprocal national visits. Elsewhere were seen, in colors of fire, the star-spangled banner, the shields of the two countries, and many other figures. Farther on, in a building hung with hundreds of lanterns, a military band was playing. The bridges of the canal which crosses the park were also illuminated; and a beautiful grotto, and fountains and cascades, lit with fires, lent enchantment to the scene. The night was cloudy, but fortunately no rain fell.

The interior of the mansion was lighted even more elaborately than the grounds around it. A distinguished company was assembled in its parlors, among whom were the Minister of the Interior, Privy Councillor Valoueff; the Minister of the Finances, Privy Councillor de Reutern; the Minister of the Demesnes, Lieutenant-General Zelenoy; Vice-Admiral Crabbe; and Rear-Admirals Lessovsky and Popoff.

Dancing began immediately after the arrival of the Americans, and was continued until midnight, when the guests were invited up-stairs to supper. Mr. Gromoff proposed the health of Mr. Fox, and of the gentlemen accompanying him, adding a few complimentary remarks, to which Mr. Fox replied:

"I drink to our host, Mr. Gromoff, whose charming entertainment has given us so much pleasure. Thick clouds are overhead obscuring the heavens, but, in looking out on these illuminated grounds, it seems as if the stars had fallen upon them, and when I cast my eyes around this table, and see the beautiful faces of the Russian ladies, I can believe that the angels have come down to bless our meeting with their presence."

The ladies waved their handkerchiefs and clapped their hands in acknowledgment of this gallant speech.

After supper more dancing took place, but it was soon interrupted by an invitation to listen to a singer from the Don, a young man who possessed a remarkable voice. He sang the Russian airs with much expression, and received frequent congratulations and applause. Mr. Gromoff himself then played on the piano our national air, when the guests again took possession of the ballroom, and danced until a late hour.

On the departure of the Americans, Mr. Gromoff begged each to accept a photographic view of his residence and a card-photograph of himself, which were gratefully received. To Mr. Fox he presented a superb malachite album.

August 21*st* (9*th*).—Tuesday morning opened cloudy, but without rain. At half-past eight o'clock Mr. Fox and Commander Beaumont[1] left, with Admiral Lessovsky, on the steam-yacht Onega to Peterhof, where, by special invitation, they went on board the Emperor's yacht Alexandria. At ten o'clock his Majesty, accompanied by his brother, the Grand-duke Nicholas, and attended by his suite, came aboard, and, escorted by the steamers Strelna, Neva, and Onega, steamed for Cronstadt. On the imperial yacht were also General Baron Manteuffel,

---

[1] Captain Murray was prevented from attending by illness.

aide-de-camp of the King of Prussia, who was on a special mission to the Emperor of Russia; Admiral Crabbe; General Milutine, Minister of War; General Todtleben; Prince Galitzine, and others.

On arriving in the eastern roadstead the Emperor was received by Admiral Novossilsky, and by the chief of the staff, who had come down by the steamer Petersburg. The Emperor and his suite, accompanied by Mr. Fox and Commander Beaumont, went on board the transport Ghiliak, just returned from a long voyage, and afterward on board the sloop-of-war Gornostay, the corvette Griden, and the clipper Vsadnik, the last three being about to sail for the Pacific.

On the Emperor's return to the Alexandria, he gave orders by signal to the monitor Lava to weigh anchor, and to attack the Smertch, a turret-ship on the Cole's system. The monitor obeyed orders, sailed around the Smertch, delivered several broadsides of blank cartridges, and returned to her anchorage. The whole manœuvre lasted only twenty-three minutes. On another signal from the Alexandria, the Lava showed how a fire on board is extinguished.

The Emperor, having expressed his satisfaction at the movements by signal, visited Fort Constantine, and thence went in the Alexandria to the little roadstead, where the party landed in small boats at the Petrovsky pier. The Admiralty docks, the steamer workshops, and the new docks, were visited and inspected thoroughly. His Majesty complimented Baron Tiesenhausen, Major-General of Engineers, in charge of the works erecting at the latter place, and took his departure amid the cheers of the workmen. The party then went to Battery No. 10, in the North Channel, where an iron turret was erecting in the fort, and at half-past three o'clock returned to Peterhof, where Mr. Fox and Commander Beaumont took leave of the Emperor and went back with Admiral Lesovsky to St. Petersburg.

August 22d (10th).—Wednesday was clear, warm, and pleasant. Mr. Fox spent the most of the morning at Levitzky's, sitting for photographs, a great demand for his pictures having arisen.

At three o'clock in the afternoon, he went by steamer to Peterhof, to attend a grand banquet given by his Imperial Majesty, the Emperor, in honor of the American mission. Accompanying him were General Clay, Mr. Curtin, Captain Murray, Commander Beaumont, Messrs. Green and Loubat, and Messrs. Post, Adams, Latimer, and Sawyer, of the Augusta and the Miantonomoh.

The banquet-hall, in which covers were set for one hundred guests, was magnificently decorated. Besides their Imperial Majesties the Emperor and the Empress, there were present their Imperial Highnesses the Grand-duchess Alexandra Josefovna, the Grand-duchess Marie Nicholaevna, the Grand-duchess Catherine Michaïlovna, the Princess Eugénie of Leuchtenberg, his Imperial Highness the Duke of Leuchtenberg, and his Grand-ducal Highness George, Duke of Mecklenburg-Strelitz.

The Grand-duchess Catherine Michaïlovna is the daughter of the Grand-duke Michael, the son of the late Emperor Paul (father of the Emperor Nicholas I.), by his second wife, Marie, daughter of Frederick Eugene, Duke of Württemberg. She is, therefore, first-cousin to the Emperor. She married, February 16, 1851, George, Duke of Mecklenburg-Strelitz.

At the table General Clay was placed between the Grand-duchess Alexandra Josefovna and the Princess Eugénie of Leuchtenberg, on the left of the Emperor, and the Honorable Mr. Fox between the Grand-duchess Marie Nicholaevna and the Grand-duchess Catherine Michaïlovna, on the right of the Emperor. Captain Murray, Commander Beaumont, Messrs. Green and Loubat, and the other officers and gentlemen of the party, occupied seats opposite their Imperial Majesties.

The Vice-Chancellor of the Empire, Prince Gortchakoff, was unable to be present on account of indisposition. Vice-Admiral Crabbe, Rear-Admiral Lessovsky, and some high functionaries of the court and of the Ministry of Foreign Affairs, were seated with the American officers.

During the dinner charming music was played by two concealed bands of regiments of the Imperial Guard. The bill of fare was written on gilt-edged paper, surrounded by an engraved border, printed in black, representing fruits, flowers, and cornucopias, surmounted by the imperial arms and crown. It reads as follows:

THE IMPERIAL BANQUET.

MENU DU 14 AOÛT.

Potage Coulis de Cailles à la Castellane.
Potage Julienne à la Royale.
Petits pâtés et Coquilles de foies gras.
Sterlet [1] à la Russe.
Filet de bœuf et cotelettes de Volaille à la Chantilly.
Timbale de Brunancaux, l'élissier.
Petits pois aux croutons.
Rotis môléa. Salade.
Savarin à la Caradoc.
Bavarois Chateaubriand.

The guests were received by the grand-marshal of the Court, and, after the customary "zakuska," entered the dining-room and stood by their respective places until the imperial family entered, when all sat down together. After dinner all arose and stood until the Emperor and the imperial family had retired.

Toward the close of the dinner, his Majesty gave this sentiment in French:

"I drink to the prosperity of the United States of America, and to the perpetuity of the friendly relations between the two countries."

At the request of the Emperor, Admiral Lessovsky, who sat opposite to his Majesty, translated the toast into English.

No other toast was given. After dinner the guests followed the imperial family into an adjoining drawing-

---

[1] The sterlet is a delicate fish of the sturgeon variety, found in the Caspian Sea and the river Volga. They are taken in nets as they go up the river to spawn, and are kept alive in tanks until needed for the table. They are esteemed a great delicacy, and fine specimens command a very high price. The best caviare is made from their roe.

room, where conversation was held for a short time, when they separated.

The following semi-official account of the imperial banquet is translated from the *Journal de St. Pétersbourg:*

"On the 10th of August the palace of Peterhof witnessed a solemnity replete with interest. These walls, where yet lives the idea of Peter the Great, developed by his august successors, 'the window opened upon Europe,' welcomed the arrival from the other side of the ocean of the delegates of a great maritime nation, charged with a mission of courtesy, the bearers of friendly words and of pledges of amity, addressed not only by the Government of the Union to the sovereign of Russia, but by the American people to the people of Russia in the august person of a well-beloved monarch, who has borne so conspicuously and so far the glory of his country, and whose precious life, providentially preserved, is considered even in the other hemisphere as belonging to all humanity.

"Their Imperial Majesties the Emperor and the Empress gave a solemn banquet to these envoys, come from such a distance to attest the brotherhood of two great peoples and the union of two worlds.

"The American mission, headed by General Clay, the minister of the United States at St. Petersburg, was conveyed to the palace in court carriages. A numerous assemblage of the high dignitaries of state and of the ladies of the court were invited to take part in the reception. The banquet-hall was sumptuously decorated, and the dinner laid for one hundred guests. Their Imperial Highnesses the Grand-duchess Alexandra Josefovna, the

Grand-duchess Marie Nicholaevna, the Grand-duchess Catherine Michaïlovna, the Princess Eugénie of Leuchtenberg, his Imperial Highness the Duke of Leuchtenberg, and his Grand-ducal Highness the Duke George of Mecklenburg-Strelitz, aided their Majesties the Emperor and the Empress in their task of sovereign hospitality. General Clay was seated between their Imperial Highnesses the Grand-duchess Alexandra Josefovna and the Princess Eugénie of Leuchtenberg, and the Assistant Secretary of the Navy, Fox, between their Imperial Highnesses the Grand-duchess Marie Nicholaevna and the Grand-duchess Catherine Michaïlovna. Captains Murray and Beaumont, the other officers of the two United States men-of-war lying at Cronstadt, and the other members of the American mission and of the legation of the United States at St. Petersburg, were placed opposite their Imperial Majesties, who talked with several of them during dinner. The Vice-Chancellor of the Empire, Prince Gortchakoff, was retained at home by indisposition. Admiral Crabbe, Rear-Admiral Lessovsky, and some high functionaries of the court and of the Ministry of Foreign Affairs, were seated among the American delegates, to do the honors of the banquet, completed by the music of the concealed bands of two regiments of the Imperial Guard.

"Near the close of the dinner his Majesty the Emperor arose and gave a toast: 'To the prosperity of the United States of America, and to the perpetuity of the friendly relations between the two countries.' The whole assemblage arose to receive with respect these words, which found an echo in every heart.

"The whole of Russia will join in the toast.

"After dinner, their Majesties passed into an adjoining room, followed by their guests, with whom they conversed in the most gracious manner.

"This *fête*, at which a perfect cordiality presided, will certainly leave happy remembrances in the minds of our American visitors, as it will among those who assisted at it and who appreciated the tact and the personal qualities which distinguished them."

In the evening the gentlemen of the mission, and the officers accompanying them, attended a ball at the English Palace. It was the third of a series of charity balls given under the patronage of the Grand-duchess Marie Nicholaevna, for the benefit of the asylum founded at Peterhof in memory of her father, the late Emperor Nicholas. The English Palace is in the English Park, on the road from Peterhof to Oranienbaum. It is so called because it is laid out in the natural or English style, instead of the geometrical or French style, introduced by Le Nôtre, the celebrated gardener of Louis XIV., who planned the Versailles gardens. It is surrounded by pretty cottages and ornamental ponds, making it a very pleasant place for a summer *fête*. The charity balls given there are usually attended by members of the imperial family and by the nobility resident in the neighborhood of Peterhof and of St. Petersburg, but they are by no means exclusive. Civilians of good standing, and foreigners in Russia who are introduced by their respective ministers, are admitted on the contribution to the charity of three rubles, for which the tickets are nominally sold.

The ball was a brilliant one, being graced by the presence of the Emperor, who shook hands with Messrs. Fox, Murray, Beaumont, and Komissaroff, on entering; the Grand-duchess Marie, the Princess Eugénie, the Dukes Nicholas and Eugène of Leuchtenberg, and other members of the imperial house. There was also a large attendance of the nobility, and of distinguished officials.

On the entrance of the Grand-duchess Marie, Captain Murray and Commander Beaumont, followed by the rest of the American officers present, approached her Imperial Highness and begged permission to present an address, which was graciously granted.

Captain Murray then read the following:

"IMPERIAL HIGHNESS: The crews of the American men-of-war in the roadstead at Cronstadt, having learned that you preside over a noble work of charity, consecrated to the memory of your glorious father, and that the ball of this evening is in furtherance of this charity, I have been deputed by them to beg you to accept this modest offering.

"Graciously permit that the distribution of it be made by your own hand, with your customary judicious generosity."

Captain Murray then asked permission to remit to her Imperial Highness the sum of one thousand silver rubles. She thanked him with much fervor.

The dancing was kept up until one o'clock in the morning. After the ball the Americans were driven in court carriages to the palace of Peterhof, where apartments had been assigned them.

CHAPTER XV.

FROM ST. PETERSBURG TO MOSCOW—THE NICHOLAS RAILWAY—GREAT NOVGOROD—THE KREMLIN—TEMPLE OF THE SAVIOUR.

AUGUST 23d (11th).—Thursday opened warm and clear. As it was the day set for Mr. Fox's departure for Moscow, the Americans left Peterhof, and returned by steamer to St. Petersburg at an early hour.

At half-past two in the afternoon they drove to the Moscow railway-station, on the Nevsky Prospect, where they were received by Messrs. Bibikoff and Kokoreff, the deputies of the municipality of Moscow. The party consisted of Mr. Fox and Mr. Loubat; General Clay, and the Secretary of Legation, Mr. Curtin; Captain Murray, Commander Beaumont, and about twenty other officers. The correspondent of the *New York Tribune*, Mr. Boreman, was also of the party. Mr. Green did not go to Moscow, he having been recalled to the United States by private business a few days before. Rear-Admirals Lessovsky and Gorkovenko, and the other Russian gentlemen belonging to the committee of reception, accompanied the Americans.

The journey was made by the regular mail-train, but in two special cars which had been prepared for the occasion by the city of Moscow. The exteriors of these coaches were draped with the American colors. A fine lunch was also spread in one of them.

The distance from St. Petersburg to Moscow is four hundred and three miles. The road, called the Nicholas Railway, in honor of the Emperor Nicholas, who built it, follows very nearly an air-line, without reference to important towns between the two points. It is said that the Emperor, after examining carefully the surveys of the engineers, and noticing that the line had been deflected at different points to subserve local interests, laid a rule on the map, drew a straight line from St. Petersburg to Moscow, and ordered the road to be built on it. It is a solid and substantial work, with all its appointments in keeping. The stations, which are of brick and stone, are uniform in style, and have carefully-kept grounds around them, planted with shrubbery.

The country through which the railway runs is generally flat and uninteresting, much of it covered with white-birch and spruce trees. More than half of it, however, is cleared and under cultivation.

At the Luban Station the travellers were invited to dinner, prepared for them in the refreshment-rooms. The deputies from Moscow proposed a toast to "the health of all our dear guests who are going to Moscow." Mr. Fox gave in return a toast "to all the Russians, America's best friends."

At the Tchudovo Station the train stopped longer than

usual. The Governor of Novgorod, the President of the Provincial Council of the government of Novgorod, the members of the council, the representatives of the corporations of the city, the bailiffs of the communes, and the chiefs of the villages, awaited the Americans on the platform of the station.

When the train arrived, the Governor, Mr. Lerkhe, read a congratulatory address, to which the President of the Provincial Council, Mr. Katchaloff, added a few words to express the gratitude of the province of Novgorod for the sympathy expressed for Russia by the American people.

"*To the Representative of the Great American People,*
    Mr. G. V. Fox:

"The undersigned, representatives of all classes of the government of Novgorod, profiting by your visit, consider it a sacred duty to express, through you, to the great American people and to Congress, their heart-felt gratitude for the sentiments which you have come across the ocean to declare.

"This sympathy for the preservation of the precious life of our Emperor-Liberator touches us to the bottom of our souls, and is the strongest proof of the good and sincere disposition of the American toward the Russian people.

"These sentiments of friendship for Russia have been before expressed in the cordial reception given to our fleet in America, for which Russia is likewise profoundly grateful.

"In this union of two great peoples, the undersigned see innumerable mutual advantages.

(Signed) "EDWARD LERKHE, *Governor of Novgorod*,
"KATCHALOFF, *President of the Provincial Regency of the Government*, etc.

"VILLAGE OF TCHUDOVO, GOVERNMENT OF NOVGOROD, *August* 11, 1866."

Admiral Lessovsky translated into English the speeches as they were delivered. When they were done, Mr. Fox, taking a glass of wine, gave a toast to the prosperity of "Ancient Great Novgorod, the oldest of Russian cities."

One of the deputation of peasants, a venerable-looking old man, with a long, white beard, came forward and said to Admiral Lessovsky: "Tell them, father, that we will always pray to God for them, because they sympathize so deeply with us and with our Emperor."

The deputation then offered to Mr. Fox bread and salt, a living fish just caught in the river Volkhoff, some biscuits which the peasants in the neighborhood of this station make for sale, an album of remarkable views and antiquities of the province of Novgorod, a medal struck in commemoration of the one-thousandth anniversary of the founding of the Russian Empire, and a large lithographic view of the monument erected in memory of the same event.

As the train moved off from the station, the crowd cheered lustily, the Americans acknowledging the compliment from the cars. Messrs. Lerkhe, Katchaloff, and several other gentlemen of the deputation, accompanied the mission as far as the Volkhoff River. As they were about taking their leave, champagne was produced, and Mr. Kokoreff toasted "the eldest brothers of the Russian land, the Novgorodians."

This visit of a deputation representing the most ancient of Russian cities, is an example of the friendly spirit actuating the whole people with regard to America. They had driven forty-five miles that day, Novgorod being that distance from the railway, simply to offer their congratulations to the Americans, and to thank them for their sympathy for their Emperor.

Great Novgorod was one of the earliest settlements made by the wild Slavonian tribes when they began to drop their nomadic life. It dates from about the fifth century. In the ninth century, its inhabitants, troubled with internal dissension and feeling the need of a strong head, sent an embassy to the Normans and invited Rurik, one of their sea-kings, to come and rule over them. Rurik came in the year 862, took up his residence in Novgorod, and founded the Russian monarchy, over which his dynasty reigned for seven hundred years. Fedor I., who died in 1598, was the last of his race.[1] In 1862, a grand celebration was held at Novgorod, and a monument erected in commemoration of the one-thousandth anniversary of the existence of the empire.

The city is situated on the Volkhoff River, about forty-

[1] According to Scandinavian antiquaries, Rurik came from a district in Sweden called Roslagen or Rodeslagen; but Prof. Kostomaroff, of St. Petersburg, one of the best Russian historians of the present day, says that Rurik (in old Slavic, Falcon) and his brothers Sineus (Blue-moustache) and Truvor (Buffalo) were chiefs of the Varangi, a Slavic tribe from the coast of the Gulf of Finland.

five miles south of the line of the St. Petersburg and Moscow railway. It contains now less than twenty thousand inhabitants, but the story of its greatness and splendor may still be read in its ancient churches, one of which, the cathedral of St. Sophia, was standing when William the Conqueror went into England. The monastery of Turyeff, two miles from the city, is still older, having been founded by Yaroslaf, the son of Vladimir. The latter monarch, enrolled by the Russian Church among her saints, was the introducer of Christianity. It is interesting to note that his eldest son, Vladimir, who died before him, married the daughter of Harold, the last of the Saxon kings of England; the issue of which marriage, a daughter, became the mother of Waldemar the Great, King of Denmark.

August 24th (12th).—At Tver, where the railway crosses the Volga, another deputation was in waiting to welcome the Americans, notwithstanding the early hour, five A. M., at which the train arrived. The usual greetings and compliments were exchanged here and bread and salt again presented.

At half-past ten o'clock in the morning the train entered the Moscow Station. A great crowd of people and a military band received the visitors with cheers and "Hail Columbia." Prince Stcherbatoff, the mayor of the city, the members of the city council, and numerous representatives of the different corporations, all with red, white, and blue ribbons in their button-holes, welcomed the mission in the most cordial and flattering terms, and informed Mr. Fox that he had been made an honorary citizen of Moscow. The travellers were driven at once to the hotel of Mr. Kokoroff, in open carriages, with gayly-dressed horses, the drivers wearing American cockades. The streets through which they passed were densely crowded with citizens, who cheered lustily and tossed their hats in air. At last the procession reached its destination. The Kokoreff Hotel, a large and imposing building opposite the Kremlin, was decorated with a profusion of American and Russian flags, with the arms of the two countries, and with the arms of the city of Moscow.

Mr. Kokoroff had munificently provided apartments, thirty-six in number, in his hotel, for the entire party. The chambers were luxuriously furnished, and every thing had been done to secure the comfort of the guests. The Americans were surprised to find in each room photographs of Messrs. Fox, Murray, and Beaumont, and in that of Mr. Fox portraits of Washington, Lincoln, and Johnson. But their surprise was greater when they saw, on the walls of the reading-room, portraits in oil of Messrs. Fox, Murray, and Beaumont. It was explained afterward that Mr. Kokoreff had employed a St. Petersburg artist, Mr. Turin, to make sketches of these gentlemen at the evening party at Mr. Gromoff's, which he accomplished without being perceived. From these sketches the portraits were painted. "When the originals have departed," gallantly said Mr. Kokoreff, "these copies will remain with us, an agreeable souvenir of our guests."

The Kokoreff Hotel stands on the river-bank, directly

opposite the Kremlin, near the bridge. It is a large building, of much architectural pretension, and contains over three hundred chambers. In its reading-room are to be found a great variety of Russian and foreign newspapers. Mr. Kokoreff, its owner, is one of the wealthy merchants of Russia. The Americans were under many obligations to him for courtesies while in Moscow.

After an official call on Prince Dolgorouky, aide-de-camp General of the Emperor and Governor-General of Moscow, the gentlemen of the mission, accompanied by Prince Stcherbatoff and others, visited the different buildings in the Kremlin, Moscow's famous citadel. *Kremlin*, a word of uncertain derivation, is a name common to the fortress around which almost all ancient Russian towns were built.

The Kremlin of Moscow is an enclosure almost triangular, surrounded by high walls, with a massive tower at each angle. From the foundation of this fortress, which existed in the middle of the twelfth century, dates that of Moscow itself. About 1170, Andreas, the son of Vladimir Monomachus,[1] Prince of Kiew, built a stone church within the Kremlin, and deposited in it the miraculous picture of the Virgin, painted by St. Luke. This picture is still shown in the Cathedral of the Assumption, which stands on the site of the ancient building. Moscow and

---

[1] Vladimir Monomachus was the grandson of St. Vladimir, and Prince of Kiew. In 1114, the Greek Emperor Constantine Monomachus sent him from Constantinople, as presents, a cross made of the wood of the true cross, an imperial crown, a splendid dalmatica, and a chain of gold. Vladimir then took the name of Monomachus, in compliment to the Emperor, and assumed the title of Czar of Grand Russia.

its Kremlin suffered much in the middle ages. It was sacked and burned by the Mongols in the thirteenth century, and again in the fourteenth and fifteenth centuries by the princes of Lithuania. The city arose the third time from its ruins in the reign of Ivan Vassiliëvitch, called the Terrible, who gave it the spoils of Novgorod, enlarged its wall, and built the towers of the Kremlin. It is now about twenty miles in circuit, and contains a population of nearly four hundred thousand. The Kremlin, the original nucleus of the city, is still its central point. From it the streets radiate, like the spokes of a wheel, but having no regular plan, and crooking in every direction.

From its situation the Kremlin commands the whole city. Its great tower of Ivan Veliky, with its gilded cupola nearly three hundred and twenty-five feet above its foundations, looks down on all the surrounding towers, and its massive battlemented walls are yet strong to defend the palace of its rulers and the sanctuary of its patriarchs. Its interior is an orderless assemblage of buildings in all styles and of different periods. There is no symmetry, no regularity, neither in the structures, the streets, nor in the spaces between the buildings. Cathedrals, chapels, palaces, built from age to age without any apparent design, of a style antique and Byzantine in character, with numerous spires, cupolas, and towers, gilded and painted with various colors, present a medley of architecture at once strange, incongruous, and attractive.

The Tower of Ivan Veliky is an octagonal structure,

five stories in height. From its summit a magnificent view is obtained of Moscow and the surrounding plain, with its hundreds of churches, palaces, and convents, its towers and steeples, its gilded cupolas and azure domes, and its mass of green-roofed houses stretching as far as the eye can see. The lower story of the tower is used as a chapel. In the next three above it are hung thirty-four bells of various sizes, the largest of which weighs sixty-four tons. But large as is this bell, it is little more than one-fourth the size of the *Czar Kolokol*, the Czar of Bells, which stands upon a granite pedestal at the foot of the tower. The great bell of Moscow was cast originally about the year 1600, but has been recast twice since, the last time by the Empress Anne in 1733. Four years after, it fell during a fire, and a large piece was broken out of one side. From that time until 1836 it lay buried in the ground, when the Emperor Nicholas caused it to be placed in its present position.[1] It measures about twenty feet in height, twenty-one feet in diameter, and weighs over four hundred and forty thousand pounds. Tradition says that when it was fused the people threw into the furnace quantities of gold and silver as votive offerings. Its metal is valued, at a low calculation, at three hundred thousand dollars.

The sacred edifices within the Kremlin walls are the Cathedrals of the Assumption (*Uspensky Sobor*), of the Archangel Michael (*Arkhangelsky Sobor*), and of the Annunciation (*Blagovestchensky Sobor*), and the Church

---

[1] It was raised and placed upon its pedestal by M. Montferrand, the architect of the Cathedral of St. Isaac's in St. Petersburg.

of the Redeemer in the Wood (*Spass na Boru*). In the Cathedral of the Assumption, formerly called the Patriarchal Cathedral, because the patriarchs officiated in it, all the Russian Emperors since the days of Ivan the Terrible have been crowned. It is a small building with a narrow and sombre nave, whose vaulted roof is sustained by four great columns that occupy almost a third of its floor. Walls, vault, and pillars, are covered with frescoes, representing in a gigantic form the figures of the apostles and the saints, with purple mantles and golden aureoles. The ikonastas is of silver gilt, covered with carved images, and resplendent with precious stones. On this screen hangs the picture of the Virgin, said to have been painted by St. Luke, and another representing St. John, attributed to the Greek Emperor Emanuel. Among the holy relics preserved with religious care is what is claimed to be one of the veritable tunics worn by Jesus Christ. The church is very rich in ornamentation, in holy relics, and in historical associations, and is one of the most venerated structures in Russia.

The Cathedral of the Archangel Michael is of nearly the same form as the Assumption, and like it is crowned with five cupolas.[1] It has also a splendid screen, and contains relics of great renown. It was built in 1505, on the site of another church erected in 1333, in memory of Russia's deliverance from famine. Up to the time of Peter the Great it was the burial-place of the imperial

---

[1] These, which are common to all Russian churches, are in honor of Christ and the four Evangelists.

family. Their tombs are still to be seen in the vaults, inscribed with their names, ages, and titles.

The Cathedral of the Annunciation is paved with jasper and agate, set with gold, and its walls are covered with figures of apostles and martyrs. In the portico are depicted the Greek philosophers, as heralds of Christ's coming. Within this church the Czars were formerly baptized and married. It contains numerous relics and treasures of priceless value.

The Church of the Redeemer in the Wood is one of the oldest buildings in Moscow. It is very small, and has little of interest about it, except its antiquity. It received its name because originally built in a wood which crowned the height of the Kremlin.

Other ecclesiastical buildings are the Miracle Monastery, the Ascension Convent, and the Sacristy or House of the Holy Synod. In the latter are preserved the sacerdotal robes and ornaments and the sacred vessels used by the different patriarchs. The most ancient of the vestments are those of St. Peter, who was Patriarch of Russia in the fourteenth century. The mitres of all the patriarchs are deposited here, as well as many other interesting sacred relics.

The palace is mostly modern, dating from the reign of Nicholas I. It stands on the site of the old palace rebuilt by Catherine II., which was burned by the French in 1812. It is no longer used as a royal residence, although suites of apartments are kept in readiness in case of an imperial visit. The interior is very beautiful. The Hall of St. George, a magnificent room two hundred feet long, has inscribed on its walls in letters of gold the names of the persons and regiments decorated with the Order of St. George. It is furnished with black and orange, the colors of the order, which was founded by Catherine II., in 1769.

Another grand hall, in pink and gold, is dedicated to the Order of St. Alexander Nevsky, founded by Peter the Great, in 1722. St. Andrew's Hall is hung with blue silk, and is decorated with the arms of all the provinces of Russia. The order dates from 1698, and was founded by Peter the Great. There are also halls dedicated to the Orders of St. Catherine and of St. Vladimir. The Order of St. Catherine, founded by Peter the Great in 1714, is a distinction conferred only upon ladies, by the Empress, who has a splendid throne at one end of the apartment. The Hall of St. Vladimir is hung with black and red, the colors of the order, which was founded by Catherine II., in 1782.[1] At one end of this hall is the "Red Staircase,"[2] used only by the Emperor in state ceremonials. The banquet-room is one of the oldest parts of the palace, dating from the fifteenth century. It is a vaulted chamber, with a single column in the centre, from which the arches of the roof spring. After the coronation ceremony in the cathedral, the Emperor dines in this room

---

[1] The other Russian orders are: the White Eagle, founded by Wladislas IV., King of Poland, in 1325; St. Anne, by Charles Frederick of Sleewig-Holstein, in 1735; and St. Stanislas, by Stanislas, King of Poland, in 1765. The Order of St. Andrew takes precedence of the others.

[2] The Red Staircase, which is of stone, is so called either because it is covered with red cloth on great occasions, or because, in ancient times, red was a synonyme of beautiful or handsome.

in state, among the great nobles and dignitaries of the empire, wearing the imperial robes and insignia.

The right wing of the palace is entirely new, having been erected only about twenty years. It is called the Treasury, and is devoted to the preservation of the curiosities, relics, regalia, and treasures, illustrative of the history of the reigning dynasty and of Russia. Here may be seen the crowns of the different countries subjugated by Russia, the globes, the sceptres, the thrones of the Czars, the robes worn by them at their coronations, the gifts brought by conquered chiefs and princes, and the golden vessels on which the people of Moscow offer the bread and salt to their sovereign when he visits their city. Among the thrones is that of Poland, and the ivory one brought from Constantinople by Sophia Palæologus, the niece of the last Greek emperor, who married Ivan III., in 1472. The latter was used at the coronation of Alexander II. The throne of Boris Godunoff, sent to him by the Shah of Persia, in 1604, is studded with rubies, pearls, and turquoises. The crown of Ivan V. contains nine hundred diamonds, and that of the Empress Anne more than twenty-five hundred. In a glass case in one of the rooms are preserved the insignia of the Order of the Garter, sent by Queen Elizabeth of England to Ivan the Terrible; and, in another room, is a large coach, with pictured panels, sent by the same sovereign to the Czar Boris Godunoff. But, amid all the magnificence of this collection, the eye, wearied with the lustre of gold and the sparkle of brilliants, turns for relief to a few relics intrinsically valueless, but priceless for the memories which they evoke. Among these is the rude litter on which the sick Charles XII. was borne from rank to rank of his army on the terrible day of Pultowa, and the sword and spurs which he wore. In another place may be seen the boots of his great conqueror, mended by his own imperial hands; and, in the room devoted to carriages, is the camp-bedstead of Napoleon, taken at the Beresina.

In another hall is preserved a collection of arms and of armor, illustrative of Russian history. Here are swords, single-handed and two-handed—plain swords for service and swords blazing with precious stones; shields, casques, and suits of armor, enamelled, gold-inlaid, and engraved; the standards of the Czars and captured battle-flags; guns of every period, from the ancient arquebuse to the modern rifle; and many a weapon that has seen historic fields, or been wielded by hands that have left their mark upon the world.

Beside the Arsenal, a massive building at the northern angle of the Kremlin, are arranged in rows nine hundred captured cannon, three hundred and sixty-five of which, one for every day in the year, were lost by the French in the awful retreat from Moscow. Austria is represented by one hundred and ninety pieces, and Prussia by one hundred and twenty-three. At the entrance of the arsenal are two very long guns of ancient manufacture; and projecting from one of the angles of the building is the Czar cannon (*Czar Pushka*), weighing forty tons, which was cast in the beginning of the seventeenth century.

The Emperor Alexander II. was born in the Kremlin, in the building called the Little Palace. This was once the residence of the Metropolitan of Moscow, but it was presented to the Emperor Nicholas about the beginning of his reign.

The walls of the Kremlin, which are something over a mile and a quarter in circuit, are pierced by five gates, to each of which is attached a religious or an historical importance. The most venerated of these gates is one over which is a picture of the Saviour, so faded that one can scarcely distinguish the features, with a large antique lamp suspended by chains before it. This time-blackened image is believed by the people to be endowed with miraculous powers. It preserved Moscow from the Tartars; it subdued the pestilence in the reign of Catherine; it turned back the tide of French invasion, and saved Russia. The gate is called the Holy Gate, and no Russian may pass through it without making obeisance and the sign of the cross, and no stranger but with uncovered head.

The gate of St. Nicholas has over it an image of that saint under glass, with a lamp before it. An inscription on the wall recites that when Napoleon attempted to blow up the tower in 1812, although the gate-way was rent by the explosion, the picture and its glass front were uninjured. All day long, the pious people of Russia's holy city cross themselves, in passing this venerated image, and burn the little tapers which take part in all their religious offices.

Although Moscow was almost entirely destroyed in

1812, and the Kremlin greatly injured, both city and citadel now present nearly the same appearance and architectural character that distinguished them before the conflagration. The streets retain their ancient sites, and most of the buildings have been restored on their original foundations. In many instances the old walls are still standing.

The Temple of the Saviour, intended to commemorate Russia's triumph over Napoleon, was founded the year of the invasion, but is not yet finished. It was begun originally on the hills from which the French Emperor first looked on the city, but, the ground proving unfit for the foundations, it was removed to its present site on the river-bank above the Kremlin. When completed, it will be one of the most splendid temples in the world.

The following account, from the Moscow *Gazette*, of a visit made to this church, by his Majesty the Emperor and the grand-dukes, August 14th, a few days after the mission, gives an interesting description of the edifice, as it is and as it will be when ready for dedication :

"His Majesty and the grand-dukes examined the work with a minute attention, and the Emperor approved and confirmed the plans made by the architect-in-chief, Tohn. These works consist, as is well known, of a mosaic pavement to cover the entire ground-floor of the temple and of the exterior peristyle, and of a number of paintings on the circumference of the cupola, after the designs of Professor Bassine.

"The mosaic pavement, judging from the design, will be superb. It will be composed principally of labradorite[1] and of porphyry, from Schokha, of which two materials the church is in great part constructed. Sienna marble and various other beautiful Italian marbles have also been used in the composition of this mosaic.

"The archbishop's seat, in the middle of the temple under the cupola, will be in plain marble, after the idea of the Metropolitan Philaret; the steps which lead to it will be in labradorite, the same as the rood-loft.

"The designs of Professor Bassine, to be reproduced on the circumference of the cupola, and which will be thirty-eight sagenes in length by three in breadth, are composed of the following figures: In the middle, on the side of the altar, Christ seated upon a throne; on his right the Virgin Mary, and on his left Saint John the Baptist; next the archangels and the figures of the apostles, the prophets, and the patriarchs, who, ever withdrawing from Christ, come to rejoin him on the other side of the cupola. Some of these figures promise to be very remarkable, judging from the design, such as those of Saint John the Baptist, of Adam, and of many other personages of Holy Writ.

"The upper part of the circumference of the cupola will be surmounted by a gallery, and an immense immovable chandelier will be suspended to light the cupola.

---

[1] Labradorite is a beautiful variety of feldspar of pearly lustre, often exhibiting a play of blue, green, yellow, and red colors. It is found in abundance in Labrador, hence its name. Porphyry (πορφυρα, purple) is a rock of a compact base of reddish feldspar, in which are disseminated rose-colored crystals of feldspar. Some varieties have a base of green, red, purple, or black. It is very hard, and susceptible of a beautiful polish. The Russians have been very successful in working it.

This chandelier is finished, but is not yet hung. The cupola is twelve sagenes in diameter; it is so high that the whole tower of Ivan Veliky, with the cross on its summit, could stand within it. The interior height of the temple is thirty-three sagenes and one and three-fourths archine above the level of the ground, and thirty-two sagenes and three-fourths of an archine above the pavement. Its exterior height, comprising the cross on the summit, is forty-nine sagenes.¹

"The paintings on the ceiling of the cupola are executed by Professor Markoff, and will be finished, it is said, by January next. They represent God the Father with open arms, and the Holy Spirit issuing from His lips in the figure of a dove; the infant Jesus, bearing on His breast the inscription '*Logos*' (the Word), is seated upon His knee.

"The head of God the Father is not painted at the zenith of the cupola, but a little lower down, so that in entering one can see the whole figure very distinctly.

"The gigantic cupola is sustained by four pillars of colossal size, four sagenes in diameter. The general plan of the interior of the church is in the form of a regular cross of four branches. The ikonastas, placed at the eastern extremity of the cross, will have, at the holy doors, the form of a tent.

¹ The archine, or arshin, is twenty-eight inches; and the sagene, or sashin, is three archines, which makes it equal to seven English feet. The cupola is eighty-four feet in diameter, and its height (interior) above the floor is two hundred and twenty-five feet and nine inches. The tower of Ivan Veliky is nearly two hundred and twenty-five feet high. The exterior height of the Temple of the Saviour is three hundred and forty-three feet.

"The grand painting, and two other paintings of the altar, the holy doors, and some pictures of the ikonastas, will be due to the pencil of Professor Neff. The artist has chosen, as a subject for the large painting of the altar, the Last Supper; the picture above the altar of sacrifice will have for its subject the prayer in the Garden of Olives; and those at the bottom of the ikonastas will be, on the one side, Jesus seated upon the throne, and on the other the birth of Christ (the Virgin Mary holding the new-born babe in her arms). The rest of the pictures covering the ikonastas, and the paintings of the walls of the temple above the choir, have been intrusted to Messrs. Reimers, Khudiakoff, Wenig, and divers other artists.

"The casing of the interior walls of the temple is advancing rapidly. The bases of the walls, which are to be covered with labradorite and porphyry from Schokha, are nearly completed. In addition, there will be arcades sustained by monolithic columns of porphyry from Schokha. Frames, also of this same porphyry, will be prepared to receive medallions in labradorite.

"Above these medallions, which form a kind of interior plinth, will be executed works in Italian marble as far as the choir, which extends above the exterior peristyle its entire length. Above the choir, up to the cupola, there will be only paintings.

"The porphyry of Schokha (government of Olonetzk) has a more homogeneous body than the labradorite; it cannot be sawn, it must be cut with the chisel.

"The cutting of the columns, the flights of steps, and the other parts of the building, is not done by machinery, but by hand, by Russian workmen, under the direction of a skilful master stone-cutter, named Theodore Philipoff.

"The work is truly of a wonderful perfection, and his Majesty paused with interest near the blocks of porphyry and of labradorite which were polishing before him. The Emperor deigned even to express, on this point, his entire satisfaction.

"When the pictures of the ceiling, which his Majesty has also honored with his approval, shall be finished, M. Tohn intends to construct under the cupola a temporary glass window, which will let in the light, while preserving the pictures from the dust, and by which the public can enter to visit the cupola. His Majesty has been pleased to authorize its construction.

"M. Tohn, desiring to be able to judge soon of the general appearance of the work which he has conceived and executed, as is very natural, not expecting to live a great while longer (M. Tohn is now very old), wishes to see begun before him all of the temple that remains to be executed; which will give him the certainty that the plan will not suffer any great change in the future.

"As to the time necessary for the completion of the work, that depends entirely on the pecuniary means placed at the disposal of the commission charged with its execution.

"If the means suffice, the temple will be done in ten or twelve years; if not, it may yet take twenty-five years. In any event, the Temple of the Saviour will be superb when finished, notwithstanding what is said of its semi-Byzantine style.

"We must not forget that this temple is built to commemorate the expulsion of the French in 1812, and that it has, consequently, an historical significance. It is surrounded by an exterior peristyle for religious processions.

"The walls of this peristyle will be covered with paintings representing the principal events of the wars of 1812, 1813, 1814, and 1815; and the trophies captured in those wars will be preserved in it.

"The entrances of this peristyle, which are reached by superb staircases in Finland granite, will be on the four sides (it is also in granite, of which is constructed the whole basement of the temple).

"The exterior walls of the temple are cased up to their top with a white stone, and ornamented with a double row of bass-reliefs (the bottom of the principal bass-reliefs is covered with stucco).

"The lower range of bass-reliefs represents biblical and evangelical subjects, which are suggestive of the principal events of Russian history during the time mentioned. The upper range is composed of medallions representing the days when the Russians achieved the victories.

"The area before the temple will be surrounded by a railing and adorned with the statues of the principal heroes of the national war. Pyramids of cannon and of cannon-balls will be erected at the grand gates. The houses which surround the temple will be demolished and a magnificent granite stairway will descend to the Moskva."

CHAPTER XVI.

PRINCE DOLGOROUKY'S DINNER—FÊTE AT THE ZOOLOGICAL GARDENS—THE BAZAAR—CHURCH OF KAZAN—AGRICULTURAL ACADEMY—REVIEW OF TROOPS—NOVO DIEVITCHY CONVENT.

AT seven o'clock, the same evening, a grand banquet was given to the members of the mission, by the governor-general, at his official residence. The Americans were received at the entrance, as they had been in Cronstadt and St. Petersburg, by the cheers of an immense multitude, and by the strains of "Hail Columbia" from a military band. The outside of the building was decorated with the flags of the two countries, with the arms of the United States and of the city of Moscow, and with garlands. The vestibule was similarly ornamented. The staircase was covered with flowers and evergreens, and lined with footmen in scarlet liveries, powdered wigs, and silk stockings. On the walls appeared again the arms of America, and over the grand entrance, at the head of the stairs, was the shield of the Russian Empire. A second band, placed in the first reception-room, also played American airs.

The great hall, in which the dinner was served, was brilliantly illuminated and decorated with flowers, coats-of-arms, and with the Russian and American flags. The portrait of the Emperor was wreathed in lilacs, and above it were draped the Russian naval and government ensigns, and the flag of the city of Moscow. The opposite wall was hung with a large American ensign.

At half-past seven o'clock the company sat down to dinner. Tables more magnificent could scarcely be devised, the Prince's exquisite service of solid silver gilt being almost lost in the profusion of exotic flowers. The walls were lined with liveried footmen, who stood like statues the whole evening; other servants, dressed in the usual black and white, waiting on the guests. An orchestra played operatic music, and the national airs of Russia and of America, during the dinner.

The bill of fare was printed in gold on tinted paper, within a colored border of fruit, flowers, and game, with the arms of Prince Dolgorouky, also in colors, at the top. It was as follows:

MENU.

Dîner du 1½ Août, 1866.

Potage tortue aux sterlets.
Consommé à la Sérigné.
Bouchées et petits pâtés.
Longe de veau à la jardinière.
Saumons de la Néva.
Foies gras de Strasbourg.
Punch Impérial.
Dindonneaux et gibier.
Fonds d'artichauts et petits pois.
Pudding Washington.
Fontaine Orientale.

After the customary toasts to the President of the United States, to the Emperor of Russia, and to the Empress and the imperial family, all of which were received with cheers and followed by appropriate music, Prince Dolgorouky proposed the health of Mr. Fox, accompanying the toast with these remarks:

"The welcome which has been given you, gentlemen, by our navy, and by all classes of the Russian people, has shown you what sympathy the citizens of the United States enjoy in our country. Believe me, you will not meet with a welcome less cordial nor less friendly in Moscow, the ancient capital of the empire, where the name of American is loved and honored as that of a great people who cherish for us a sincere friendship. You, gentlemen, have shared with us our joy at the miraculous preservation of our beloved sovereign. The congratulations expressed by you in the name of the people of the United States have touched our hearts deeply, and the whole nation gives you its thanks."

Mr. Fox replied:

"If the toast in which my name has been pronounced had been addressed to me personally, I should feel some embarrassment in replying; but it is offered to all the Americans present, and also to those who, though inhabiting the other side of the globe, had their sympathies aroused by the danger which menaced your sovereign. This feeling has found expression in the resolution of Congress and the dispatch of the monitor Miantonomoh with this mission to your country. If the hearts of the Americans present could be uncovered, there would be found what I now behold, the flags of Russia and of America intertwined. May these two flags in peaceful embrace be thus united forever!" (All arose and cheered.)

Prince Dolgorouky then proposed the health of General Clay, and of Captain Murray and Commander Beaumont, accompanying the toast with these remarks:

"The brilliant reception given by the United States to the Russian squadron in 1863 and 1864 has left in Russian hearts an ineffaceable remembrance of gratitude, and has drawn together still more closely, if possible, the ties of love and of sympathy which unite the two nations."

Captain Murray thanked Prince Dolgorouky in behalf of himself and of Commander Beaumont, and proposed "The Russian Army and Navy."

General Clay then toasted the Governor-General of Moscow, who replied as follows:

"The Russian and American people are attracted toward each other by resemblances which it is impossible not to acknowledge. This is one of them: At the time when you fought so energetically for the grand principle of the abolition of slavery, our well-beloved monarch gave liberty to twenty-two millions of serfs, who now bless their liberator. The electric telegraph, that powerful instrument of civilization, has annihilated the distance which separates the two continents. It will transmit to the other side of the ocean these mutual congratulations of nations whose hearts beat in unison. It will tell your countrymen that these are the congratulations of nations sincerely attached to each other. I drink to the health of the American Army and Navy, and to all the American people. Long live America and Americans!"

During the progress of the dinner a military band was heard playing in front of the house, and loud and frequent cheers proclaimed the presence of a great crowd of the citizens of Moscow. Prince Dolgorouky conducted Mr. Fox to the balcony, in answer to the popular appeal. As far as could be seen, the open space in front of the palace was packed with human beings. As soon as the American envoy was descried, the air rang with loud and prolonged hurrahs. It seemed as if the shouts would never end. It was a grand, spontaneous, popular ovation, and proved that the people of Russia's ancient capital were as profoundly touched by the proffered sympathy of the United States as were those of St. Petersburg. The occasion was a most gratifying one to both host and guests.

At ten o'clock the company visited the Zoological Gardens, the president and directors of the society having left invitations in the morning to a *fête* to be given in honor of the Americans. The grounds were splendidly illuminated and filled with people. The directors met the party at the gate, and conducted them, preceded by a military band playing our national march, to the lower pond in the botanical garden, where a second band received them with American and Russian airs. The loud cheers of the people forced several repetitions of the national music. The night was clear and bright, and the appearance of the gardens, lit with lanterns, different-colored lights, and transparencies, was most beautiful.

The names of Washington, Franklin, Lincoln, and Johnson, were prominently displayed.

When the military bands had finished, a company of Tyroleans, dressed in their picturesque national costume, entertained the party with some of their sweet songs and dances. The Americans were invited next to the pavilion, from the gallery of which they witnessed a display of fireworks on the shore of the lake. This exhibition was something really remarkable. The principal piece represented the Temple of Liberty, with the inscription " Hail Columbia " in letters of fire; from columns on each side was the Genius of Russia, in the act of flying, with outstretched arms toward it. Another piece represented a battle between an old-fashioned three-decker and a monitor—ending in the former being blown into the air, amid immense applause by the spectators. Afterward swans sailed over the lake, breathing streams of fire of various colors, flashing rockets and variegated lights from their wings, and finally disappearing in a whirl of serpents and balls of fire, with a beautiful effect.

The fireworks being over, the guests were invited to the lower terrace, where a supper was prepared, with tea and punch. Before the departure of the gentlemen of the mission and their escort, the president thanked them for their visit, and begged Messrs. Fox, Clay, Murray, and Beaumont, to accept the title of honorary members of the Imperial Society of Acclimatization, for which those gentlemen expressed their gratitude.

The grounds of the society cover about thirty acres, and are very prettily laid out. Ice-hills and skating-ponds furnish amusement in winter to the people, a small admittance fee being charged.

August 25th (13th).—Saturday opened as bright and beautiful as the preceding day. At ten o'clock the deputies of the city called on the Americans to invite them to visit some other of the remarkable sights of the city. As an excursion into the country was proposed, open carriages were provided, harnessed *à la yamstchik*, some with three and Mr. Fox's with four horses abreast; all the teams being decorated with red, white, and blue cockades, and shining silver plates, and hung with little bells which jingled merrily as they moved. Prince Stcherbatoff, who speaks English perfectly, rode in the first carriage with Mr. Fox.

The first halt was made at the round stone tribune, near the Church of St. Basil, in the Kitai Gorod, outside the wall of the Kremlin, called the Lobnoë Miesto. Popular tradition says that this was the ancient place of execution, but it is more probable that it was used as a rostrum from which the Czars addressed the people on state occasions. It is not known when nor by whom it was built, but records prove its existence in the reign of Ivan the Terrible, in the middle of the sixteenth century.

The Kitai Gorod, or Chinese city, is a quarter contiguous to the Kremlin, on the east side. In it is the famous Gostinnoy Dvor, or Bazaar of Moscow, where the greater part of the trade of the city is centred, and where may be found goods of every description, gathered from all parts of the world. The great building covers three squares, and is intersected by hundreds of passages, the sides of which are lined by the shops. Each business has its own department or street: the silversmiths occupying one row, the cutlers another, the furriers a third, and so on. The shops are all small, but the store-rooms above them contain vast quantities of goods. Over seventy-five millions of rubles are invested beneath its roof.

As the Americans passed through this labyrinth of streets, guided by an officer of police, all the shopkeepers and their assistants stood at their doors with cap in hand, to greet them. The alleys were crowded with streams of buyers and sellers, and it was not without some difficulty that the party made its way through.

The Cathedral of Kazan, or of St. Basil, on the square between the Bazaar and the wall of the Kremlin, is a most remarkable structure, noticeable even in this city of strange sights. It is a building of two stories, surmounted by a dozen or more domes and cupolas, of different color, form, and height. This one is like an incipient bell-tower, that one is slim and pointed, a third resembles the folds of a turban, a fourth is an honest tower, a fifth is a globe crowned with a Greek cross on a crescent, a sixth is a cupola with pillars; and all these domes are painted in bright colors — some red, some blue, some gilded, giving to the whole a most grotesque appearance. It appears to be without any plan, but to have been put together piecemeal, as chance or some crazy imagination directed. It was built in 1554, by Ivan the Terrible, over the tomb of St. Basil, to commemorate his capture of Kazan, the great stronghold of the Tartars, on the Volga. The Czar was so pleased with the work, says tradition, that he had the eyes of the architect put out, for fear lest he should enrich another land with a similar architectural wonder.

Having inspected the different chapels and the shrine of the saint, the party reëntered the carriages and drove through the Tver Gate to Petrovskoë Razoumovskoë, about ten miles from the city, where is situated the Imperial Agricultural Academy. The flags of the United States and of Russia were flying from the several buildings, and Mr. Geleznoff, the director, the professors, and a large number of students, were in readiness to receive the guests. Mr. Geleznoff made a brief address of welcome, after which the visitors were shown over the buildings and grounds. The class-rooms, the chapel, the chemical laboratory, the departments of the natural sciences, of veterinary science, of comparative anatomy, etc., were inspected and every thing explained. Lastly, the company were conducted to the splendid gardens of the academy, where, in a building decorated with flags, a lunch was found prepared, for which the morning's excursion had provided ample appetites.

The party drove next through the park of Petrovsky, viewing the palace in passing, and thence to the plain of Kudinskoë, where thirty thousand troops were in camp. Aide-de-Camp General Güldenstaube, commander of the military district of Moscow, had the men drawn up in line, without arms. He himself, surrounded by his staff, received the Americans, the bands meanwhile playing

"Hail Columbia." After a brief interview, the general called from the ranks a number of singers, who chanted some of the Russian soldiers' songs. The time grew gradually faster, and some of the men struck into a wild dance, holding in each hand a stick to which ribbons and bells were attached. Their movements were rapid and exciting, somewhat resembling our Indian dances.

The songs and dances ended, the visitors drove down the entire line of troops, the officers and men of each regiment saluting, and the bands playing our national air. The camp of the Military Academy of Alexander was next visited, after which the train started for the city, returning by the Prisnensky Gate.

At the plain of Novo Dievitchy the calico print-works of the Messrs. Ganechin was visited. The proprietors received the Americans at the door, presented them with the customary bread and salt, and a drawing of the works, through which the visitors were shown in detail. Mr. Fox was also given a large number of the Messrs. Ganechin's patterns, which he distributed, on his return home, among different New-England mills. They were used very extensively, and had the effect of changing almost entirely the styles in this country. These patterns were similar to those worn by the Tartars, the most of the calicoes made here finding a market in Bokhara.

The workmen and the country-people near these mills were greatly interested in Commander Beaumont's negro steward, Cæsar, whom they surrounded and examined with unrestrained curiosity, having probably never before seen a black man.

The Convent of Novo Dievitchy next opened its hospitable doors to the strangers, the abbess receiving them in person at the entrance with bread and salt, and conducting them into the church, where vespers were then singing. After the service, the five other churches and the various buildings within the walls were shown. The nuns did not appear to be kept so secluded as in the Roman Catholic convents, but were seen everywhere, and looked as if they enjoyed the sight of the visitors. The convent was founded in the beginning of the sixteenth century, in commemoration of the taking of Smolensk. It has been a favorite resort for the imperial princesses who have renounced the world. Sophia, the ambitious half-sister of Peter the Great, was imprisoned here, being forced to take the veil and live in rigid seclusion to the time of her death. She is buried within its walls, as are several others of the imperial family. The lady-abbess presented Mr. Fox with a large number of interesting photographs.

After a visit to the calico printing-works of Mr. Hübner, where a lunch was served, the party returned to the city to make preparations for the municipal banquet, to take place the same evening. It is almost superfluous to state that throngs of people attended the Americans and greeted them with cheers wherever they went; and on their return to the hotel the open space in the front of the building was densely crowded. Indeed, the enthusiasm of the citizens of Moscow over their guests appeared to be unbounded, and created an impression on the minds of the Americans not easily effaced.

CHAPTER XVII.

BANQUET OF THE MUNICIPALITY OF MOSCOW.

THE municipal banquet took place in the Town Hall, a building well adapted for such a purpose. Its front was illuminated and festooned with flags. The visitors were received at the grand entrance, the avenues to which were crowded with people, by the officers of the city government. The staircases were aglow with lights surrounded by plants and flowers, and the walls were decked with shields and national emblems. The four great rooms had been converted into magnificent conservatories of rare flowers and shrubs, illuminated with hundreds of wax-tapers. The ornamentation of the dining-room was particularly beautiful. Flags, banners, and shields of arms, were displayed with great skill amid wreaths and garlands of green. At one end, on a ground of green leaves, was hung a full-length portrait of the Emperor, surrounded with Russian flags; and portraits of Washington, Lincoln, and Johnson, and of Messrs. Fox, Clay, Murray, and Beaumont, decked with wreaths and colors, graced the other walls.

The company, numbering nearly four hundred, sat

down to the tables at seven o'clock and arose at eleven. The service was magnificent, befitting the great and wealthy city of Moscow. A splendid band played during the dinner, giving the national airs of the two countries. There were many toasts and speeches, all of which were received with cheers that found an echo from the people in the street.

The *menu* was as follows:

GRAS.	MAIGRE.[1]
1. Potage tomate Américaine. Consommé royale.	1. Pureé de "lottes."
2. Pâtés Russes: "koulebiaka."	2. Pâtés Russe: "koulebiaka."
3. Sterlets à la Russe. Soudaks, sauce régence.	3. Sterlets à la Russe. Soudaks.
4. Roast-beef.	4. Mayonnaise de saumon.
5. Crême de gélinottes aux truffes.	5. Pâté chaud de torchis aux truffes.
6. Punch Impérial.	6. Punch Impérial.
7. Chouxfleurs et artichauts.	7. Chouxfleurs et artichauts.
8. Rôts: faisans et gibier divers.	8. Rôts: poissons divers.
9. Pudding: Moscovite.	9. Pudding: Moscovite.
10. Fruits glacés à l'Américaine.	10. Fruits glacés à l'Américaine.

A card containing the programme of the music played during the evening was also placed beside each plate:

ORCHESTRE DE M. SAX.

Marche du Prophète	*Meyerbeer.*
Ouverture de l'opéra "La Vie pour l'Empereur"	*Glinka.*
Fantaisie sur le motif, "Yankee Doodle"	
Air de l'opéra "La Vie pour l'Empereur"	*Glinka.*
Quadrille, "Amerikanische"	*Gungl.*
Potpourri sur "l'Africaine"	*Meyerbeer.*
Valse, "Die Peather"	*Lanner.*
Polka, "Electrofor"	*Strauss.*

---

[1] The day was a fast day of the Greek Church, therefore a second bill of fare (*maigre*, literally, lean) was provided for those who could not eat meats.

Prince Stcherbatoff, the Mayor of Moscow, gave the first toast. He said:

"The great nation of the other hemisphere sends us her greeting—that glorious nation which has lately triumphed over her painful trial, and astonished the world by that new demonstration of her gigantic power. Powerful through her inexhaustible resources, still more so by her undaunted spirit, and full of faith in her future, the great North American nation has attained in the space of a few years what to others would have been the work of whole centuries, and has taken her place among the leading nations of the civilized world.

"Distant lands and the ocean divide us, but the spirit of man cares not for space, and our two peoples have long since united in thought and in feeling.

"With a loving interest do we follow each other's successes, with mutual sympathy do we sustain each other in the hour of danger, and we unite to praise the glorious names of the great men whom Providence in mercy sends in the times of great nations' trials. The name of Lincoln is one of those illustrious names. Untiring warrior for a sacred cause, he pressed forward, never losing sight of his guiding star; and his death was the last tribute of his loyal service to his country and to humanity. But the great immortal idea did not perish with his life. Lincoln bequeathed the accomplishment of his work to his people, to his successor, and his last will is now nearly fulfilled.

"May God Almighty help you to reap the harvest of your glorious labors and endeavors; may He strengthen the ties of the revived Union of your great nation; may the American people, blessed by peace, advance steadily onward to the realization of its glorious historical calling, with its chosen leader at its head!

"We drink to the welfare of the North American United States, and to the health of President Johnson."

Prince Stcherbatoff's speech was received with loud and protracted cheering, again and again repeated, the band meanwhile playing "Hail Columbia." The scene was one of the most inspiring that had been witnessed since the arrival of the mission on Russian soil, and proved how deeply the people of Moscow were touched by the unexampled course pursued by our country in sending her congratulations to the Emperor.

As soon as the applause had subsided, Mr. Fox arose and gave the health of his Imperial Majesty in the following words:

"To him whose empire extends from the Atlantic to the Pacific, and from the Arctic to the Mediterranean, but who possesses a greater empire in the affection and devotion of a valiant people—to the Emperor of all the Russias."

A like applause followed this toast, the band playing the Russian national hymn.

Mr. Clay spoke next:

"I have now been in Russia six years, and I think, therefore, that I speak not without a knowledge of the sentiments of those present when I propose to bear in memory, next to our great and good friend whose health has been drunk with so much feeling, her whose virtues outshine the lustre of the Russian throne, him who inherits the features, the temperament, and the auspicious name of his imperial parent, and those who are as ready to perform the duties as to share the honors of the house of Romanoff: I propose the health of her Imperial Majesty, of the Hereditary Grand-duke Alexander, and of all the imperial family."

Mr. Liamin, president of the Exchange Committee, followed:

"Gentlemen, we would wish not only to efface from the memory of men, but to suppress entirely from the series of events, the misfortune which had nearly happened to us this year. The criminal hand of a murderer was raised toward the Russian sovereign, the sovereign who has abolished slavery in his vast empire, who has adopted as the problem of his reign the establishment in his dominions of an impartial and complete administration of justice, and the bestowal upon all of liberty of thought and of speech, the highest rights of man.

"At the first news of his safety, came from every quarter congratulations for the happy preservation from the danger that menaced the life so priceless to us. We have a firm and steadfast belief in the sincerity of this joy, for the blackest wickedness itself would vainly seek even the shadow of justification for such a repulsive attempt. But neither the sincerity nor the fulness of that joy has prevented those who have congratulated us from the use of the habitual forms of diplomacy.

"Pardon the exactions, excessive perhaps, of the Russian heart; but it seems to it that the grandeur of the safety, the impossibility not to love the reforming monarch, in a word, the greatness of the transports of seventy millions of men, would awaken echoes out of the customary forms of congratulation.

"At this moment, gentlemen, a person is before you who has brought that unusual echo awaited by our hearts, who has rejected the rigor of diplomatic receptions, and in the excess of sympathy has discarded all the rules of the code of conventional compliments.

"Not one person alone, but the whole Congress of the United States has chosen Mr. Fox as the eloquent interpreter of the congratulations to our sovereign and to all of us—to all the Russian people.

"An entire squadron has been equipped and has traversed half the world to bring to us, by the mouth of our dear guest, the joyous congratulations. We see not a simple form of diplomacy, but that open effusion coming from the heart.

"Can there be found a single Russian who will not proclaim aloud with me the cordial toast to the representative of the great Congress—to its envoy, the Honorable Mr. Fox?"

Mr. Fox replied in these terms:

"I do not understand the language in which these congratulations have been spoken, but the melody of friendly words reaches the heart without an interpreter. Visiting for the first time Holy Moscow, whose monuments were gray with age when America was discovered, we find ourselves strangers among you; strangers in language and in origin, but, in the presence of Him who of one blood made all nations, we are brothers (applause). Welcome blossoms upon every lip. Whence arises this affinity between the two great powers of the East and of the West? How is it that a modest villager, threading his way through the crowd, advanced, the first, to his sovereign, just at the proper moment to arrest the hand of an assassin? Divine Providence directs all things. (Prolonged cheers.) Russia and America are both proceeding along a path to which no limit can be perceived. Russia, led by a resolute monarch, of a benevolent mind, inspired from above (loud cheers), advances toward the East, spreading the light of Christian civilization among the ignorant races of vast provinces that come under her sway. America, receiving with joy the surplus population of Europe, and fusing these with her own sons, into one nationality, moves without leadership toward the West, like the shadow of an eclipse, which covers by degrees the disk of the moon, and guided, like it, by the same omnipotent Hand. The diverse systems of the two nations are human; their tendency to the improvement of mankind is Divine. From this similarity of endeavor springs our relationship, with its sacred impulses, yielding to which we contribute our effort to the Divine purpose." (Long-continued applause.)

Mr. Rezanoff, the dean of the Corporation of Moscow Merchants, after a short but pithy speech, gave a toast "to the health and long stay in Russia of General Clay and Mr. Curtin."

Mr. Clay responded:

"I propose a toast to him who, always serving so

courageously and so wisely the interests of his country, has known how, at the same time, to preserve a strong interest for other countries; a man born in Russia, but who by his liberal principles belongs to all nations; to a statesman, a diplomatist, and, above all, a philanthropist— to Prince Gortchakoff."

Mr. Curtin then spoke in the Russian language as follows:

"I thank you profoundly for the honor you have done me by the toast just given. In reply, permit me to propose another toast dear to my heart. There is in Russia a city around which clusters many great memories of Russian history and of Russia's life. It was in this city that the grand idea of the unity of the Russian empire was born. In this city was always found the living source of Russian strength, which has borne gladly all reverses, and supported all losses to create, strengthen, and cause to flourish a great and united Russian empire. This great thought has animated all the Russian people, and the desired object has been attained. When I remember that this city, during so many centuries, has been the rampart of Russian power, and that in those sorrowful days when others lost courage she remained steadfast; when I remember how she received her enemies, and when I experience how she welcomes her friends, I cannot help exclaiming: 'Great Moscow! I render thee homage!' Gentlemen, I have the honor to give a toast to the mother of the Russian land."

Mr. Curtin's speech was followed by loud and continued applause, the company pressing around to clink glasses with him and to clasp his hand; and the enthusiasm did not abate until he had been tossed in the air, in true Russian style.

Mr. Jakuntchikoff then spoke:

"Gentlemen: A Russian merchant, I arise, with peculiar gratification, to offer a toast that has an intimate connection with the success of commerce. There is a power which is both military and civilizing. The development of this power extends, without conquest, the boundaries of nations possessing it—in war, serving as the most powerful bulwark of national independence, and, in peace, as the most effectual means of commercial development. This power is the navy. This power is recognized by the civilized world, which now must confess that the mightiest naval power of the earth is the great American Republic, whose disinterested friendship we possess. The arrival of our honored guests has shown the depth of their sympathy for us, and has been the means of solving a great naval problem. This wonder of naval architecture, this vessel unique in structure, this floating fortress, hitherto considered as only fit for shore defence, the monitor Miantonomoh, after sweeping through the vainly-opposing waves of the ocean, and proudly showing its impregnable towers in the Thames, and on the shores of France, has come to us and united our Russia and America by a bridge which no artillery can destroy. To our enemies this bridge is inaccessible, for its foundations are laid in the waves of the ocean. I propose a toast in honor of Captains Murray, Beaumont, and the officers of the American squadron."

Captain Murray replied for himself and brother officers. He said:

"In behalf of the little squadron, insignificant in point of guns and numbers, but, if taken in connection with events and the future, pregnant with significance; in behalf of the officers of that squadron I return my thanks for this complimentary toast. Our officers heard, long before they came to Russia, of your hospitality. They now feel it in their very hearts, and they thank the Russians. When they return they will carry with them the most grateful recollections of the few days they have spent in Russia. I have the honor to propose a toast to the health of the Governor-General of Moscow, Prince Dolgorouky."

Mr. Pogodine next spoke:

"As an old Muscovite, thoroughly Russian, one whose life has been entirely devoted to the study of history, I ask the president to permit me to address a few words to our dear and honorable guests. Russia and America are near to each other in spite of the enormous distance between them. It is, as we say in Russia, 'to be reached with the hand.' The telegraph has accelerated our communication, but there is another wire more rapid than the electric; there is another tie stronger than any metal or any diplomatic art, a tie that is expressed by our common saying, 'The heart understands the heart.' By a kind of instinct, by a second sight, like that we read of in Scott, we Russians and Americans have great consideration for each other, are equal in reciprocal love, and wish well each to the other, without any other thought, not being able to explain even the reason of our mutual sincerity and warmth. The sympathy of our Government, as well as that of our people, makes itself loudly heard as soon as an opportunity presents.

"For instance, I will mention two events of a recent date. An insurrection broke out in North America All of us Russians were heartily grieved, and, without wishing any material harm to the South, we hoped that the Union might rise from the struggle, as soon as possible, complete and unharmed; that the work of Washington might not lose one particle of its greatness and splendor. The Emperor expressed this general feeling in words which were accepted with enthusiastic gratitude in America. Russia was menaced not long ago by a great calamity, from which God miraculously preserved her, visibly extending His hand. The United States have shown their lively joy at this happy event, so near to the feelings of our own people; and now, in order to express it before the Emperor, there comes to us across the sea, by order of the American Congress, a special ambassador, our honored guest now present, to whom we testify our heart-felt gratitude.

"I will add that this sympathy is increased by the resemblance of our institutions, by our connections with Europe, and history generally. I do not speak of the likeness as regards the extent of our territory, our power and means; nor of the abundance of our natural productions. As regards institutions, the United States is a republic, and Russia an absolute monarchy; but here, as well as on the map, extremes meet. In the Russian absolute monarchy there is a democratic stream that flows uninterruptedly throughout its history. As regards the forms, all of them have lost much of their original meaning, and our honorable guests have justly remarked, in one of their speeches, that under our form one may progress; and they now hear in Moscow what they heard in St. Petersburg, that the Russians, thanks to our gracious Emperor—who marks a new era in our history —may express their ideas and reason as freely as people do in New York.

"I have but to speak, in conclusion, of the resemblance between Russia and the United States in reference to the Old World. It is impossible not to agree that Europe looks on the New World with some apprehension, some suspicion, some jealousy. I believe I make no mistake in asserting that the principal European governments, influenced severally by their own views and particularities— and I do not blame them—did not look at the American conflict so impartially and disinterestedly as we did. They rather wished that there should be two Unions instead of one. They regard with the same eyes the other New World—I mean Russia. For fifty years, during the reigns of Alexander I. and of Nicholas, Russia was the chief supporter of peace in Europe, without regard to her own interests; but, as soon as there was an opportunity, all this was forgotten, and Europe, without cause, leagued with Turkey against us, with the only aim of weakening our power by attacking us suddenly. Where are we to look for the cause of such a disposition? Perhaps in the jealousy of her old age, in the general and involuntary conviction that America and Russia will have as much in their future as she has had in her past.

"Yes, it is evident, by all the combinations of the science of history, that to Russia, as well as to America, a great future is reserved, to which we are now drawing near, thank God, with hope and faith. Let us wish that the friendly union between the two governments may pass from an ideal to an actual one, so that we may advance hand-in-hand; that both the nations may develop, ripen, and strengthen this idea of mutual coöperation on this glorious road as far as possibility will permit.

"Allow me, gentlemen, to propose a toast that, with the help of the Almighty, Russia, as well as America, may grow in strength and prosperity, and at the same time that Europe may know peace, that all her questions may be resolved for the real good of all her people, including the unhappy and forgotten Slavonians, for the welfare of humanity at large—white, black, red, and bronzed." (Loud applause.)

After a toast to the American ladies, proposed by Mr. Gorboff, Mr. Sukhotine read Mr. Maikoff's version of the poem written by Oliver Wendell Holmes, which was recited first at the Merchants' Dinner in St. Petersburg. It was received with deafening applause, and with nine cheers for its author.

Prince Stcherbatoff then gave the health of the translator of the poem and Mr. Potemkine, the attorney to the Synodal Board of Moscow, spoke of the proposal to erect a Russian church in New York City, for which, according to a communication received from Mr. de Stoeckl, the Russian minister at Washington, a subscription in America had produced already seven thousand dollars. Mr. Potemkine added that Russian merchants had already answered to the appeal of the attorney-general of the holy synod on this subject, and that the other classes of the population would answer without doubt equally to this appeal; and he showed, as a new proof of the sympathy of the Americans, the interest and the share taken by them in the construction of this church.

Mr. Curtin expressed, in the name of General Clay, his entire concurrence in the remarks of Mr. Potemkine, and the hope that the Russians would soon find, in coming to New York, an orthodox church worthy of the Greek religion. Mr. Clay, he said, would subscribe five hundred rubles, and Mr. Fox as much; and he believed that private subscriptions in New York would yet yield twenty-five thousand more. He was certain, too, that twenty-four thousand rubles, additional to the thousand given by Messrs. Clay and Fox, would be raised in Russia.

After dinner a subscription-paper was started by Mr. Samarine, who himself headed it with one thousand rubles.

Mr. Gorboff spoke next, closing with these words:

"Let us hope, gentlemen, in ending this banquet, for the prompt and complete development of the material well-being, the moral prosperity, the civilization in the same degree, of all our Russian brethren, lately serfs, and of the emancipated negro race of North America."

After a few remarks by Mr. Janovsky, Mr. Kokoreff paid the following tribute to the memory of Lincoln:

"The greatest of all forces on earth is the force of thought and will, bestowed by Providence on the happy few. This force has had three gigantic utterances in the New World. By this force Columbus discovered the New World, Washington founded its civilization, and Lincoln gave equal rights to his countrymen, by abolishing slavery. Sentiments of thankfulness and gratitude at the name of Lincoln, for what he did for the good of mankind, are felt as a duty by every Russian. All the actions of Lincoln, as our mayor, Prince Stcherbatoff, has observed, sprang from the force of his character, from his steadfast aspiration toward the proposed aim, in spite of every obstacle. When a youth in poor circumstances, in New Salem, Lincoln used to say: 'Failures ought not to deprive us of courage; on the contrary, they are the means of exciting the activity of the brain.'

"Here is one of the many facts of the life of Lincoln, which may give us a clear notion of the force of his convictions: Lincoln established, in connection with one of his friends, a grocery, but the enterprise did not succeed, and his associate deemed it necessary to add to their business the sale of wine and tobacco. Notwithstanding his friendship for his partner, and the bad state of his affairs, Lincoln declined the proposal, for he stoutly defended the principle of temperance. His refusal occasioned the loss of his fortune, and brought him, proportionately to his means, largely into debt. This failure obliged him to study—what would you think? Grammar and law!

"Lincoln's own life was for him the best intelligence-book in the many branches of popular activity into which he drifted. Before he attained his twenty-eighth year, he had passed through the following occupations: farm-laborer, wood-cutter, carpenter, workman on railways and steamboats, ship-carpenter, boatswain, clerk in a shop and a mill, grocer, captain of militia, postmaster, and surveyor. In all these employments Lincoln showed an unswerving devotion to the truth, but his great intellectual powers needed a wider career. He passed his examination, and became a lawyer. In this profession his veracity became so celebrated that people called him 'Honest Abe.' With a great store of knowledge in almost every branch of human life and pursuits, Lincoln served several times as a member of the Legislature, and as a presidential elector. In these positions, and as a lawyer, he led for more than twenty years a remarkable public life. On every occasion possible he obstinately pursued his favorite idea of freeing his fellow-man from slavery. He was deeply devoted to this idea, because it was his heart and the grandeur of America that wanted it, and because he had been in his youth a witness of the trials of the slaves.

"Although he began his grammar studies late, in his twenty-fourth year he acquired such eloquence that all America listened to his speeches with enthusiastic approbation. His illustrations had the particular and rare quality of being taken from practical life. Strange to theoretical allurements, they were founded on experience acquired on the farm, in the shop, in the wood, on the steamboat, in the courts, and in political and legislative assemblies. The value which the North American States attached to the all-comprehensive capacities of Lincoln, and the sincerity of his words, is shown by the fact that the edition of his speeches published in 1858 sold to the number of nearly a million volumes. This acknowledgment was followed by another: Lincoln was elected President of the United States, and under what circumstances? The election took place at the time when the Southern States were preparing for secession, when they had in store a large quantity of arms, and when, after having taken a fortress, they had led their army against Washington, where there were not even a thousand soldiers to meet their attack. Lincoln's popularity and his ability carried all obstacles before him. It attracted to Washington troops from all the Northern States, and saved the capital from danger. A year later five hundred thousand soldiers were in the field. At the end of four years Lincoln was again elected President. We may easily imagine the triumph of his people on this occasion, when even in Russia there was an outbreak of universal jubilation at the news. We all saw in this reëlection the pledge of the triumph of the Northern over the Southern States.

"Rumors of threats, and of attempts made against the life of Lincoln, produced the greatest sorrow in Russia. We feared for a life not only indispensable for the New World, but precious for all mankind. The gloomy apprehensions were not dispelled, when our whole country was astounded by the shocking news that on the 15th of April, 1865, the traitorous hand of a murderer cut short the life of him who called up to an independent life millions of slaves, who during the whole war travelled without any guard, who received every one without announcement, who could have been killed at any moment, but who was guarded by Providence for the fulfilment of His decrees. But when the great deed of Lincoln's was done, and mankind stretched out its hands to put the laurels of merited glory upon his head, the Most High called him up to Him, to receive a higher, heavenly reward. Men are not able to reward the deeds of a life which was entirely devoted to acts of philanthropy and of truth. Only He who was crucified for the benefit of mankind, the Almighty Son of God, can reward such deeds.

"Then with the profoundest reverence let us lift our hands to Heaven, and express our sincere gratitude, and the wish of an eternal memory to the name of the friend of mankind, and the defender of truth—Abraham Lincoln!"

The toast was drunk with every mark of respect for the memory of the "Martyr President," after which Mr. Kokoreff continued:

"Having given utterance to our mournful feelings in commemoration of Lincoln, I propose, gentlemen, another toast—to the health of his widow and two sons, and to the prosperity of all the inhabitants of Springfield, where was brought up, in our own time, this great man, the glory of America and of all mankind, of the Old and of the New World." (Applause).

Mr. Schipoff, one of the leading merchants of Moscow, followed. He said:

"The presence here of our esteemed guests is full of

significance. In their persons, a nation, occupying a foremost place in the civilized world, greets us with sympathy and good-will, encouraging us in our labor of regeneration, joining in our rejoicings at the fortunate deliverance of our beloved monarch—of him who has done so much for the happiness and welfare of mankind. Such an expression of good-will by a great nation we prize most highly, and we entreat our esteemed guests to convey to their fellow-countrymen the assurance of our most hearty thanks and warmest sympathy. Between the United States and Russia there have never been any hostilities; but at no time hitherto has the mutual good-will between the two countries found such strong utterances as of late.

"With unexampled energy and valor the North American States fought for the abolition of slavery at the same time that Russia was accomplishing the emancipation of twenty million serfs. In the United States self-government is developed in the highest degree; and Russia, too, is introducing it in her municipal corporations. In the United States the courts of justice are open; Russia is establishing the like system, and already the people rejoice at the beneficial effects of its institution. Both countries are great in territory, both contain inexhaustible treasures; but these treasures require development, and this development can only be attained by means of adequately remunerated capital and labor. Of this the United States are fully convinced, and, consequently, in their commercial policy, maintain strictly the principle of protection, not suffering themselves to be misled by the plausible theories of certain economists. Russia, too, is beginning to understand that in strict protection of national labor, in connection with a full development of the resources of a country, lies the secret of national wealth. And by no one has this truth been so clearly and so convincingly put as by that highly-respected American political economist, Carey, and by our esteemed guest, now for the second time in Moscow, General Clay. Like them, we believe that love toward mankind begins with love toward one's own country, and a proper encouragement of national labor. In whatever direction we turn, we see everywhere that Russia and America are so directed by the hand of Providence that their individual interests not only do not impede, but, on the contrary, promote their mutual development; consequently, the more Americans and Russians love their country, the nearer they draw toward each other. Such, then, being the case, gentlemen, can a Russian, devoted to his country, heart and soul, do less than propose a toast to the everlasting and ever-increasing friendship between Russia and America? Here, in our ancient capital, replete with true Russian life, let us raise our glasses to the welfare, prosperity, and power of the two nations whom a great future surely awaits."

A toast to the health of the Mayor of Moscow, Prince Stcherbatoff, was then given, after which Prince Dolgorouky closed the long series of toasts with one to "the health of our dear guests, and of all those who have spoken so feelingly and so fervently on this memorable occasion."

After the dinner, the company adjourned to another

room, where tea and punch were prepared, and engaged in friendly conversation until long after midnight.

Each of the Americans was presented, in remembrance of the visit, with the first volume of Martinoff's edition of "The Remarkable Historical Monuments of Moscow." To Mr. Fox was also given an album of ten photographic views of Moscow.

CHAPTER XVIII.

KUZMINKI — PRINCE GALITZINE'S FÊTE — THE FOUNDLING ASYLUM—THE ROMANOFF HOUSE—SOKOLNIKI PARK.

AUGUST 26th (14th).—The charming weather which had thus far accompanied the mission, changed on Sunday morning, and heavy clouds threatened rain.

Mr. Fox called on Prince Stcherbatoff, the mayor, and afterward attended services at the English chapel in Tchernichefsky Péréulok. There is a numerous colony of English and American residents in Moscow, and the chapel is well sustained.

At half-past three o'clock in the afternoon the party started in carriages for Kuzminki, the estate of Prince Galitzine, distant about twelve miles from Moscow. It is one of the most beautiful places in the environs of the ancient city. Its proprietors, who have long been among the wealthiest of Russia's princes, have often entertained crowned heads at their residence, as is attested by numerous monuments erected in the magnificent park.

A drizzling rain had set in as the gayly-decked carriages, with horses harnessed *à la yamstchik*, and drivers with American cockades in their hats, passed through the

Petrovsky Gate, and took the road for Kuzminki, but
did not dampen the ardor of the people. The villages o
the route wore the air of a holiday, and the roadsid
were thronged with peasants, who took off their hats a
hurrahed as the train of vehicles dashed by.

On arriving at the park gate, which was decorate
with the American shield and with the intertwined colo
of the two countries, Prince Galitzine, wearing the scarl
uniform of the hussar regiment of his Majesty's guar
rode out on horseback and welcomed his guests. At t
same time a military band, stationed in the shrubber
struck up "Hail Columbia," and a crowd of peasar
cheered lustily. The Prince, who was a young m
of twenty-four years, rode beside Mr. Fox's carria
through the park to the château, where the who
party alighted.

Kuzminki, formerly a shooting-lodge of Peter t
Great, was given to the Galitzines by the Empress Aur
The park, which is surrounded by a flat, arid country,
as beautiful as an oasis in the desert. A small stree
runs through the grounds. The monuments erected
commemorate the visits of different sovereigns of the E
pire are of cast-iron, from the Prince's foundries in
beria. Over the entrance to the stables, which are wort
of royalty, are two large cast-iron horses, also made
the Prince's works.

The Americans were first invited to a part of the pa
where a deputation of peasants of the commune of
khotskaïa, ancient serfs of the Galitzine family, awai
them. At their head was the mayor of the neighbor

village, Ephim Vassilieff Gvozdeff, also an emancipated serf, who presented Mr. Fox with bread and salt, on a silver salver, with these words:

"We wish to tell the envoy that we are come to congratulate him on his arrival, and to present him with bread and salt, and also to say that we love him, and that we shall remember the love of his people for our country and our sovereign."

Struck by this simple speech, and the unexpected deputation of peasants, Mr. Fox accepted the bread and salt, and thanked the mayor in sympathetic words.

After an hour's stroll through the beautiful grounds, the guests of Kuzminki were invited to dinner, which was served in the rotunda of the château. Portraits of the Emperor and the Empress, of Washington, Lincoln, and Johnson, and of Messrs. Fox, Clay, Murray, and Beaumont, hung on the walls, decked with flowers, greens, and flags. The table glittered with the magnificent family plate, with golden candelabras, and vases of Sèvres porcelain, among the rarest of exotic flowers. Bands, concealed from sight, played the airs of the two countries. The *menu*, written in black and gold on glazed paper, with the Galitzine arms in relief at the top, was as follows:

DÎNER DU 14 AOÛT, 1866.

1. Soupe Talleyrand.
2. Consommé garni.
3. Petits pâtés divers.
4. Filet de bœuf à l'Africaine.
5. Steriet à la Russe.
6. Fromage de gibier.
7. Punch glacé.

8. Volailles diverses.
9. Petits pois et artichauts.
10. Baba Parisien.
11. Timbale New York.

Among the invited guests at the dinner was the emancipated serf, Gvozdeff, the mayor of the commune.

When the champagne appeared, Prince Galitzine gave the first toast, in the following words:

"Excuse me, gentlemen, if I cannot find words to express my thanks for the honor you confer on me, although I ought to recollect that I owe this honor to the ancient masters of this château, my ancestors. Citizens of a powerful republic, I thank you for having desired to see a house in which, more than once, its faithful and zealous subjects have received the visit of the reigning sovereign, whose true greatness has inspired your people with so touching a sympathy. You, gentlemen, my countrymen, I thank you with all my heart for honoring the memory of my ancestors. I have the honor to propose a toast to the President, Mr. Johnson, and to the Congress of the United States of America."

This was received with applause by the guests within and with tremendous cheers by the crowd assembled in the park, with the firing of artillery, and with music by the band.

Mr. Fox replied:

"Prince Galitzine is probably the youngest person sitting at our table, but the idea of uniting beneath this historical roof the representatives of Russia and America, to enable them under such charming influences to strengthen their mutual sympathies, is worthy of more mature years, and is in accord with the traditions of that eminent family of which he is the representative. Let us, gentlemen, follow the example which he has just given to us, in drinking the health of our President and Congress, and unite in offering the sincerest wishes of our hearts for the happiness of Alexander II."

This was received with great enthusiasm, the band playing the Russian national hymn.

Prince Galitzine next toasted Mr. Fox, and General Clay followed with the health of the Empress, the hereditary Grand-duke, and the Imperial family. The Prince then toasted General Clay, Captain Murray and Commander Beaumont, and all his guests, to which Captain Murray replied by giving the health of the host. After a toast to Prince Dolgorouky, General Clay closed the series of healths with one to the absent lady of the mansion.

After dinner the guests were shown to the drawing-rooms and balcony, before which a band of music was playing. A large number of ladies from the country about Kuzminki awaited the coming of the gentlemen, and, the most of them speaking English fluently, the conversation soon became animated.

The music of an orchestral band in the rotunda presently announced that the punch had been lighted, after partaking of which, the party returned to the balcony to witness the fireworks. Although the evening was still damp, the rain had ceased, and the display was a fine one. The guests were invited next to the landing-place of the lake in the park, where firework swans floated on the water, and a grand triumphal arch, bearing the initials of Washington, Franklin, and Lincoln, in letters of fire, was exhibited. After the fireworks, the garden was beautifully illuminated with Bengal lights.

When the company returned, they found the rotunda filled with peasants. An affecting scene took place. Mr. Fox presented an American flag to the mayor, Gvozdeff, who was at the head of the villagers, all of whom had been serfs, with these words:

"Accept this flag of my country. The colors are the same as those of Russia, though disposed in a different manner. This flag has often been displayed in battle, but is this day the standard of peace and good-will. Preserve it, that you, the emancipated Russian peasants, may recognize the emblem of a friendly nation, that will always sympathize with the struggles of your class to place yourselves on a level with the benefits of civilization and freedom, conferred by your well-beloved sovereign."

Tears stood in the eyes of a number of the old men as the mayor took the flag.

"Say to your countrymen," said Gvozdeff, "that we esteem that friendship, and that, if misfortune menaces one of us, both peoples will be united against the enemy."

The peasants then marched away in procession, bearing the American flag at their head.

The party did not break up until after midnight. Prince Galitzine escorted his guests on horseback to the borders of his estates, through rows of bonfires, built on each side of the road, and bade them farewell at the gate.

August 27*th* (15*th*).—Monday being the annual feast-day of the Greek Church, the embassy attended services in the Cathedral of the Assumption, the most sacred church of Russia. The splendor of this ancient building, the historical associations connected with it, and the magnificence of the Greek ceremonial, rendered the scene a most solemn and impressive one. This service was celebrated by the Vicar of Moscow, his Eminence the Archbishop Leonidas.[1]

The Foundling Orphan Asylum was visited next, and afterward the Nicholas Institute. The former dates from the year 1763, in the reign of Catherine II. About twelve thousand children are admitted into this institution, and more than two thousand women enter the secret wards of the lying-in hospital connected with it yearly. The infants receive the best of medical attendance, and the most careful nursing. If strong and healthy, they are sent, at the end of a month, together with their nurses, to the surrounding villages, where the physician of the district takes charge of them. On the visit of the mission, the nurses, dressed in the national costume, and each holding a babe in her arms, were drawn up in lines in the different wards. The sight of three or four thousand infants thus exhibited, with probably not one of their mothers present, was an interesting one. The effigy, in silver, of the great Empress Catherine, the founder of this magnificent institution, was presented to Mr. Fox.

The Nicholas Institute is attached to the Asylum, but

[1] He was formerly an officer in the Imperial Navy.

no foundlings are admitted. Its inmates are all female orphan children of the servants of the crown, the boys being cared for elsewhere. About eight hundred girls receive a good education here annually, and are obliged to serve the government for six years after graduation, as governesses and teachers, receiving a small salary for their services.

The Americans were then shown the Romanoff house, the ancient building in which the Czar Michael, the first of the dynasty of Romanoff, was born, and where also his father, the Boyar Theodore, afterward Philaret, Patriarch of Moscow, was brought up. The house was burned in 1812, and the thick stone walls are all that remain of the ancient structure. It was entirely restored about fifteen years ago, and now represents a Russian dwelling-house of the sixteenth century, being ornamented and furnished in the style of that period.

In the afternoon, the Zoological Gardens were again visited, and the animals inspected by daylight. An address of welcome was presented to the mission by the directors, and Messrs. Fox and Clay, at the request of the members of the Society of Acclimatization, each planted a tree in memory of their visit.

In the evening, the party went in carriages to the Hawk Park, Sokolniki, several miles out of Moscow. The weather was delightful, and the road thither was filled with vehicles and pedestrians, all on their way to this great public promenade. Many beautiful villas, belonging to wealthy citizens, line the way. On arriving at the park, the carriages were left, and the party walked through its beautiful avenues and glades. Everywhere they went immense crowds greeted them. It was calculated that more than sixty thousand people were present. After a time the pavilion of the rotunda was reached. All the grounds about it were illuminated with colored lamps. A band played our national air, and the people cheered, as Prince Dolgorouky and suite received the visitors at the entrance. After tea and refreshments, a company of gymnasts and rope-dancers gave an entertainment, and the evening ended with music and a splendid display of fireworks.

CHAPTER XIX.

TROITZA MONASTERY — ST. SERGIUS — THE RUSSO-GREEK CHURCH — THE METROPOLITAN PHILARET — AMERIKAN-SKAÏA AVENUE — DIPLOMA OF HONORARY CITIZENSHIP — NIJNY-NOVGOROD.

AUGUST 28*th* (16*th*).—On Tuesday morning, which opened bright and clear, Messrs. Fox, Loubat, Clay and Curtin, Captain Murray, Commander Beaumont and other officers, and the accompanying Russians, went in a special railway-train to the celebrated Monastery of St. Sergius, at Troitza (Trinity), distant about forty miles from Moscow.

This holy place has existed since the middle of the fourteenth century. It has not only a religious history, but also a record glorious in the country's annals. The people name it with reverence, as one of the sanctuaries of the faith, and with love as one of the ramparts of the land. Three times has it turned back the tide of invasion and saved Russia. Mongols, Poles, and the insurgent Streltzi, were foiled by its embattled walls, and more than once have the vast riches of its cloisters helped the country in its extremity.

St. Sergius, its founder, whose baptismal name was Bartholomew, was born about the year 1304, in Rostof, of noble parentage. He was noted for his piety from his childhood, and many miracles are attributed to his earliest years, but at the request of his mother he did not take monastic vows until after the death of both his parents. He lived the life of an anchoret on the site of the present monastery for many years, suffering every privation. His reputation for sanctity at last drew around him a little colony of followers, and about the year 1342 a monastery, with Sergius as abbot, had grown up about his cell. The holy man led a simple life, laboring with his own hands, and crowning his work with deeds of charity. He was favored on several occasions, we are told, by visitations from on high, even the Virgin appearing to him once in person. In 1382, at the age of seventy-eight, St. Sergius was laid to rest beneath the church which he had founded. At the time of his death, the monastery had become rich and powerful, having vast estates and many dependants, but he retained his abstemious habits to the last. Thirty years afterward his relics were withdrawn from the tomb, in the presence of an immense assemblage of people, who had gathered from all parts of the empire to do honor to his memory, and placed in the splendid silver shrine, where they are to be seen to this day.

At half-past eleven the Americans arrived at the Troitza railway-station, which was gayly decked with flags in honor of their coming, where they were received by the authorities and the representatives of the corporations. The party drove at once to the hotel opposite the monastery, the road thither being lined with people from the neighboring villages, who cheered loudly as they passed. After a lunch, the Geothismansky Skit, or Hermitage of Gethsemane, the summer-residence of his Eminence Philaret, the Metropolitan of Moscow, was visited, the venerable prelate having expressed a desire to receive his transatlantic friends in his cell.

The Hermitage, which occupies a very pretty site, about a mile and a half from the monastery proper, was built in the year 1845. It, as well as the church connected with it, is remarkable for its simplicity. The altar and all of the sacred vessels used in the service are of wood.

The Metropolitan of Moscow is one of the chief ecclesiastics of the empire. The Russian Church, while agreeing in doctrine with the nine other branches of the orthodox Greek Church, is entirely distinct in its administration. In 1588 the spiritual supremacy which the Patriarch of Constantinople had exercised was abolished, and Russia became an independent patriarchate. In course of time, its head assumed an authority almost equal to that of the Czar himself, and, on the death of the patriarch, in the reign of Peter the Great, that monarch abolished the patriarchate, and transferred the government of the Church to the Holy Synod.

The ecclesiastics of the Russo-Greek Church form two classes—the black clergy, so called from the color of their dress, who are bound by monastic vows, and the white or secular clergy. The higher ecclesiastics, the metropolitans, archbishops, and bishops, are chosen almost exclusively from the monks. A convent of monks is presided over by an archimandrite, or abbot, under whom are friars, priests, and deacons. The white clergy, who perform all the common offices of the religion, are protopopes or archpriests, popes or priests, deacons, subdeacons, and readers. The black clergy are celibates; the white clergy are allowed to marry once, but must do so before they enter the religious state. If the wife of a priest die, it is customary for him to give up his priestly functions, or to become a monk. There have been, however, of late years, some notable exceptions to this rule.

The Holy Synod, which was instituted in 1721, has its seat at St. Petersburg. It was presided over, in 1866, by Isidore, Metropolitan of Novgorod, St. Petersburg, Esthonia, and Finland. Its members were: Arsenius, Mettropolitan of Kiew and Galicia; Philaret, Metropolitan of Moscow and Kolomna; Joseph, Metropolitan of Lithuania and Wilna; Eusebius, Exarch of Georgia, and Archbishop of Karthli and Kakhetie; Eugenius, Archbishop of Moscow; the Protopope Basil Bajanoff, Almoner of their Imperial Majesties; the Protopope Michael Bogosslovsky, Grand Almoner of the Army and Navy; Philotheus, Archbishop of Tver and Kachine; Platon, Archbishop of Riga and Mitau; Philaret, Bishop of Ufa and Menselinsk; Innocent, Archbishop of Kamtchatka; and the Procurer-General, the Privy-Councillor Count Tolstoy, Minister of Public Instruction.

This body, in which is centred the government of the Russo-Greek Church, is dependent on the Emperor, who is nominally the head of the Church in all matters pertaining to administration; in questions of dogma and of rites it is independent. The Emperor is always represented at its sittings, and its decrees have to be sanctioned by him before they become valid.

The Metropolitan Philaret, who was seventy-four years of age at the time of the visit, received Mr. Fox with a short but touching speech, in which he assured him of his sincere and profound sympathy with his mission of peace. He concluded by wishing that all Christian nations might entertain toward each other feelings as friendly as those which existed between Russia and the United States. His Eminence then offered the American envoy his blessing, and, in memory of his visit, presented him with a picture of the Hermitage and of the shrine of St. Sergius. Notwithstanding his great age,[1] the Metropolitan lived in a narrow, scantily-furnished cell, with almost as much austerity as the founder of Troitza himself. He accompanied the visitors to the Church of the Assumption, and explained to them, through the intermediation of Admiral Lessovsky, every thing of note within it.

The party went next to the subterranean grottoes, or catacombs, dug by some of the more austere monks, who have made vows of seclusion from the light of day forever, and live a life of fasting and prayer. Two churches are connected with these cells, one above and one under

---

[1] Philaret, Metropolitan of Moscow and Kolomna, died in 1868, and was succeeded by Innocent, a priest who had won success as a missionary in Kamtchatka. This appointment was a noteworthy exception to the general custom of selecting the higher ecclesiastics from the monks.

ground. About three or four miles from the Hermitage of Gethsemane is a miniature desert called Paraclete, inhabited by thirty monks, who live a still more secluded life, shutting themselves out from all connection with the world.

On arriving at the monastery, the Americans were received with the ringing of all the bells. The subprior, his Eminence the Archimandrite Anthony, met them at the gate and conducted them first to the shrine of St. Sergius, in the Cathedral of the Trinity.

The walls of Troitza, which are twenty feet thick, and from thirty to fifty feet in height, enclose, within their circumference of about seven-eighths of a mile, ten churches and a number of other buildings. They have nine massive towers and two gate-ways. Vehicles pass through only one of the latter. The other, which is called the Holy Gate, is accessible only to those on foot, and is used for processions and for receptions of the Emperor and members of the imperial family, and of the Metropolitan of Moscow, who is also prior of the monastery. In one of the towers are studios for photography and lithography, and in another is a reservoir for the water which supplies the whole convent. In old times the towers and the walls bristled with cannon.

The principal church, that of the Holy Trinity, was built in 1422 by St. Nikon, the successor of St. Sergius, and contains the relics of the latter. The shrine in which they are exposed to view is of solid silver, and weighs nine hundred and thirty-six pounds. The church is of stone, decorated in the interior with paintings of the same date, but which show many signs of modern restoration. The ikonastas is covered with paintings adorned with gold, silver, and precious stones, all gifts of different donors. Over the altar is a baldachin of silver gilt, supported by silver columns, that weighs four hundred pounds. A candelabrum with seven branches, on the altar, weighs nine pounds of gold and thirty-two of silver.

Among the more remarkable of the paintings on the ikonastas is one which was ornamented with gold and jewels by the Czar Boris Godunoff, and afterward by the Czar Michael, the founder of the Romanoff dynasty. A single emerald on this picture, engraved with a figure emblematic of the Trinity, is valued at twenty thousand rubles. Among the gifts are a number of valuable ones from the present Emperor and from different members of the imperial family.

In the Church of St. Nikon the relics of that saint also are exposed in a silver shrine. Over the holy door in the ikonastas is an ancient picture of Our Lady of Jerusalem, said to have been brought from Greece by Prince Vladimir, the propagator of Christianity in Russia.

In the Church of the Assumption of the Virgin is a large two-headed eagle, carved in wood, said to have been placed there by Peter the Great to commemorate his concealment under the altar during the revolt of the Streltzi.

The great belfry near this church is two hundred and ninety feet in height, and contains forty bells, one of which weighs sixty-five tons. The building is of five stories, and is surmounted by a gilded cupola.

To describe all the curious objects in this ancient monastery would require a volume. All the emperors have vied with each other in the richness of their gifts, and its churches exhibit a wealth of precious metals and stones almost incalculable. Every thing of interest was shown to the party, the churches and chapels, the vestries, the refectories, the academy, with its library, and all the sacred and the historical relics.

On leaving, Mr. Fox was presented with a picture of St. Sergius by the subprior, who twice kissed and blessed him.

At half-past three o'clock a special train took the party back to Moscow. In the evening all visited the theatre by special invitation, Messrs. Fox, Clay, Murray, and Beaumont, occupying the Governor's box. The entertainment consisted of one act from the ballet of "The Peri," one from the ballet of "Pharaoh's Daughter," and, by order of Prince Dolgorouky, one act from Glinka's opera of "Life for the Czar."

On the same day, at Cronstadt, a dinner was given to those of the crews of the American vessels who were unable to attend the first banquet on account of duties on board ship. The dinner was served, like the former one, in the great alley of the summer garden, and was like it also in all its details. The feast passed off pleasantly, and a large crowd of people, who had gathered to see the jolly tars, appeared to enjoy it as much as the participants.

August 29*th* (17*th*).—On Wednesday morning, at half-past ten o'clock, the mission left Moscow for Nijny-Novgorod. Before his departure, Mr. Fox was invited to name a new avenue which had just been opened in the suburbs of the city. He called it the American (*Amerikanskaia*) Avenue, a name which will commemorate forever the mission of peace in which he was the chief actor.

The diploma of honorary citizenship presented to our envoy by the city of Moscow is very elaborate and beautiful, both in design and in execution. It is exquisitely drawn in water-colors, on heavy board, thirty-six by thirty inches in size. The border is architectural, in the Byzantine style, and comprises a broad base, enclosing a view of the Kremlin and the bridge leading to it; a tower and minaret on each side, the two connected at the top by an ornamental arch, and shadowy battlements behind. At the base of each minaret is a medallion; that on the left representing the churches in the Kremlin, that on the right, the bronze monument of Minin and Pojarsky, near the Kremlin. The peasant Minin is standing in a commanding attitude, with upraised arm, calling on the boyar Pojarsky to aid in driving the Poles from his country. In the centre of the arch is a shield, displaying St. George and the Dragon,[1] the arms of Moscow; and above all, the

---

[1] This was the cognizance of the Grand-dukes of Russia until the marriage of Ivan III. with Sophia, the daughter of the last Greek Emperor, when that monarch, hoping to make Moscow the heir of Byzantium, then in possession of the Turks, adopted for the national arms the two-headed eagle. This imperial symbol is said to have been first adopted by Constantine, to denote that, although the empire seemed divided into East and West, it was yet but one body.

imperial arms, the double-headed eagle surmounted by the crown.

The inscription within the arched border is in the Russian language. Translated, it is as follows:

GUSTAVUS VASA FOX,

Who presented to his Imperial Majesty the congratulations of the North American Congress, on the occasion of deliverance from the danger which menaced his Majesty and all the Russian people, by the resolution of the Municipal Council of Moscow, approved by his Majesty on the 25th of August, 1866, and in token of the particular regard of the citizens of Moscow for him as a worthy representative of the great North American people, friendly to Russia, is acknowledged

HONORARY CITIZEN OF MOSCOW.

The Mayor of Moscow:
(Signed) PRINCE VLADIMIR TCHERCASSKY.

Aldermen:
(Signed) PRINCE DMITRY GALITZINE,
CONSTANTINE GILDBACH,
VASSILY BOSTANJOGLO,
VASSILY TORGASHEFF,
JACOB BUSHANOFF.

Assistant Aldermen:
(Signed) MICHAEL BIDICOFF,
VLADIMIR VICHNIAKOFF,
IVAN BACLANOFF,
ALEXANDER GORBUNOFF,
GREGORY ORLOFF.

The diploma is enclosed in a splendid portfolio of embossed leather, ornamented at the corners and in the centre with silver filigree-work, Byzantine in style, after designs by Sazikoff, the famous silversmith of St. Petersburg. It is of a single piece of leather, and is embossed by a plate of the full size.

The work required several months for its execution. It was retained in Russia some time for exhibition, and sent to Mr. Fox, after his return home, through the State Department.

When the news was received in Nijny-Novgorod that Mr. Fox contemplated visiting that ancient town, a deputation, consisting of Messrs. Gubino and Volkoff, representing the city, and Messrs. Losseff, Korniloff, and Kotoff, appointed by the merchants of the fair, came at once to Moscow with a special invitation, which was accepted with thanks, and the day of departure was fixed for the 29th (17th) inst. One of the deputies, Mr. Korniloff, remained over to accompany the party. A special car attached to the regular train was used until the arrival at Vladimir, where a special train was provided for the remainder of the journey.

A number of the principal inhabitants of Moscow, who had become acquainted with the Americans during their brief visit, called to bid them farewell at the hotel and accompanied them to the railway-station, where a crowd of people had gathered to witness the departure. When Mr. Fox and party entered the station accompanied by Prince Dolgorouky, Prince Stcherbatoff, and many other officials, a band played our national air, and the crowd cheered enthusiastically. Mr. Fox thanked them for the cordiality of his reception and for the hospitality he had received, and left the ancient city amid the expressed regrets of her citizens. Mr. Clay did not go to Nijny-Novgorod, but returned to St. Petersburg.

The journey from Moscow to Nijny-Novgorod, two hundred and seventy-three miles by rail, was a pleasant one, though the country is not very attractive to the eye. The same flat sandy soil, with occasional swamps, as that between St. Petersburg and Moscow, stretches away on each side as far as one can see. These plains, however, are rich in agricultural products. The railway-stations are large, commodious buildings of brick and stone, laid in alternate courses, and every thing is provided within them for the comfort of travellers. Crowds of people from the neighboring villages were collected at almost all of them along the route, who greeted the Americans with cheers, music, and the display of flags.

At Vladimir the party found a dinner prepared for them in the railway-station, at the city's expense. The machine-shops of the company, located here and carried on by French capitalists, were visited. The town, which has a population of about fifteen thousand inhabitants, is an ancient one, having been founded in the twelfth century.

At Kovroff, the mayor and other officials awaited the arrival of the train. It is a small place of about four thousand inhabitants, situated, like Vladimir, on the river Kliasma. Mr. Fox received here a telegram announcing the arrival at Nijny-Novgorod of their Imperial Highnesses the Hereditary Grand-duke Alexander and his brother, the Grand-duke Vladimir.

At Viazniki, a town celebrated for its linen manufactures, the party took tea. The people there were particularly enthusiastic in their reception, strewing the way with flowers and evergreens.

Nijny-Novgorod was reached about midnight. The railway terminus was illuminated, and a band played our national air as the train entered. The station-house was filled with people, and a vast crowd occupied the neighboring streets. A large number of the principal merchants, headed by a body of committee-men in full dress, greeted Mr. Fox as he stepped upon the platform. Short speeches of welcome were made by the marshal of the nobility of the province and by the mayor of the city, to which our envoy replied fittingly. The guests were then conducted to carriages in waiting, and, preceded by Cossacks, who cleared a passage through the crowd, were driven to the residence of Mr. Jouravleff, who, like Mr. Kokoreff at Moscow, had proffered the hospitalities of his house.

In crossing the long bridge of boats over the Volga, which is two-thirds of a mile wide at this point, an enchanting picture came into view. The hundreds of vessels on the river and the houses along its banks were illumined with lamps and lanterns, and the mountain, with Minin's tower on its summit, blazed with Bengal lights. All were lighted at once by electricity, producing a startling and beautiful effect. The house of Mr. Jouravleff was also hung with Russian and American flags. The illumination was in honor of the Grand-dukes, who had arrived that day.

Nijny-Novgorod, or Lower Novgorod, so called to distinguish it from its more ancient namesake, Great Novgorod, contains ordinarily about forty thousand inhabitants; but, during its annual fair, its population numbers usually nearly a quarter of a million. At the time of the visit of our mission, it was estimated that more than three hundred thousand souls were in the town. The number is always calculated by the amount of bread sold by the bakers on each day.

CHAPTER XX.

OFFICIAL VISITS—TOMB OF MININ—VIEW FROM THE KREMLIN—THE GREAT FAIR—THE VOLGA—THE TEA-TRADE—THE MERCHANTS' DINNER—RUSSIAN GYPSIES.

AUGUST 30*th* (18*th*).—Thursday opened bright and clear. At ten o'clock Mr. Fox, Captain Murray, and Commander Beaumont, accompanied by Admirals Lessovsky and Gorkovenko, paid their respects to their Imperial Highnesses, the Cezarevitch Alexander Alexandrovitch and the Grand-duke Vladimir Alexandrovitch. They afterward made official calls on the governor, Lieutenant-General Odintzoff, and the temporary governor (appointed during the fair), Aide-de-Camp-General Ogareff. The official quarters were in the Kremlin, which, like that at Moscow, is a hill crowned with a massive wall, with towers at the angles, and with battlements and loop-holes for musketry. Within the enclosure are a church, the government palace, the courts of law, barracks, arsenal, and other buildings. On the esplanade stands the tomb of Minin, the Russian patriot, who was a native of Nijny-Novgorod. It is a handsome chapel, with an octagonal tower, capped with a pyramidal steeple and a pointed dome. Minin, in the early part of the seventeenth century, roused his countrymen against the Poles, who had overrun Russia. He persuaded Prince Pojarsky to take the command of the forces raised, and the enemy were driven from the land. His victorious banner, which is religiously preserved in the chapel, was brought out at the time of the French invasion, and again borne against the foe, creating the utmost enthusiasm among the Russian troops.

The governor, General Ogareff, received the visitors surrounded by a numerous staff of officers; and, after welcoming them to the hospitalities of Nijny-Novgorod, invited the party to visit the porch of his residence, where, he remarked, he would show them the Russian Mississippi and Missouri. The gentlemen followed him to the broad stone platform in front of the palace, whence a view was had of the whole surrounding country for thirty or forty miles. In the distance was the vast alluvial plain, across which the Volga, like a ribbon, stretched away to the horizon amid cultivated fields and occasional woods, while, in the foreground below, spread over the triangle where the Oka and the Volga meet, was the Fair, with its endless rows of shops, its streets thronged with the people of two continents, and bordered with a forest of masts and of steamboat-chimneys. The vessels and barges lay so thickly on the river that the water was nearly hidden, and the long bridge of boats appeared almost a superfluity. There were barges that had come down the Kama from Siberia and the Ural, and steamers up from Astrakhan and the Caspian Sea; boats that had floated with the current

of the Kliasma from Moscow, or through Lake Onega
and the Schcksna from St. Petersburg; and queer-looking
Asiatic craft, with colors and ornaments strange to
Western eyes. Most of them were flying their flags,
some the American as well as the Russian, for the arrival
of the Grand-dukes had made it a gala-day.

Nijny-Novgorod lies on the right bank of the Volga, at
its junction with the Oka. It is the eastern terminus of
the European railway system, which makes there a connection
with the vast net-work of rivers that intersect all
parts of the Russian Empire. From its unique position,
being, as it were, the frontier post of Europe and of Asia,
it gathers yearly a greater variety of produce and of customers
than any other town in the world. In its bazaars
the goods of London, Paris, and Berlin, are exposed beside
the products of all the Asiatic countries, and in its
streets may be seen and heard all complexions, costumes,
and languages.

The great annual Fair, which attracts this motley
throng of merchants, begins on the 1st of July and lasts
two months. During its continuance, trade is carried on
to the amount usually of more than a hundred million
rubles. All the traffic is by direct purchase and sale,
the commodity bargained for being delivered on the
ground. This necessitates the collection of immense
quantities of goods, which, when the shops are filled, are
stacked in piles in the open air, and covered with mats to
protect them from the rain. The advance of the Russian
railways into Asia will probably soon affect seriously this
great mart of exchange, which has been the meeting-place

of the merchants of Europe and of Asia for more than five hundred years.

The bazaar and the surrounding shops were erected in 1824, when the Fair was removed from its old position at Makarief, seventy-two miles below, to its present site. The governor's house occupies the centre of the Fair, which is laid out in squares separated by broad avenues. The governor lives here only during the Fair, his permanent residence being in the upper town. From the rear a wide boulevard, lined on each side by shops, with rows of trees in front, leads to a cathedral. The lower story of the official mansion is devoted to stalls for the sale of manufactured goods and fancy articles. There is also a restaurant there. The bazaar, containing more than three thousand stalls, is surrounded by a canal, as a protection against fire. The system of drainage is very perfect. The sewers, built of cut stone, are arranged in regular streets, are lofty and well ventilated, and are entered by stairways through towers placed at intervals along the upper avenues, each of which is in charge of a Cossack. These sewers are flushed several times a day with water raised from the river by pumps.

The Fair has long since overflowed the bazaar, and extends now to the banks of the Volga and the Oka, along which the lines of wharves stretch for ten miles. It has trespassed even upon the river itself. On a sand-bank in the middle of the Oka is a row of sheds, painted blue, more than a mile in length, where is stored in immense piles the iron brought from the Siberian mines. This is the most important article of traffic, and vessels are continually loading and unloading at these storehouses. The iron is in all forms, from bars and sheets, to every variety of household utensil.

Along the Volga are warehouses of cotton, tea, mill-stones, hides, dried fish, rags, and other bulky merchandise. All day long the contents of these vast stores are changing and being shipped from the wharves on vessels bound for all parts of the empire and the East.

Four hundred steamers, to say nothing of the countless barges, scows, and sailing-craft, ply on the Volga, and thence through its vast system of tributaries, that covers Russia like a net-work from the regions of pines and snows to the shores of the Caspian. Steam navigation on the Volga begins at Tver, where the railway from St. Petersburg to Moscow crosses it. Tver is from two and a half to three days' journey above Nijny-Novgorod. From the latter place to Astrakhan, at the mouth of the Volga, is about six days by steam. The whole navigable length of the Volga is about two thousand miles. The Oka is navigable for nearly a thousand miles. The trade of all the countries bordering on the Caspian comes up the Volga; but the most important of all the products sold at the Fair come down the Kama, another affluent of the Volga, joining it fifty miles below Kazan. This river drains the markets of Siberia, of the Ural, and of Central Asia. All the iron and the tea reaches Nijny-Novgorod through this channel.

Tea was formerly the most important article of merchandise at the Fair, the annual sales amounting to over fifteen million pounds, but the cheaper sea-carriage *via* Canton has impaired this trade of late years. The tea sold at Nijny-Novgorod is brought from Kiakhta, on the borders of Siberia and China, on camels and sledges across the country to Perm, on the Kama, where it is shipped on steamboats for the Volga. Kiakhta, in the government of Irkutsk, is the great emporium of trade between Russia and China. Annual fairs are held there, where caravans from both countries meet to barter their respective goods, Russian furs, broadcloths, linen and woollen goods, ironware, etc., being exchanged for teas, rhubarb, Chinese silks, and other products and manufactures of the Celestial kingdom, the greater part of which goes directly to Nijny-Novgorod. Other smaller fairs are held along the borders of Siberia and China, but they are chiefly of local importance, the greater part of the Western trade being carried on through Kiakhta.

All varieties of teas, from the delicate yellow tea to the coarse tea pressed into bricks, enter Russia through this channel. The yellow tea, which sells at Nijny-Novgorod generally as high as twenty dollars the pound, is the choicest of the crop, the first picking. The leaf is of an amber yellow, and the infusion almost colorless. It is drunk without either milk or sugar, has an exquisite odor and flavor, and is very exhilarating in its effects. It is served at the tables of the wealthy in small cups, after dessert, the same as coffee. It comes from China in small chests, each containing about four and a quarter pounds, covered with raw-hide. A number of these, usually about eight, are packed together in a bullock's skin, fastened with raw-hide, and thus transported to their destination on camels, sledges, boats, etc.

The brick tea is the refuse of the crop, pressed into solid cakes. It is used by the peasantry, and notably by the Calmucks and Tartars of the steppes, who boil it with mare's-milk, and sometimes make a kind of soup of it by mixing with it mutton-fat and parched millet. Great quantities of black and green teas, for general consumption, are also sold at the Fair.

The Americans, in company with a number of the officials, visited all parts of the Fair. The heat was oppressive, and the dust blew in clouds, but the streets were thronged with people. The most of the peasants were dressed in holiday costume in honor of the Grand-dukes, presenting a very picturesque appearance. Whenever the carriages stopped, they were surrounded at once by a curious crowd of gazers, so that progress was at times exceedingly difficult. Among the most interesting of the shops are those where the silver-gilt ware of Tula is exposed for sale. It is exquisitely wrought in the pretty forms of the "Renaissance." The fur-shops, too, are attractive, and contain treasures seldom seen elsewhere. After a long drive through the different rows, the party partook of a lunch at the restaurant of Nikita Egoroff, and returned to their quarters in time to rest before the festivities of the evening.

At seven o'clock Mr. Fox and party attended a grand dinner, given in his honor by the merchants in the great building in the middle of the Fair. The dining-hall was ornamented with evergreens, flowers, Russian and American flags, and with portraits of the Emperor, and of Washington, Lincoln, and Johnson. A gallery in the room was filled with ladies.

About one hundred and fifty sat down at the tables, among whom were representatives of all the different nationalities, Russians, Persians, Tartars, Armenians, and merchants from the Caucasus and from Siberia. Mr. Schipoff, the president of the Fair, presided, and gave the first toast. He said:

"I thank our dear American visitors for the kind reception their country gave our Russian naval officers. When Russia was experiencing a dark hour, America showed her sympathy in unmistakable signs, and Cronstadt, St. Petersburg, and Moscow, have been trying to return similar evidences of friendship. The friendship of America has transformed more than one of the old enemies of Russia into friends. The appearances alone of sympathy between Russia and America have sufficed to bring about such a result. Though Moscow, the first city of the empire and the heart of the country, had rivalled Cronstadt and St. Petersburg, the demonstrations of those three cities would not have sufficed, because they are only cities. Here, on the contrary, is represented the entire Russian Empire, north, south, east, and west; and Siberia and Central Asia participate in the proceedings. If the merchants of Nijny-Novgorod give the Americans a whole-hearted reception, if they understand and appreciate the fact that Russia and America are friends, it means more than a superficial observer at the dinner to-night would imagine. These merchants are gathered in

Nijny-Novgorod for only a few weeks, and cannot make the same splendid outward show in proportion to the degree of their friendship, but you may be assured of the warmth and unanimity of their feelings. In a few days the Fair will close, and they will carry home with them, to every corner of Russia and Asia where Russian trade and politics have sway, the enthusiasm which this happy occasion has called forth, and tell the story of how Russians and Americans met and recognized each other as the best of friends. America, differing from European countries, is a friend which every Russian feels will continue to be such. It is a long time since the two countries first showed a mutual attachment; and this fact and their several missions prove to me that their friendship will be enduring. When the merchants return to their homes, the simple steadfast people, who cannot read nor write, will learn that Russia possesses a friend across the ocean, on the other side of the world, and the story will become a tradition handed down from father to son. All the people of Russia will second the toast—To the prosperity of the people and to the health of the President of the United States."

Mr. Schipoff was interrupted in the course of his speech by frequent and loud applause. The band played our national air at the conclusion.

Mr. Fox, then directing attention to the portrait of the Emperor, said:

"To that Sovereign through whom the Divine purpose reaches the people of Russia, his Imperial Majesty Alexander II."

All the company arose and drank the toast, the enthusiasm culminating in loud cheers, the band joining in "God save the Emperor!"

A toast given by Captain Murray, "To the health of the Empress and of the Imperial Family, and of her who will soon become a member of that august family," was received with similar applause. He referred to the Princess Dagmar of Denmark, the betrothed of the Cezarevitch, who was married to him with imposing ceremonies at St. Petersburg, the 9th of November following.

The next toast was in honor of the "envoy of Congress, the Honorable G. V. Fox," which was greeted with the same hearty enthusiasm.

Mr. Fox replied: "It has been explained to me that the mayor refers to the warm reception tendered us in the various cities of Russia, and also at this place, where so many merchants are congregated. It is true that we have been welcomed at Cronstadt, at St. Petersburg, and at Moscow, as he describes; and the same generous hospitality meets us here. Like a bee wandering among flowers, we have tasted everywhere the delights of a Russian welcome, and shall return to our country laden with the sweets which have been gathered from the hearts of the Russian people. But the search of the bee in the corolla of the beautiful flowers is not for its own gratification; it extracts therefrom the honey which becomes food and refreshment for man. Its humble course is directed by an infinite wisdom, and here, near the centre of Russian life, where merchants and representatives from the remotest provinces and tribes meet for the interchange of material interests, have we not a right to believe that our footsteps hither are the result of the same guidance? Then let us be thankful for the influences which are drawing still closer the traditional bond which exists between the two empires, rivals only in the development of great ideas, such as your beloved sovereign continues to promulgate. (Cheers.) In this eventful year, on this historic ground, shall we not form a 'Holy Alliance,' not on parchment as a menace, but a moral alliance that in the interest of peace will merit God's blessing, and stand as an example to other nations?—I drink to the Governor, the Mayor, and the Merchants." (Great cheering.)

Mr. Ogareff responded briefly, making some very complimentary allusions to Mr. Fox, which elicited much applause from the merchants.

Mr. Osipoff followed. He thanked the Americans for the degree of consideration which had influenced them to send the congratulatory mission on the happy escape of the Emperor, and begged to remind them that not only the cities where they had been, but every town in Russia, thanked them. He proposed a toast to the prosperity of the American and Russian merchant marine and navies, and, as the representative of the American Navy, to Captain Murray. He hoped to see none but Russian and American ships engaged in carrying the products which are exchanged between the two countries.

Captain Murray responded as follows:

"No eloquence can express the sympathy with which we have been welcomed in Russia. What mean these star-spangled flags suspended here? Why are our oars

saluted by the music of the cheers which fill the air?
Why does the eye light up with pleasure, the hand press
ours with warmth? Why this generous hospitality, these
complimentary toasts and speeches to us, humble Americans? We are undecorated [applause] and simply clad.
We are American citizens, without pretension." Captain Murray then answered his own questions by referring to the love of country which characterized the two
nations, and mentioning some of the things in which
they harmonize. He spoke of the mutual interests of the
two nations in the construction of the Russo-American
telegraph, which should bind the two hemispheres together, as a first step toward realizing the pleasing picture
of the future, when Russian and American commerce
should whiten the dividing ocean, and commercial cities
should dot its shores.

The health of Commander Beaumont was then given
by Mr. Maschnin. Mr. Beaumont replied briefly, and
proposed a toast to the Russian Navy.

Mr. Ter Akapoff, an Armenian merchant, then made
a speech in his native language.

"The Americans," he said, "had scarcely set foot on
the soil of Russia, and made known their mission, when
enthusiastic acclamations of welcome were raised in all
parts of the empire. They meet with a like reception
here at the Fair, where many different nationalities are
met like one family, under the wise direction of a reforming sovereign, enjoying peace and happiness.

"Permit me to bid you welcome, and to say to you,
in the name of all the Armenians, that your mission of

friendship is received with enthusiasm in all the distant borders of Russia, and by every people that enjoys the benignant sway of our great sovereign, Alexander II."

Mr. Fox replied:

"As soon as we had crossed the Russian frontier, we were struck by the deep and sincere devotion of the people for their sovereign. It seemed to us that, in proportion as we advanced into the interior of the empire, this feeling became stronger and stronger. But now we learn from this citizen, newly arrived from the extreme East, that there also it is equally strong. Deeply impressed by this discovery, the source of your unity, power, and progress, I desire to propose again the health of him who has inspired such feelings — his Imperial Majesty, the Emperor."

A second time the national hymn of Russia was drowned in the tumultuous applause of the company.

Other toasts were given by Messrs. Egoroff, Veretenickoff, and Schipoff. The latter spoke of Lincoln, and praised the financial ability of Mr. Chase. He compared the status of the Russian paper currency with the American, greatly to the advantage of the latter. The reason why Russian paper-money was below par was not because there was too much of it, and the cause of the rising of American currency to nearly what it should be was owing to the ability of our secretary's management. He drank to the memory of Lincoln, and to the health of Mr. Chase.

After the dinner a band of gypsies, men and women, clad in their picturesque costumes, entertained the company with their songs and dances.

These Bohemians, as they are called, although none who see them can doubt their Indian origin, are met with in all the chief cities and towns of Russia. Their complexions are tawny, their hair black, and their eyes dark and piercing. The men have a Jewish cast of countenance, like the Karaim Jews of the Crimea, but it is not so observable among the women. Many of the girls are very beautiful, both in face and figure, but the older women do not exhibit the delicacy of outline which characterizes them in youth. They dress gaudily in bright colors, and wear many ornaments.

Their music is very fascinating, having about it a strange and savage harmony almost impossible to describe. Sometimes their songs, which are accompanied usually by the guitar, are low, sweet, and plaintive; sometimes loud and boisterous. Now we have a romance of passionate love, sung by a beautiful girl whose flashing eyes wander coquettishly among her audience; now a wild chorus of cries bursts from the whole band, like a harsh, sardonic laugh; and now a song, measured in rhythm and defiant in its tones as the war-cry of a proud and unconquerable race, is sung by a man with an energy and a spirit that insensibly affect all who hear him. The solo-songs are generally followed by choruses in which the whole band join, making a most striking contrast. Men and women spring of a sudden into action, with loud cries and halloos, clapping their hands and snapping their fingers, pirouetting and dancing and setting the whole body in a quivering motion, like the dancing-girls of the East, all the while keeping perfect time and following the air sung by their leader with endless variations. To look upon these strange figures clad in their bright-colored costumes, and decked with ornaments, to see their faces marked unalterably with the evidences of their Asiatic origin, their flashing eyes and passionate glances, the graceful *abandon* of their movements, one seems to be transported to the fervid regions of the East, of which poets sing, where soft airs loaded with perfumes benumb the senses and invite to sweet repose.

It is worthy of mention that the Russian gypsies, although possessing the same general characteristics of the wandering Bohemians seen in other countries, are more circumspect in their behavior, and are, as a rule, virtuous. This is remarkable, considering the free life they lead, and the temptations by which they are surrounded. Many of them have inspired serious passions in the breasts of Russia's noblest scions, and occasionally one has become the wife of some man of high rank. But, despite the seductions of the gay world, they seldom separate themselves entirely from their people, preferring the free and independent life to which they have been accustomed from their youth, to wealth and luxury in what is to them a prison.

At the conclusion of the gypsy songs and dances, Mr. Fox was invited into another room, and toasted again before a portrait in oil of himself, which hung upon the wall. Punch was then lighted and the company engaged in general conversation until eleven o'clock, when the very agreeable entertainment came to a close.

CHAPTER XXI.

THE VOLGA STEAMERS—A PEASANT WELCOME—DEPARTURE FROM NIJNY-NOVGOROD—SHIP-BUILDING ON THE VOLGA—KOSTROMA—THE CZAR MICHAEL—SUSANIN—A LADY'S WELCOME.

AUGUST 31*st* (19*th*).—In the morning, which was pleasant, the party again visited the Fair, and afterward, accompanied by Mr. Moschnin, went on board of a number of the Volga steamers, lying at the quay. Almost all of them are manned by Tartars, who make good sailors. They work cheerfully, lightening their labors generally with their wild songs, and appear to be as happy as children at play; but they have to be watched closely, else they do not accomplish much.

The steamboats are small and sharp, and draw more water than is necessary. Some of them were built in England and transported hither in pieces, to be put together in the ship-yards here. Some, however, are piloted through the maze of lakes, canals, and streams, that connect the Volga with the Gulf of Finland. Boats built on the American system, like those of the Mississippi, would be more serviceable, and would be preferable on many accounts.

The Cathedral of the Transfiguration was visited next, in the upper town. It was founded in the year 1221. Near it is shown the place where the patriot Minin stood when he harangued the people in 1612, and incited them to rise against the Poles.

At two in the afternoon, a deputation of peasants from the village of Bezvodnaïa, about twenty miles from Nijny-Novgorod, called on Mr. Fox, and presented him with specimens of their manufactures in iron and brass, consisting of sieves, hooks and eyes, chains, and fine netting. These articles, which are all made by hand, are the work of the women of this village, who are noted in the surrounding country for their beauty. They made a very pretty appearance in their picturesque costumes—polisses of red silk and high head-dresses profusely ornamented.

Mr. Fox thanked them for their kindness in coming so far to see him, and offered them, in remembrance, some of his card-photographs, with which they appeared greatly pleased. More than twenty thousand of these card-photographs of Mr. Fox were sold during the stay of the mission in Nijny-Novgorod.

At five o'clock the Americans and their Russian companions dined at the Lebedeff Hotel with the president of the Fair and a few prominent merchants. Much good feeling was manifested, and toasts were given to Mr. Fox, to Mr. Schipoff, and to Admiral Lessovsky. In reply, the last-named gentleman spoke of the reception he had met with in America, and of the friendly relations existing between the two countries. He referred also to the commercial ties which ought to bind Russia and America, and said that the Imperial Navy would always protect and foster the merchant service. Mr. Osipoff said that it was desirable that Russian commerce should be freed from the great expense of freight and commission, and wished that direct relations might be opened with the Americans.

After dinner, the party walked to the upper town to see the illumination in honor of the grand-dukes, which took place every night during their presence in the city. All the houses and shipping were lit with lamps and lanterns, as on the night of the arrival of the Americans, and in many places were seen transparencies showing the initials of the imperial visitors, surmounted with the crown. The streets were crowded to such an extent that the way was sometimes blocked with carriages and footpassengers, so as to be almost impassable.

The following is the translation of a dispatch sent on this day by Prince Gortchakoff, Vice-Chancellor of the Empire, to Mr. de Stoeckl, the minister of Russia at Washington:

Peterhof, August 31 (19), 1866.

Sir: The mission intrusted by the Congress of the United States of America to Mr. Fox, Under Secretary of State, has met with a reception by the Imperial Court, the public, and I may say the Russian nation, which you have already been able to appreciate from the notices in the public journals.

I need not dwell on these manifestations of the mutual

sympathy between the two countries. It reveals itself in full light. It is one of the most interesting facts of our time—a consolatory fact in the face of the recent complications which have just awakened in old Europe sentiments of hate, of ambition, of rivalry, bloody struggles, appeals to force, so little in harmony with the progress of humanity; a fact which sows between two great peoples, almost between two continents, the seeds of mutual good-will and friendship, which will bear fruit, become traditional, and inaugurate between them relations founded on a real spirit of Christian civilization.

In a letter which our august master addresses to the President of the United States, and which I request you to transmit to its destination, his Imperial Majesty begs Mr. Johnson to convey to Congress the assurance of the sentiments which he has already expressed to Mr. Fox.

I annex hereto a copy of the letter for your information.

You will also, sir, express yourself to the same effect both to the President and to the members of the Federal Government, as well as to other influential personages.

In face of a movement of national sympathy so spontaneous on both sides, the task of the Government is simply to fall in with the current, to promote it, and to direct it in actual practice to the good of both countries.

In this aim we count upon the coöperation of the Federal Government, as it may count upon ours.

The Emperor has been most favorably impressed by Mr. Fox. The tact with which he has acquitted himself of his mission has been highly appreciated in our official circles, as well as by the public of all classes with which he has come in contact, and he has been ably seconded by the distinguished *personnel* who accompanied him. It would have been difficult to commit to better hands the measure of cordial courtesy prescribed by Congress.

You are directed to bear witness to this sentiment. Receive, etc., etc.

(Signed) GORTCHAKOFF.

Mr. de Stoeckl, etc., etc., etc.

THE EMPEROR OF RUSSIA
TO
THE PRESIDENT OF THE UNITED STATES.

Peterhof, *August* 17, 1866.

I have received, by the hands of Mr. Fox, the resolution of the Congress of the United States of America on the occasion of the Providential favor of which I have been the object.

This mark of sympathy has touched me deeply. It is not merely personal to me—it is a new attestation of the sentiments which unite the American nation to Russia.

The two peoples find in their past no recollections of old grievances, but, on the contrary, memorials only of amicable treatment. On all occasions they add new proofs of mutual good-will. These cordial relations, which are as advantageous to their reciprocal interests as to those of civilization and humanity, conform to the views of Divine Providence, whose final purpose is peace and concord among nations.

It is with a lively satisfaction that I see these bonds

continually strengthening. I have communicated my
sentiments to Mr. Fox. I pray you to express them to
Congress and to the American people, of which that body
is the organ. Tell them how much I, and with me all
Russia, appreciate the testimonials of friendship which
they have given me, and how heartily I shall congratulate
myself on seeing the American nation growing in power
and prosperity by the union and continued practice of the
civic virtues which distinguish it.

Accept, at the same time, the assurance of the high
consideration with which I am

Your good friend,

(Signed)   ALEXANDER.

September 1st (August 20th).—On Saturday morning,
at ten o'clock, Mr. Fox and the accompanying gentlemen
visited the foundery and machine-shops of Mr. Koltchin,
one of the largest establishments of the kind on the
Volga.

At eleven o'clock the party embarked on the steamer
Sarapoulets, belonging to Mr. Koltchin, and started up
the Volga for Kostroma. Besides Mr. Koltchin, they
were accompanied by the mayor and other officials, and
by a large deputation of merchants. A band on board
played our national air as the steamer left the wharf, and
the people on shore responded with loud hurrahs.

After the steeples and the forest of masts of Nijny-
Novgorod had disappeared from sight, the company were
invited to sit down to a breakfast laid in the cabin. The
occasion was enlivened by the presence of a band of gyp-

sics, mostly women, about two dozen in number, who sang their wild songs to the accompaniment of guitars. Speeches and toasts alternated with the music, and the time passed merrily away, until a point about twenty miles above the city was reached, when the Sarapoulets drew up in mid-river, alongside the Depecha (Dispatch), a smaller steamboat, drawing only three feet of water, and transferred the Americans to her. Before the separation parting toasts were drunk, each man draining his glass and then throwing it overboard, in accordance with the Russian custom. Hand-shakings and mutual regrets followed, the gypsies sang a touching farewell song, and the steamers, each flying the American flag, separated with "Hail Columbia" by the band, and loud hurrahs. The Sarapoulets returned to Nijny-Novgorod, and the Depecha took her course up the Volga.

The river at this point is nearly two-thirds of a mile in width, with low banks like the Mississippi. The steeples and gilded domes of churches are seen everywhere. Indeed, churches appear to be a Russian specialty, and are built in commemoration of almost every thing. There are sixty in Nijny-Novgorod alone, and every town is as well supplied in proportion to population.

A large business is done along the Volga in shipbuilding. Nearly all the steamers are now Russian-built. The most of them are tugboats, used for towing barges, and they are not very highly finished; but the quality of the Russian iron is good, and they are put together strongly, so that they make very serviceable craft. The immense trade of the river and its affluents, increasing every year, makes a continual demand for more boats, and all the ship-yards are full of work.

At Katunki, a town above Nijny-Novgorod, are extensive tanneries. As many as fifty thousand cat-skins are dressed here annually. A great deal of flax is spun in the surrounding country, and great quantities of linen are manufactured in Kineshma and other towns beyond. Near Kostroma is a Tartar village, founded in the sixteenth century, whose inhabitants still retain their national looks and manners.

September 2d (August 21st).—Sunday opened with fine weather. At about ten and a half o'clock the cupolas of the Cathedral of the Assumption, in Kostroma, were descried across a bend in the river, and soon after the city came into sight. The view of Kostroma from the water is highly picturesque. All Russian cities look larger than they are, being the reverse of compactly built; and, having a profusion of churches, whose cupolas and steeples rise in every direction, they present an imposing appearance from a distance.

At eleven o'clock the Depecha reached the pier, which was decorated with flags and covered with carpets. At the landing-place stood Lieutenant-General Rudzevitch, Governor of Kostroma, in full uniform, who came on board the steamer and welcomed Mr. Fox to the hospitalities of the city. The boat had not been expected before two o'clock, and the customary crowd was absent; but the news of the arrival spread like wildfire, and in a few minutes all the avenues leading to the river were filled with people hurrying to the pier.

The party landed at once, in company with the governor, and proceeded in carriages to make the usual official calls. The governor's residence was first visited, and afterward those of the marshal of the nobility of the province, Mr. Kartzoff, and of the mayor of the city, Mr. Akatoff. After these ceremonial calls, the gentlemen returned to the steamer, where lunch was prepared under an awning on the deck. They had scarcely arrived when the city dignitaries came to return the visits, and were invited to partake of travellers' fare.

The landing was now black with people. Some barges near by were crowded also, and many row-boats, filled with men and women, covered the river around the steamer. Whenever an American was seen enthusiastic cheers went up, which were echoed and reëchoed by the thousands behind them. One man standing upon a barge attracted Mr. Fox's attention by his loud shouting, and by the distinctness with which he pronounced his name. On sending for him to come on board he proved to be a painter, Ivan Ratshkoff by name, who had formerly been a serf. Mr. Fox wrote his name on the back of one of his card-photographs and gave it to him. The worthy man was so moved at this simple gift that tears came into his eyes. He immediately went ashore, and returning after a time brought Mr. Fox a small picture of St. Nicholas, painted by himself, on the back of which, at our envoy's request, he inscribed his name. This little episode aroused the people to fresh enthusiasm.

After the lunch, the party, under the guidance of Mr. Kartzoff, rode out to view the city and the many objects of interest in it.

Kostroma is situated on the left bank of the Volga, at its junction with the Kostroma River, and has a population of twenty thousand. It dates from the twelfth century, having been founded about 1150, by George, the son of Vladimir Monomachus. It suffered various vicissitudes in the early centuries, from plague and famine, Tartars and Poles; but its chief historical interest lies in the fact that it was the ancient home of the Romanoff family, and that near it occurred the incident, in the life of the first sovereign of that illustrious race, on which Glinka founded the plot of his well-known opera of "Life for the Czar."

The election of Wladislas, the son of Sigismund, King of Poland, to the Russian throne, in 1610, aroused an intense national feeling. Minin, a citizen of Nijny-Novgorod, of whom we have already spoken, called his countrymen to arms, and gave the command to the Boyar Pojarsky. Siege was laid to Moscow, the city taken, and Wladislas driven from the country. Pojarsky, a vigorous statesman, succeeded in establishing some degree of order in the distracted country; after which he sought out the real heir to the throne, Michael Fedorovitch Romanoff, a youth of sixteen, and invited him to accept the crown. The prince, who was the son of the Metropolitan of Rostof, had been educated in a monastery, and was loth to leave his studies for the more important duties to which he was summoned; but the nobles and the military leaders, who had ratified Pojarsky's choice, and elected him Czar, at last persuaded him to accept the throne, and he left the monastery of Ipatieff, where he had taken refuge, and took up his abode near Kostroma.

The Poles, still intent upon seizing the country, determined to murder the young Czar, as the easiest way of ridding themselves of his accession, and secretly dispatched a party of men to Kostroma to accomplish their purpose. On reaching the neighborhood of the city, they separated into small bands, to avoid suspicion, and planned to meet at the Czar's house, on the Romanoff estate. One of these bands fell in with a peasant of the neighboring village of Domnino, named Ivan Susanin, and inquired the way to Prince Michael's house. They told him they had been sent to the Czar on important business, and would reward him liberally for acting as their guide. Susanin detected their Polish accent, and suspected foul play. They were then but a short distance from the estate, but he told them it was a long way off, and, as a terrible snow-storm was then drifting, persuaded them to go to his cottage for food and rest. He gave them refreshment and strong drink, meantime sending a trusty messenger to the Czar, to warn him of the impending danger.

The Poles slept for several hours. A little after midnight, guided by Susanin, they started in the blinding storm to accomplish their mission. The faithful peasant conducted them by by-paths into the thickest depths of the forest, and, after thoroughly exhausting them by the difficulties of the way, declared that he had missed the road. As day dawned they lost patience, and accused him of treachery. Susanin, feeling that the Czar was then safe, and knowing that the Poles could not find their way out of the wood, boldly avowed that he had purposely led them astray. Their rage was unbounded, and they literally chopped him into pieces with their swords. His last words were:

"I would rather die than be a traitor, and God will receive my soul."

Most of the party died in the forest, of cold, hunger, and fatigue, and the few that crawled out alive narrated the story of Susanin's heroism. The Czar Michael richly rewarded his family, and gave a large tract of land to his daughter and her husband (he had no son), and their heirs forever. Great privileges and immunities were bestowed also on his descendants, who now number over four hundred persons; but they have lately been forfeited.

In the reign of the Emperor Nicholas, a splendid monument was erected in the square at Kostroma in memory of Susanin and his noble act of self-sacrifice. This was the first object visited by the Americans. A granite column, rising from a massive pedestal of the same stone, is surmounted by a bust of the Czar Michael, crowned and clad in imperial robes. Beneath the bust is the double-headed eagle of Russia, and lower down, surrounded by a wreath, are the arms of Kostroma. At the base of the column kneels Susanin, and on the pedestal is a bass-relief representing his noble sacrifice of his own life to save his sovereign's. The monument is a fine work of art, worthy of the subject which it commemorates.

The party went next to the Monastery of Ipatieff, on

the banks of the Kostroma, without the city. It dates from the fourteenth century, and contains many interesting relics of antiquity. The young Prince Michael took refuge within its walls when the crown was offered to him in 1613. His rooms are still preserved, furnished as they were when he occupied them. The Americans were shown through the church, the vestry, the library, and other parts of the monastery, so celebrated in Russian history, and were requested to write their names on a special page of the visitors'-book as a memorial of their call.

The ancient house of the Romanoffs, where the family lived before its elevation to imperial dignity, is also still to be seen near Kostroma. It is remarkable for its thick stone walls, small rooms, and narrow doors, and looks as if built to stand a siege.

The Cathedral of the Assumption is one of the most ancient specimens of ecclesiastical architecture in Russia, having been founded in the year 1239, in commemoration of the miraculous appearance of the Holy Virgin to Prince Vassily. It is remarkably well preserved, having undergone but few alterations in the past six centuries.

The extensive steam machine works of Mr. Schipoff, then recently established, were inspected next, after which Mr. Fox went, in company with the governor, to call on Madame Linachoff, a young married lady, who had visited the steamer and left a bouquet of flowers, tied with a silk band of stars and stripes, and the following note, written in English, addressed to the American Envoy:

"Permit me, sir, to greet your arrival, and, in offering this nosegay, may you remember that you have met at

Kostroma a person who, with her family, fully appreciates the sympathy your nation has shown to Russia. Long live America and her union with Russia!

"*Proprietor in Kostroma,*

"CATHERINE LINACHOFF, *born* POLTORATZKY."

Both Madame Linachoff and her mother spoke English, and the interview was an exceedingly pleasant one.

CHAPTER XXII.

AN EMBARRASSING HONOR—THE BANQUET AT KOSTROMA—RECEPTION BY LADIES—MR. FOX AN HONORARY CITIZEN OF KOSTROMA—RIBINSK.

AT six o'clock Mr. Fox and the accompanying gentlemen were invited to the House of Assembly of the nobility, where a dinner was given in their honor by the city of Kostroma.

When Mr. Fox landed from the steamer, some young girls presented him with flowers and offered him a welcome in English. As he stepped up the bank a peasant took off his overcoat and threw it down before him. Our envoy leaped over it. The open pathway to the top of the river's bank was immediately covered with clothes, and the immense throng waited in silence to see what he would do. Hesitating for a moment at accepting so unusual an honor, reserved generally for a beloved member of the imperial family, Mr. Fox, seeing there was no way of avoiding it, stepped forward on the garments cast in his way. Tremendous cheers greeted the action, and hats and handkerchiefs were waved in every direction. At the top of the bank the people endeavored to detach the horses from his carriage, and would have effected their object if the animals had not been beyond control in consequence of the hurrahs.

The Assembly House of the nobility is a fine building, with marble halls. The front was decorated with flags, shields, and emblems expressive of the friendship of the two nations. A military band played at the entrance, where the managers met the guests and conducted them up the staircase, decorated with flowers and evergreens, to the great hall, where a large company was assembled. All classes of society were represented, including the peasants, among whom were a number of the relatives of Komissaroff.

The dinner was served in a spacious and beautiful saloon, with walls of white marble. At one end was a portrait of the Emperor, wreathed with flowers, and under it the bust of Komissaroff, crowned with evergreens. Opposite were shields bearing the names of Washington, Lincoln, and Johnson. The galleries of the second story were filled with ladies, and an orchestral band was stationed in the choir.

The opening speech was made by Mr. Kartzeff, the marshal of the nobility. He said:

"The presence among us of the honorable Mr. Fox, the representative of the powerful North American nation, is not only a proof of the sympathy of the people of the United States, who participate in Russia's joy at the preservation of the precious life of her sovereign, but it is also a pledge of the continuation of the friendly alliance between Russia and America, which is now as strong and firm as the union between countries of such a similarity of interests can be.

"Gentlemen, Russia and America, travelling in different paths, have attained substantially the same results. Both countries have insured to all their citizens, without exception, the freedom of labor, founded on the rights of man. In Russia, the great reform which gave liberty to twenty millions of bondmen was effected by the nobility, who have aided to establish the new social order which our beloved sovereign has built up in so short a time, with the concurrence of the whole people, and without any disturbance of order. The sympathy of the Americans for this national work is most precious to us, and the consideration of our guests for Kostroma, in which they honor the personification of Russian patriotism, is equally appreciated. We are all grateful to the honorable Mr. Fox, representative of the friendly nation of North America, for the visit which he and his travelling companions have made to our province, the birthplace of the reigning dynasty and of two saviors of Russian sovereigns.

"I have the honor to congratulate the honorable Mr. Fox, and to propose a toast to the health of the President of the United States and to the prosperity of the great North American nation."

In answer to this speech, which was received with cheers, Mr. Fox gave the following toast:

"To that illustrious Romanoff, the Liberator, who has inherited the benediction given by a pious mother at Kostroma to the chief of this dynasty, and to whose heart that blessing has been transmitted, producing the divine fruit manifested in successful efforts for the benefit of his people—Alexander II., Emperor of Russia."

Enthusiastic applause followed this toast, the orchestra playing the Russian national hymn.

Lieutenant Commander Pritchett, of the Augusta, gave, in the absence of Captain Murray, who was detained by indisposition, a toast to the health of the Empress and the imperial family, and Governor Rudzevitch one to the Cezarevitch, both of which received the usual cheers and music.

Mr. Prokhoroff, President of the provincial board of the government of Kostroma, then made an animated and eloquent speech, concluding with a toast to the prosperity of America and her national institutions, and to the prosperity of Russia and her well-beloved sovereign.

When he had finished, the following telegram was dispatched to Washington:

"Kostroma, the cradle of the House of Romanoff, in congratulating Mr. Fox, expresses its wishes for the happiness of the American people."

Mr. Boschniak then offered a toast to "the Congress of the United States and to our dear guests, the representatives of the American Navy."

Mr. Fox responded:

"Kostroma has surrounded us on all sides with compliments of welcome. Outside these walls a compact crowd of her citizens chant the inspiring national songs of Russia. Inside, the melodies of the two nations are mingled; and those glorious flags, consecrated by victory, are here joined together. In the galleries, alas! too far removed, the angels of Russia smile upon us. (Applause.)

"Pilgrims from the New World, we have come hither desiring to connect our country with your glorious history, to plant on this sacred soil the sympathies which our people have commissioned me to express on the occasion which menaced your beloved sovereign; and we pray that the seed thus sown may bear a perennial harvest of fraternal feeling between the two nations forever. I give a toast to the governor, to the marshal of the nobility, to the mayor, and to all the people of Kostroma."

Mr. Boschniak gave a toast to "Admiral Lessovsky, who, during his visit to America, has bound such sympathetic relations between Russia and the United States;" to which the admiral replied by giving the health of "all the Russians who accompanied him in his voyage."

Mr. Curtin, secretary of the American legation, then spoke in the Russian language as follows:

"There are places so hallowed by glorious and sacred memories that our hearts, at sight of them, are involuntarily filled with emotion. In one of those places, sacred to the past, we find ourselves to-day. In a time of suffering and trial, when Russia, without a Czar, was harassed by enemies who hoped to ruin and destroy her, Kostroma had a youthful boyar [nobleman] worthy to be chosen the Czar and deliverer of Russia at the universal call of her people. When the life of the newly-elected chief was in danger, in Kostroma was found a peasant who gladly laid down his own life for his native land. Centuries later, when the guilty hand of an assassin was raised against the descendant of Michael Romanoff, Providence, watching over the destinies of Russia, prevented the accomplishment of the crime; and by the hand of a Kostroma peasant was the land again saved from calamity. Such is the significance of Kostroma. She once gave and twice preserved to Russia a Czar. Therefore it is that she is honored, and therefore it is that we Americans are standing here to-day at the cradle of the house of Romanoff, having come from our distant fatherland to bring you our greetings and to congratulate you, her inhabitants, on the preservation of your Emperor's life, and on the heroism and virtue of your illustrious townsmen, Susanin and Komissaroff, the saviors of Michael Romanoff and of Alexander II. I beg leave to propose a toast to the prosperity of beautiful Kostroma."

This speech in their own tongue so delighted the Russians that Mr. Curtin had to submit to a tossing, in addition to the cheers which he received.

Mr. Curtin was followed by the peasant Finikoff, a relative of Komissaroff's and member of the provincial assembly. "Permit me also, honorable Mr. Fox," he said, "to congratulate you, as the representative of the peasants freed from serfdom by our good Emperor. You see yonder on the wall the likeness of one of our class who saved the life of our sovereign, to which act we are indebted for your dear presence among us. Accept, in my person, the expression of sincere gratitude on the part of the peasants of Kostroma, who will always remember your friendship and your love for our country and for our Emperor, the Liberator; and allow me to give a toast to the mutual friendship of Russians and Americans."

Toasts followed to Komissaroff-Kostromsky and to the Russian and the American ladies. As soon as dinner was over and tea had been drunk in the assembly-rooms, the company adjourned to a beautifully decorated and illuminated pavilion in the public garden, where a large number of ladies awaited their coming. Twelve beautiful young ladies, dressed in white, offered the Americans flowers as they entered. The daughter of the governor, who led them, presented to Mr. Fox a bouquet tied with red, white, and blue ribbons. Our envoy had the honor of leading the dance with the wife of General Rudzevitch, the governor. After the dancing, there were more toasts and speeches, music, and a rustic concert, by some red-smocked shepherds, on pandean pipes.

From the ballroom Mr. Fox and some of the party went to visit a hemp-yarn factory, where very young children were at work; and thence to the owner's house, where wine and cigars were proffered, and all were asked to write their names in an album.

At midnight the party bade adieu to Kostroma, and returned on board the Depecha. The governor and other officials accompanied them to the landing, where they were followed by crowds of people, who sang national songs and cheered. The streets were brilliantly illuminated, and bonfires and blue-lights lit up the river's bank. Much warmth of feeling was expressed by the citizens at parting, and the Americans bade them good-by with many regrets that their visit was necessarily so short a one.

After Mr. Fox's return to the United States, he received, through the State Department, letters-patent, conferring on him the honorary citizenship of the city of Kostroma.

The diploma is on heavy Bristol board, thirty by twenty-four inches in size. At the top are the arms of Kostroma, a green shield quartered by two intersecting lines of gold; in the first quarter a silver cross, in the fourth a silver crescent, inverted. Beneath the shield are two circles, that on the left enclosing the letters "M O" (Michael Czar) and the date "1613," the year of the accession to the throne of Michael Fedorovitch Romanoff, the founder of the present dynasty; that on the right, "O K K" (Osip Komissaroff-Kostromsky) and "1866," the year in which he preserved the life of the latest Romanoff. The four corners of the diploma contain views in Kostroma: at the top, on the right, the principal cathedral and the convent where Prince Michael lived; on the left, a scene in ancient Kostroma; at the bottom are two views of the city from the river. At the middle of the left side is the monument of Susanin, and opposite it, on the right, is a picture of the lower cathedral (Uspensky). The seal of the city is appended at the bottom.

The inscription, which is in both Russian and English, reads as follows:

The citizens of Kostroma, penetrated with the feelings of the deepest esteem for the famous American nation, for the sympathy expressed by it on account of the wonderful deliverance of our beloved monarch from the wicked attack of the murderer, and sincerely grateful to the American Embassy for the high honor bestowed upon Kostroma by their visit, resolved to immortalize this event, momentous for our city, by offering to the representative of the great nation, the Vice-Secretary of the Navy of the United States, Mr. Fox, the title of

CITIZEN OF NOTE OF THE TOWN OF KOSTROMA.

The Minister of the Home Department has informed us, on the 30th of October, 1866, that our gracious sovereign has approved and confirmed the resolution of the City Council of Kostroma, in consequence of which we have the honor of forwarding this diploma, with the signatures of the City Council of Kostroma, and the seal thereof affixed to the act.

To the Honorable Mr. Fox.

September 3d (August 22d).—Monday opened bright and clear. The Volga grows narrower above Kostroma, and there is little to be seen, excepting a few scattering villages and occasional church-steeples, until Yaroslaf is reached at the confluence of the Kotorosl River. It is a place of considerable business importance, having a large trade in grain and iron. With a population of about thirty thousand, it has seventy-seven churches. It dates from the beginning of the eleventh century.

At one o'clock in the afternoon the steamer reached Ribinsk, a place of eleven thousand inhabitants, at the junction of the Sheksna with the Volga. A landing was made just above the town, and the rope-walk of Mr. Juravlyeff visited. He employs nineteen hundred persons in rope-making, doing all his spinning by hand. He is also a large dealer in lumber and timber, employing a great many barges in his business. After visiting the different buildings on his place, the party dined with him.

Although Ribinsk is a comparatively new town, dating only from the end of the last century, it is a place of great commercial importance. The canal-system which connects the waters of the Volga with the Baltic begins here, and from seven to eight thousand vessels arrive at and depart from it yearly. Great quantities of grain and tallow, brought from below, are transshipped here into smaller vessels for St. Petersburg.

CHAPTER XXIII.

UGLITCH—KEMRA — KORTCHEVA — RECEPTION AT TVER—A SOLDIER OF BORODINO—ST. PETERSBURG BAZAAR—THE GREAT THEATRE—BREAKFAST AT GRAND-DUCHESS CONSTANTINE'S.

SEPTEMBER 4*th* (*August* 23*d*).—The fine weather continued. The river grew still narrower, and the banks higher. Churches were seen in every direction. At Uglitch, a town of five or six thousand inhabitants, there are twenty-seven, some of them of much architectural beauty.

This city, which dates from the middle of the tenth century, was once large and populous. Dmitry, the younger son of Ivan the Terrible, was confined here, during the reign of his feeble brother Fedor; and here, in 1591, he met a violent death, which was attributed to the treachery of Boris Godunoff, the brother-in-law of Fedor, who hoped, by cutting off the heir, to succeed to the sovereignty himself. Fedor, the last of the house of Rurik, died in 1598, and Boris accomplished his ambitious designs. Dmitry's murder was denied afterward by pretenders, who assumed his name and rights, it being claimed that another child had been substituted in his place. One of these was successful in his imposture, and was crowned Czar at Moscow in 1605, Fedor II., the son and successor of Boris Godunoff, having met a fate similar to that of the true Dmitry. Even after the accession of the house of Romanoff in the person of the Czar Michael, in 1613, the convulsions caused by the tragedy at Uglitch still affected the peace of Russia, and were with difficulty suppressed.

At Kaliachin the steamer stopped to wood, and the Americans seized the opportunity to walk through the village. The chief industry is starch-making. Little worthy of note was seen, excepting a church on the river-bank, with a handsome Greek tower.

At eight o'clock in the evening, the Depecha again stopped for wood, at the village of Kemra. A deputation of the inhabitants, with the mayor of the town at their head, came down to the landing, and presented the following address to Mr. Fox:

WELCOME TO THE REPRESENTATIVE OF THE AMERICAN NATION FROM THE PEASANTS OF KEMRA.

SIR:—Your presence in our country is evidence of a mutual sympathy, and betokens an everlasting peace between the two great nations, America and Russia.

This warm friendship sprung up in the days of similar hardships experienced by two great peoples: by the Americans in a civil war, by the Russians in the Polish rebellion. But these great afflictions were triumphantly overcome, and each country fully restored to its unity.

The whole of Russia and the Russian nation greet you, our honored guests. We, the peasants of Kemra, beg permission to be numbered among them, and to express to you our warmest sympathy, and to welcome you, high representatives of the great American nation.

In the name of the people of Komra, elected head of the village, BUGREENOFF.

     Peasants: MICHAEL MATOVIN.
          IVAN BUGREENOFF.
          ALEXANDER STELIAROFF.
     Merchant: IVAN SOBTSOFF.
          IVAN MALINTCHIN.
     Merchant: ANDREAS MIROFSKOY.
          SIMEON RAWGUNOFF.
          PETER SDUNEN.
  Merchant's son: NICHOLAS SOBTSOFF.
          IVAN BOGOMOTCHEFF.

KEMRA, *August* 23, 1866.

The deputation that presented this address was composed entirely of peasants, no government officials being present. The authorities of the town were all elected by the body of the people, under the new system of self-government authorized by the present Emperor.

After the address of welcome, the gentlemen of the mission were invited ashore to visit the church and to take tea. The church is a fine building, in imitation of the patriarchal church at Moscow. It was lighted instantly by means of a combustible thread running from candle to candle.

After a walk through the village, the party took tea with the officials and some of the principal inhabitants. Champagne was produced freely, and a few toasts were given. When the Americans left, the people accompanied them to the river-bank with torches and lanterns. Some of the houses were illuminated, and a long line of torches was planted on each side of the road, making a very pleasing effect. Almost the whole population of the village crowded the landing, and cheered lustily as the steamer pushed off.

Kemra contains about twenty-five hundred inhabitants, whose chief occupation is the manufacture of boots and shoes. Men only are employed in this work, the women laboring in the fields. Mr. Fox asked to see some of their products. This request appeared to please them much, and in a few minutes a great number of boots and shoes, of all shapes and sizes, were brought in and exhibited.

September 5th (August 24th).—Wednesday opened bright and pleasant. The steamboat had been obliged to anchor the greater part of the night, on account of the shoalness of the water, so that but little progress had been made. At half-past seven in the morning, she stopped at Kortcheva to wood. A deputation, consisting of the mayor, the chief of police, and the principal personages of the town, came on board and requested an audience with Mr. Fox, to announce to him that he had been elected an honorary citizen of Kortcheva. They also invited him and the other gentlemen to land, and partake of tea and refreshments. At the entertainment which followed, Mr.

Fox toasted his new fellow-citizens, which elicited much enthusiasm from the good people.

Kortcheva is a town of about three thousand inhabitants, engaged mostly, like Kemra, in the boot and shoe business. There were no government officials there, which made the welcome tendered by its people the more significant. Wherever our mission went, it was received by the peasant-class with the utmost enthusiasm; and heart-felt expressions of love and gratitude to the United States were heard in every little village.

At the next stopping-place for wood, the peasants brought on board presents of fresh-caught fish.

At half-past five in the afternoon, Tver, the end of the voyage, was reached.

The city, which has a population of about twenty-five thousand, occupies a commanding site, on the left bank of the Volga, one hundred and seventy-five feet above the water. The railway from St. Petersburg to Moscow crosses the river at this point on a fine bridge built on the American plan.

Mr. Fox was received at the steamboat-landing by Prince Mestchersky, marshal of the nobility of the province, by Prince Bagration, the governor, by the mayor, and representatives of the corporations, and by many of the principal citizens. The railway-station was gayly dressed with flags, and a band played "Hail Columbia." After the formal congratulations, the party were taken in carriages to the principal points of attraction in the city, and afterward to dinner in the railway-station.

Tver dates from the latter part of the twelfth century,

but the most of its public buildings belong to a more modern period. In one of its churches, which has a handsome three-storied belfry, are buried the ancient princes of the province. The Church of the Holy Trinity is a well-preserved specimen of early Russian architecture.

There is a large business done at Tver in grain and iron, and there are a number of nail-factories there. The iron is brought down the Kama from Siberia, and much of it is shipped back again in its manufactured state. There is also a considerable trade with Astrakhan, at the mouth of the Volga, more than two thousand miles distant, and with the ports in the Caspian.

The dinner in the railway-station was an elegant affair, notwithstanding the haste with which it had been prepared. The hall was hung with flags, and decorated with flowers and evergreens. Portraits of Lincoln and Johnson were on the walls.

The Americans were greeted with cheers and music as they entered, and Prince Bagration, the Governor of Tver, welcomed them in a few appropriate words.

The governor also gave the first toast, "To the President of the United States of America," which was received with applause, and followed by our national air.

Mr. Fox responded:

"To him, who belongs entirely to Russia, but is recognized as a leader wherever the principles of Christianity and civilization are in the ascendant—his Imperial Majesty Alexander II."

Similar enthusiasm followed this toast, and the music, "God save the Emperor!"

Prince Mestchersky then gave a toast "to the health of the Honorable Mr. Fox, the Envoy of the United States of America," which was received with loud cheers.

Glinka, an aged soldier who fought at Borodino and Moscow, arose as soon as the applause had subsided, and read a poem of his own composition, celebrating the friendship of Russia and America.

When he had finished, Mr. Fox spoke as follows:

"During my journeys in Russia, I have met everywhere an extraordinary and universal sympathy. This feeling, maintained in its strength, will conduct the two nations to a closer union for their mutual welfare and happiness. But, in speaking of the future, the past should not be forgotten—the past, in which the principles advocated by Russia, and carried by her to a successful issue, have raised her to the height of power and of glory. The governor and the marshal of the nobility will pardon me, I trust, if, instead of a response to their kind toast, I propose one in honor of that glorious epoch for Russia and her representative" (pointing to Glinka), "an epoch when Russia, rising like one man, drove from her territory such numerous and powerful enemies. May the same fate overtake those who, in the future, invade Russian soil!" (Great applause.)

After a toast to the governor by Captain Murray, Mr. Curtin proposed one to the health of the marshal of the nobility, of the vice-governor, and of the mayor. Others followed to the prosperity of America, and to the health of Admiral Lessovsky, but time pressed, and the arrival of the train from Moscow brought the festivities to a close.

Prince Bagration gave the final toast. He said:

"Gentlemen, there is an end even to joys. We must separate from the eminent guests whom we have received with sincere enthusiasm, and whose memory we shall always preserve. In accompanying them on their journey with our cordial wishes for their happiness, let us not forget those in a distant land who await their return with love and impatience. I drink to the health of the families of our dear guests, and of all the American ladies."

The members of the mission departed for St. Petersburg on the train at seven o'clock, the crowd cheering and the band playing as they left the station.

September 6th (August 25th).—After a pleasant night-ride, unattended by any noteworthy incidents, the party reached St. Petersburg at nine o'clock the next morning, and reoccupied their rooms at the Hôtel de France. Mr. Fox attended to private business during the day, and dined informally in the evening with Admiral Popoff and family.

During the night, Acting Volunteer-Lieutenant Wheeler of the Augusta was taken ill with the cholera at the Hôtel de France. Much uneasiness was felt at his condition by his friends, and the Russian officials exhibited their anxiety concerning him by the most unremitting attentions. Admiral Lessovsky sat up all night with him, and did not leave his bedside until the physicians on the following day pronounced him to be out of danger.

September 7th (August 26th).—Various parts of the city were visited, especially the bazaars, where purchases were made of articles peculiar to Russia and her manufactures. The Gostinnoy Dvor, or Great Bazaar, of St. Petersburg, is on the Nevsky Prospect, and extends over several squares. It is two stories in height, the lower of which is occupied by retail shops of almost every variety of merchandise, while the upper is devoted to the storage of goods and to wholesale dealing. The numerous lanes and alleys by which it is intersected are crowded by day with purchasers; but at night, after business-hours, the great building is deserted by all excepting the watchmen, none of the merchants living in their shops, as is the custom in Constantinople.

Almost every thing can be bought within the bounds of this colossal fair, but the purchaser should understand the Russian language well enough to bargain and know something of the actual worth of the articles wanted, if he would expend his money to advantage. There are many shops, however, where the English language is spoken, and where all goods are sold at undeviating prices.

In the evening Mr. Fox and several of the other gentlemen attended the opera at the Bolchoy (Great) Theatre. This house, which is under government patronage, is unsurpassed in any other of the European capitals for size and magnificence. It will seat over three thousand persons, and has five rows of boxes. The scenery, costumes, and stage accessories, are as near perfection as can be attained by the lavish expenditure of money, and its troupe of actors, singers, and ballet-dancers, is unexcelled. There is a government school in St. Petersburg for the education of actresses and ballet-dancers, for which large sums are appropriated yearly. At the Bolchoy Theatre the operas and ballets are given with great splendor and perfection of detail. Glinka's beautiful opera, "Life for the Czar," was produced on the night of Mr. Fox's visit. It is a great favorite in Russia, and never fails to arouse the patriotic enthusiasm of the audience.

At its conclusion, the party went to the club-grounds of the Merchants' Society for Mutual Assistance. There was a general illumination, and the remainder of the evening passed very agreeably with dancing and music.

On this day a telegram was received from Perm, a town on the Kama River, near the borders of Siberia. It was addressed to Prince Gortchakoff, and was as follows:

PERM, August 26, 1866.

The society of Perm, in all its classes, at the dinner given on the occasion of the solemnity of the anniversary of his Imperial Majesty's coronation, welcomes with a unanimous toast the worthy and highly-honored representatives of the American nation, our friends and guests, and most respectfully begs your Excellency to communicate it to them.

In the absence of the Governor,
    The President of the Board of State,
        NIKITINE, and
    The Mayor of the town, KAMENSKY.

Mr. Fox acknowledged the receipt of the friendly missive, and thanked the citizens of Perm for their welcome.

September 8th (August 27th).—At ten o'clock on Saturday morning, Mr. Fox, Captain Murray, Commander Beaumont, and Mr. Loubat, went to Strelna, a palace of the Grand-duke Constantine's, about twelve miles from St. Petersburg, to be presented to her Imperial Highness the Grand-duchess Alexandra Josefovna, the wife of the Grand-duke Constantine.

The gentlemen were shown into a drawing-room, where, much to their surprise and gratification, they found the maids of honor, the two young Countesses Keller and the two young Countesses Komarovsky, and the Baroness de Rantzau (of an old and distinguished Württemberg family, and governess to the Grand-duchess Olga, daughter of the Grand-duke Constantine, and now Queen of Greece), all clad in white, with sashes of red, white, and blue, and with ribbons of the same colors in their hair. The grand-duchess entered in a few minutes with her daughter Olga, each dressed in a similar manner to the maids of honor. Her Imperial Highness led by the hand her little son, who wore a sailor's costume complete in all its details. A more strikingly handsome and more queen-like woman cannot be conceived of, and her daughter was scarcely less beautiful. The grand-duchess was born Princess of Saxe-Altenburg, and is sister to the ex-Queen of Hanover.

The Grand-duke Constantine, who was absent in the

Caucasus at the time of this visit, is grand-admiral of the Russian Navy. He is one of the most intelligent and most learned princes in the world, and his merit would have given him fame and a distinguished position even if he had not been so near a throne. His father, the Emperor Nicholas, placed him early under the tuition of Captain (now Admiral) Lütke, a good scholar and excellent seaman. The Grand-duke displayed great aptitude for study, and soon became an adept in naval science, and in kindred branches of knowledge. He paid much attention to languages, and now speaks with fluency, besides his native tongue, the English, German, French, and Turkish. He is a proficient also in music, and takes especial delight in classical authors.

In 1845 he paid a visit to Constantinople, being the first prince of the imperial house of Russia that had set foot in that city since it fell into the hands of the Moslem. He was received by the Sultan, Abdul Medjid, with distinguished honors, notwithstanding that it was whispered among the Greek subjects of the Sublime Porte that he was the Constantine destined, in accordance with a prophecy, to restore to its ancient faith and glory the city of Constantine, which was lost under a Constantine.

Two years after, he cruised in the Ingermanland, a ship-of-the-line launched under his directions at Archangel,[1] in the Baltic, the North Sea, and the Atlantic; and,

---

[1] Archangel, the city of the Archangel Michael, named from a monastery built there in the sixteenth century, is the capital of the government of the same name, the most northern in European Russia. It is situated about

in the Pallas, in the Mediterranean. After this cruise, in which he was accompanied by Admiral Lütke, he visited most of the principal cities of Europe, and returned home by land. It was at this time that he became betrothed to a princess of Saxe-Altenburg, whom he married the year following (1848), and who, in accepting the Greek faith, took the name of Alexandra Josefovna.

The Grand-duke Constantine is also a soldier of merit, and of tried courage. In 1849 he accompanied Field-Marshal Paskevitch in his Hungarian campaign. Although but twenty-two years of age, he greatly distinguished himself, and received the cross of St. George for gallantry on the field of battle. At one time an engagement was won by the Grand-duke, who brought a battery into position at a critical moment, and directed its fire so accurately as to rout the enemy.

During the war with the allied powers, he was intrusted with the defence of the Baltic, a duty which he performed most successfully. In 1853 the Grand-duke's yacht was capsized off Cronstadt by a sudden squall, and he was nearly lost. He sustained himself in the water on a broken spar for over an hour, encouraging his companions with great coolness and presence of mind, until all were rescued from their perilous position.

Under his direction, the Russian Navy has made great and rapid progress of late years. He was much interested in the emancipation of the serfs, and aided the Emperor

forty miles above the mouth of the river Dwina, which empties into the White Sea. There is a navy-yard there, and the surrounding country abounds in the best of ship-timber.

materially in bringing about the enfranchisement which has added so much to the glory of his reign.

Her Imperial Highness, the Grand-duchess, expressed regret at her husband's absence, and invited the gentlemen to breakfast with her.

Strelna is prettily situated on high ground overlooking the waters of the Gulf of Finland. It is surrounded by neatly-kept gardens in the Dutch style. Peter the Great built the palace originally for his daughter Elizabeth, but it has undergone many changes since his time. It was burned in the reign of the Emperor Alexander I., who rebuilt it almost entirely.

The breakfast was laid in a piazza in front of the palace, whence was obtained a beautiful view of the grounds and of the waters of the gulf.

Besides the Americans, the following persons were present:

Grand-duchess CONSTANTINE.
Grand-duchess OLGA, *her daughter, now Queen of Greece.*
Countess MARIE KELLER,
Countess NINA KELLER,
Countess ANNETTE KOMAROVSKY,
Countess ELIZABETH KOMAROVSKY,
} *Maids of Honor.*
Baroness DE RANTZAU.
Mr. TENGOBORSKY, *Master of Ceremonies of his Imperial Highness.*
Mr. BIBIKOFF, *Equerry of his Imperial Highness.*
Count ARMFELT, *Gentleman of the Chamber of his Imperial Highness.*

Colonel KIRCOFF, *Aide-de-camp of his Imperial Highness.*

Vice-Admiral CRABBE, *Minister of the Navy.*

Rear-Admiral Prince MICHAEL GALITZINE.

Major-General GRABBE,[1] *of the suite of his Imperial Majesty.*

Captain EULER, *commander of the Strelna, the Grandduke's steam-yacht.*

Captain KITKINE, *commander of the Grand-duke's sailing-yacht.*

Lieutenant PELENG, *gentleman attached to the young Grand-dukes.*

Captain HANIMOGLO (*wounded at Sevastopol*).

Mr. KOUDRIAVTZEFF, *of the Imperial Household.*

The breakfast passed off in the most agreeable manner, the pleasures of the table being enhanced by music from a concealed band. Mr. Fox and the gentlemen accompanying him took leave of her Imperial Highness at half-past two P. M., and returned to St. Petersburg in Admiral Crabbe's yacht.

[1] Major-General Grabbe is commandant of one of the regiments of the Imperial Horse Guards. His regiment is mounted entirely on black horses, and it is one of the finest in the service. General Grabbe was for many years in the Caucasus, where he greatly distinguished himself.

CHAPTER XXIV.

BANQUET OF THE ENGLISH CLUB—SPEECH OF PRINCE GORTCHAKOFF.

At five o'clock of the same day, Mr. Fox, Mr. Loubat, General Clay, Mr. Curtin, Captain Murray, Commander Beaumont, and other officers, attended a grand banquet given in honor of the mission by the English Club of St. Petersburg. This is the aristocratic club of Russia, among its members being many of the highest officials of the government. It was founded in 1770 by an English gentleman on the club-system of his native country; hence its peculiar name, which no longer serves to characterize it, as it is now intensely Russian.

The banquet was semi-official in character, and intended as a public declaration of the friendship between Russia and the United States. As such, it was regarded as an event of unusual significance.

The dinner was a model one in every respect, and entirely free from any thing like a popular demonstration. There was no crowd in the street, and no band at the door. The guests were met in the reception-room, and, after the usual "zakuska," were conducted to the grand dining-hall of the club, where the greater part of the company had already assembled.

About two hundred and fifty persons were present. Prince Gortchakoff was seated at the head of the principal table, with Mr. Clay at his right and Mr. Fox on his left. There were no speeches at the dinner, and but three toasts. They were as follows:

1. The health of the Emperor.
2. The health of the Empress, of the Cezarevitch, and of the Imperial family.
3. The prosperity of the American people, and the health of the President and of the Representatives of the United States, ordinary and extraordinary.

The bill of fare was printed in gold, on glazed board, within a gilt border. At the top, a shield, surmounted by a crown, bore two clasped hands, with the motto, "Concordia et Lætitia." Above the hands was "1770," the date of the club's foundation.

The *menu* was as follows:

DÎNER

du 27 Août, 1866,

PAR LA SOCIÉTÉ ANGLAISE DE ST.-PÉTERSBOURG.

1. Potage Tortue à la Chambord au vin du Rhin.
2. Consommé aux légumes à la Saint-Phard.
3. Boudins de volailles. Petites bouchées en corbeilles.
4. Truite froide à la Néva.
5. Filets de bœuf piqués à la Béarnaise.
6. Poulets sautés aux truffes à la Mortalaise.

7. Punch à la Romaine.
8. Rots: Bécassines, coqs de bruyère et doubles.
9. Petit pois et fonds d'artichauts.
10. Pains d'abricots à la Parisienne et fromage glacé garni de fanchonettes.

After dinner a quiet hour was passed in an adjoining room, with coffee, tea, and cigars. Then, in accordance with the ancient custom of the English Club at its extraordinary meetings, the company returned to the dining-room and placed themselves once more about the table, upon which the punch was already blazing under the superintendence of General Grabbe.

As soon as the glasses were filled, General Tolstoy, a director of the club, turning toward Prince Gortchakoff, spoke as follows:

"Prince Alexander Michaïlovitch, our assembly begs you to communicate to our guests from America the sympathy we have for them; we thank them for accepting our invitation; we rejoice that they have had once more an opportunity to witness the expression of the sentiments which Russia entertains for America." ("Bravo!")

Prince Gortchakoff arose in response to this request, and addressed the meeting at length, speaking in the French language. He said:

"GENTLEMEN: Our friends from across the Atlantic understand the sentiments with which their presence and the object of their coming inspire us. These sentiments have been expressed to them by every class in the social scale—where mind illustrates thought, and where the heart knows but a primitive tongue. They have been heard like the echo of a single voice; mine can add but little to it.

"The exceptional act, unique in history, by which Congress has conveyed a message of affection to our sovereign; the choice of the person who has been charged with its delivery, whose high position and dignity, united to a warmth of heart, we fully appreciate; the skill and courage of those who brought the monitor across the ocean, solving a problem which till now has baffled modern science; and, finally, the fact that among us is found a representative of that nation which, during a series of years and under all circumstances, has given us proofs of a strong desire to preserve a good understanding between the two countries—all this, gentlemen, constitutes a complete and harmonious whole, without a discord.

"I rejoice at the presence of these gentlemen, for I believe that Russia loses nothing by being looked at closely. Distance rounds the lines of a far-off horizon, but only a near inspection can give a thorough knowledge of details.

"I congratulate myself that practical minds, strangers to prejudice, have come to judge us as we are. They will be able to appreciate both the sovereign, who is the greatest glory of the country, and the people, which constitutes its strength. ("Bravo! hurrah!")

"It is said that good reigns furnish blank pages for history. This saying is not absolutely true. If there is a reign of which every page is fruitful in reforms of a high character in the interest of internal organization; if there is a reign devoted to a care for the present, in view of a grand future—it is that which unites to-day all the affectionate and devoted sentiments of the nation, because we all have the absolute conviction that every moment of that noble existence is consecrated with an unlimited devotion to the welfare of our country. (Enthusiastic applause.)

"I will cite among these numerous works the grandest of them all—that of emancipation—and here I beg of our American friends permission to speak frankly. The resolution of Congress contains an error, which distance only can account for, where it mentions an enemy of emancipation. The madman to whom it alludes belongs to no nationality. He had no personal stake in the destinies of the country; he represents the blind chance of birth only. (Applause.)

"In Russia, gentlemen, there exists not a single enemy of emancipation. The class upon which this measure has imposed heavy sacrifices has welcomed it with the same enthusiasm as those who owe to it their liberty. This testimony our sovereign has been the first to render to his territorial nobility, and I believe, gentlemen, that in this circle, which represents both intellect and property, no voice will be raised to contradict my words. (Applause.)

"There is no need to dwell on the manifestations of sympathy between the two countries. They shine in the broad light of day. It is a fact the most interesting of our epoch, a fact which creates between two nations—I will say rather between two continents—germs of reciprocal good-will and friendship which will bear fruit, which create traditions, and which tend to consolidate between them relations founded upon the true spirit of Christian civilization. This understanding does not rest on geographical proximity—the gulf of oceans separates us. Nor does it rest on parchment—I have not found any trace of it in the archives of the ministry confided to me. It is instinctive; nay, more, I dare to call it providential. I rejoice in its existence; I have faith in its duration. In my political position, all my care shall tend to its consolidation. I say care and not efforts, because efforts are unnecessary when the attraction is spontaneous and reciprocal. ("Bravo!")

"Another motive which induces me to proclaim emphatically my appreciation of this good understanding is, that it is neither a menace nor a peril to any one. It derives its inspiration neither from covetousness nor from any sinister design. God has given to the two countries such conditions of existence that their grand internal life suffices for them. (Applause.)

"The United States of America are invulnerable at home. This state of things is founded not only on the fact that the rampart of ocean guarantees them against European complications, but upon the public spirit which rules them, and upon the personal character of their citizens. America cannot experience any evil that she does not make for herself. We have draped with mourning the sad pages of these latter times. We witnessed with deep regret the struggle between the brothers of the North and of the South; but we always had faith in the final triumph of the Union, and we hope for its permanent consolidation through the efforts of the present President, whose policy, inspired at once by firmness and moderation, has all our sympathy.

"I find, also, a certain analogy between the two countries. Russia, by her geographical position, may be drawn into European complications; the chances of war may bring us reverses. Nevertheless, I think that Russia possesses a like invulnerability, which she will make manifest whenever her dignity and her honor shall be seriously menaced (bravos); for then, as in all the crises of our history, the true power of Russia will show itself; it does not lie simply in her territorial extent, nor in the number of her population; it is in the intimate and indissoluble bond which unites the nation and the sovereign, and which confides to his hands all the material and intellectual forces of the country, and centres in him every sentiment of love and of devotion. (Unanimous applause.)

"I thank you, gentlemen, for the indulgence which you have accorded to my words, while regretting that the sentiments which animate us have had so imperfect an expression." (Unanimous cries, "On the contrary, they are perfect.")

"Before concluding, as I do not wish to leave any thing unsaid with which our friends from America would have the right to reproach us, let me not forget to consecrate a few words of respect to the memory of President Lincoln—that great citizen, who sacrificed his life in the performance of his duty. (Applause.)

"Permit me, then, returning to a sentiment that we have already given, to propose a toast to the prosperity of the United States, to the success of the work of pacification, to the present President, to Mr. Fox, to whom has been confided a task which could not have been put into better hands; to Captains Murray and Beaumont, whose intrepidity and skill insured the success of that long voyage, and to all of those collectively who participated in it. I should be guilty of ingratitude did I forget the present representative of the United States now among us, who has constantly given proof of his affection for Russia. (Cheers.)

"When our friends from America return home, I trust that they will take with them and preserve the sentiments which they leave behind with us; that they will tell their countrymen that a great nation will never forget the proof of sympathy offered to its sovereign; that it will never forget that there was a moment in the history of the two nations, when we and our friends from America lived the same life, when they shared our sorrows as well as our joys."[1]

Prince Gortchakoff's speech closed amid a murmur of approbation, which soon broke into enthusiastic and prolonged applause. The gentlemen present crowded around to congratulate him on the expression of sentiments which coincided so exactly with their own. The cheering culminated in "Hail Columbia" by the band, after which Mr. Skripitzine pressed forward to the table and spoke as follows:

[1] Appendix D.

"Gentlemen, let us thank Prince Alexander Michaïlovitch for having abstained until to-day from taking part in the public manifestations. By so doing, the Prince has given to all the Russian people the opportunity to express freely their sentiments, to prove freely their sympathy, which no one could doubt. The eloquent discourse of the Prince has confirmed the sincerity of all the mission has heard and seen among us." ("That is true.") "At the same time, the Prince has proved that the government of our great sovereign, like that of the United States, is never at variance with popular feeling. This union of the two governments and of the two peoples constitutes their great strength. Permit me to propose a toast to the health of Prince Alexander Michaïlovitch."

Cheers several times repeated greeted this sentiment, after which Mr. Fox spoke:

"In the presence of him who has spoken in the name of Russia, I ought not to open my mouth. My mission was accomplished when I placed in the hands of his Majesty the Resolution of Congress. But there has been another mission to fulfil. In remaining in Russia to accept its hospitality, I assumed a very difficult and delicate part: that of representing day by day the spirit which dictated that resolution. Until my return to Washington, where I must receive the approbation or censure of my government, I shall not know whether I have satisfactorily performed that obligation. What I am sure of is, that everywhere in Russia, from the highest to the most humble, there has been unanimity in the welcome given to us. In the course of a reception without precedent, even in this empire, the great people on whose broad shoulders rests the national unity, have cast their sympathies before us like a garment thrown in our path. If there has been any thing wanting in these interchanges, I have been in fault, not any Russian.

"And now, to the word of welcome and the bright sunshine that accompanied it, have succeeded sad farewells and the sombre clouds of winter. But beyond shines the eternal sun. Human passions may, in the future, raise threatening clouds between the two countries. God grant that they who shall then have the control of affairs may see, like Saint Paul, a light from heaven shining round about them, a divine light emanating from the sympathies of these days! When the dark night of civil war was spread over America, there was one great statesman in Europe whose prophetic eye saw the dawn of final victory. (Bravos and loud applause.) His sympathetic words fell on our hearts and grew there, like pearls. He has attained the evening of his days; the glories of the setting sun, emblematic of his life, surround him. As the sun, by Divine permission, stood still for Joshua, so may he abide for the eyes of both nations to look up to! (Great applause.) America gives the health of Prince Gortchakoff." (Loud cheers, and the Russian Hymn.)

When the applause which succeeded Mr. Fox's speech had subsided, Mr. Maikoff read a poem in the Russian language, written by Mr. Rosenheim, which he had translated previously, line by line, to the Americans. It was a farewell to the mission, and it was received with cries of "Bravo!" "Good!"

The next speaker was Count Orloff-Davydoff. He said:

"GENTLEMEN: After the numerous speeches made in honor of the American deputation at Cronstadt, at Moscow, and elsewhere, after the address made this evening by the minister who represents before our contemporaries and before history the present policy of Russia, it seems to me that I ought to be particularly modest in my remarks. But there is a word which I wish to speak, because it sums up, in my judgment, the character of the honorable deputation which we have the happiness to see among us, and that of the great power which this deputation represents.

"This word, gentlemen, is—*initiative*.

"There is not a power that has not given proofs of sympathy to the Russian nation on the occasion of the attempt of the 4th of April. There is but one power that has sent to us a whole deputation, with one of its chiefs of state at its head. And it is this solemnity, not of form, but of composition, not of the squadron, but of the persons that it brought, that I can justly designate by the name of *initiative*.

"This deputation, the interpreter of peaceful and of amicable sentiments, has brought with it a great marine monster—the Miantonomoh. It exhibited it in England, brought it into our waters, and allowed it to be visited by the multitude with a generous indifference, justified, however, by the assurance that America need not fear any imitation of her invention. In fact, the imitation of a new engine of war can, at the best, establish an equality between the inventor and the imitator who is behindhand, but cannot give any superiority to the latter. For an engine of destruction, to be all-powerful, must be original, and a monopoly which belongs to its author. Then, like gunpowder, as long as it was known only to a single power, the new arm is assured of a force equal to that which defeated the brave knights sung by Ariosto, who lamented that the new invention reduced the brave man to an equality with the coward.

"But it is not alone by engines of destruction; it is also by those of construction and of public utility that most of the *initiatives* are due to the Americans. The American plough, the application of steam to agricultural work, American bridges, and a host of other inventions, have been adopted by us, preserving in them the name of the nation that is their author. *It is all very well to follow a good example, but the glory is to him who gives it.*

"May we also see erected among us establishments like the great penitentiary prisons of America, in which the sublime inspired idea is not to stop at the punishment, but to bring about also the reform of the criminal!

"I have not yet named the most sacred of all the *initiatives* taken in the New World. It was in the course of the last war in America, that we saw established, through immense pecuniary sacrifices, a society to succor the wounded and the dying. The combat scarcely ended, the apostles of consolation spread themselves over the field of battle, never asking whether it was a Southerner or a Northerner that stretched toward them his imploring hand. It will be one of the glories of the conqueror Lincoln, it will be the supreme consolation of the vanquished Jefferson Davis, that he patronized this holy and beneficent institution.

"Once more has the example borne fruit, and it was in a republic of our ancient Europe that a similar brotherhood was organized in the course of the war just ended in Germany. I will say then to our illustrious guests: Rejoice in having again imitators; glory in your *initiative*, and, as a poet, whose name and works are familiar to you, says:

"'Indulge your honest pride, and say—how well!'

"I have the honor to propose to you, gentlemen, to drink to the prosperity of the charitable Christian societies in the United States of America." ("Bravo! Bravo!")

Captain Murray followed. He thanked Prince Gortchakoff for his compliments, and expressed his gratitude for the gracious hospitality which had been extended to the officers of the squadron wherever they had been in Russia, and which had made an impression that time cannot efface.

"It has been justly remarked here," he said, "that the sea has its dangers; but we have overcome them only *to expose ourselves to far greater dangers on land*. Shall we be able to triumph over them also after having struck on the rock of Russian hospitality?

"Gentlemen, permit me to offer a toast to the prosperity of this magnificent club, which in its organization presents so many things worthy of admiration. Long live the English Club!" (Applause.)

The next speaker was General Clay, the United States minister. He said:

"GENTLEMEN: I am not insensible to your kindness, but after the able and conclusive speeches of my distinguished friends, Prince Gortchakoff, Count Davydoff, and the Assistant Secretary of the Navy Fox, nothing remains for me but to express my thanks to my eminent friend the Minister of Foreign Affairs for the compliments he has paid to me.

"Having always been the friend of Russia, because she has always been the friend of my country, I will hazard a word in the spirit which has governed all my official and my personal relations with this great nation. Peace is judged here, as with us, to be the true policy of nations. With a population of seventy millions of the same language and religion, strong in the love of her father and sovereign, Russia can treat with indifference the little questions of the balance of power, and devote all her energy to the development of her civil, social, and material well-being.

"I give, then, a toast to trade, agriculture, education, and manufactures, more powerful than arms for maintaining the independence and liberty of nations." (Cheers.)

Commander Beaumont also thanked Prince Gortchakoff for his flattering attention. He would have wished to drink to the prosperity of this hospitable association, but, as every thing had already been said on that subject, it only remained for him to wish with all his heart the prosperity of the company.

Admiral Crabbe followed:

"I will not renew," he said, "the expression of our feelings. On our side, and on that of these gentlemen, our guests, we have heard enough of them. But I will propose a toast to the health of my comrades in the service who were the first to win the love of the Americans, and who knew how to cultivate good relations with them." (Cries of "Lessovsky! Lessovsky!") "Permit me, gentlemen, to give a general toast to our Navy."

After Admiral Crabbe, Mr. Skripitzine drew, in the warmest language, a parallel between Russia and America, comparing their native forms of government, the independence of their religious administrations, and their historical existences. He mentioned also the respect felt in Russia for the memory of Lincoln, and of the pious visit of the Americans to the tomb of Minin. In closing, Mr. Skripitzine gave a toast to the constant, indissoluble, and firm union of the two nations for the general progress and development of their peoples. ("Bravo!")

Mr. Curtin then spoke as follows, in Russian, as usual:

"I did not expect to have the honor of addressing you to-night. I knew that to-day he through whom Russia has spoken for so many years would speak. ('Bravo! bravo!') We are met here in a family reunion; in this family circle we all remember that recently, by a stroke of his powerful pen, Prince Gortchakoff dispersed the clouds that menaced Russia. ('Bravo!') I do not find my insignificant and inconsistent voice—" ("No! very good! too modest! bravo!") "His Excellency said there had been a *misunderstanding* (spoken in a whisper), and I rejoice that he has condescended to speak of it. The American Congress, on the reception of the mournful news, was eager to express the interest it took in it. I, who have lived nearly two years in Russia, I know well that there is no discord ('bravo'); that Russia is like a single man in feeling ('bravo! bravo!'); that if there is any rivalry in Russia, it is only in the devotion of Russians to the sovereign of Russia. ('Bravo!')

"Europe and the whole world do not yet entirely appreciate the sacrifices that the nobility have made in this great reform ('bravo!'); and if, in history, Alexander II. has the glory of having freed instead of having conquered men, history will not forget that he was aided by Russia's nobles. The world does not yet appreciate this act, because it is the first example in history where a class has made such a sacrifice ('bravo!'); do not forget what the labor of twenty millions of men signifies. It is a great capital in our avaricious age. ('Bravo!') The most notable feature of this reform, of this reorganization, is that all classes have advanced with the Emperor, hand-in-hand. ('Bravo!') The Emperor made the plan, the nobility executed it, and the peasants enjoy all the benefits of which they were deprived. ('Bravo!') Gentlemen, in this assembly, which includes the learning and the statesmanship of Russia, where are united the best of Russia's nobles, permit me to propose a toast to the Russian nobility: may its glory be eternal!" ("Bravo! bravo!")

Mr. Suchkoff followed. He said:

"GENTLEMEN: We have assembled to express our gratitude to the American people for the sympathy they have shown for Russia. The mutual sympathy of the two nations needs no proof. That is a fact; that is an axiom. But I ought, in the profound joy that my Russian heart feels, to express gratitude to him who, although belonging to a nation separated from us by oceans, unites with us in our common sentiments, in our common tendencies, by the expression of these feelings in our dear language; to him who, loving Russia, knowing its sympathy for America, knowing the ties which exist between the two nations, has devoted his time to the study of our national language, and not only of our language, but also of our history.

"From the words spoken by Mr. Curtin, we see that he understands Russia well, and that he has established fully the fact that the sole direction, the sole feeling which unites Russia, is her devotion to her sovereign, which he correctly expresses by calling it a tendency toward the same objects. Permit me to propose the health of Mr. Curtin. (Applause.)

"Gentlemen, a toast has been given to the health of the Russians who were in America, and who established the foundations of our friendship, which, though they may have existed before, have now been strengthened and put upon more solid bases. Sympathizing deeply with this sentiment and accepting it with pleasure, in all the strength of the word, it is impossible for me not to speak of those individuals, and not to propose a toast to the health of him who was at the head of our fleet—to the health of Stephan Stephanovitch Lessovsky, who has gained the cordial good-will of both Russians and Americans." ("Bravo!")

One of the company proposed to drink again to the health of Prince Gortchakoff, which elicited unanimous and loud applause.

Prince Gortchakoff replied:

"GENTLEMEN: I cannot find words to express how much I am moved; but I ought to say that your personal kindness with regard to myself goes beyond what I have any right to expect. It has only fallen to my enviable lot to be the faithful executor of the august will and orders of my sovereign. ('Bravo!') I am happy in having understood the Russian people; but you all know how well and how truly our sovereign understands and esteems them." ("Hurrah! to the health of the Prince!")

Mr. Tolstoy then proposed a toast to "our good Stephan Stephanovitch, who received so excellent and unanimous a welcome in America. To his health! It is he who has effected our present amicable relations with America, and has brought us so happily together." (Cheers.)

A gentleman next gave the health of Admiral Crabbe, who responded:

"Let us close worthily this noted day, and drink cordially to the health of our sovereign; let us wish him a long reign, for our own happiness and for the confusion of our enemies." (Unanimous and prolonged cheers.)

Admiral Lessovsky followed. He said:

"GENTLEMEN: Allow me to tell you why success attended us when we were in America. We found there a brilliant and friendly welcome prepared for us. That welcome we owe to the words of Prince Gortchakoff, who, as you all know, had refused at that time, in the most unmistakable terms, to intervene in the civil war in America, leaving entirely to the glory, the strength, and the wisdom of the United States Government the care of ending the struggle as it thought best. Such is the reason of the success, or of the foundation of the success, which our expedition met with. In every citizen we saw a friend, made by the words of Prince Gortchakoff.

"Afterward, gentlemen, these excellent judges of naval construction visited our ships, and saw in them the most splendid specimens of marine architecture." ("We believe it!") "This is why, gentlemen, I ask permission to join with you in the expression of a universal gratitude and of the highest respect for the chiefs of our navy; and first for his Imperial Highness the Grand-duke, who has endowed Russia with such magnificent ships. We had orders to cruise on the coast of Courland. All at once we received orders to make a voyage around the world. We did not delay for an instant, for we were provided with every thing necessary. I had the honor to command the squadron.

"Gentlemen, let me here say a word for our brethren, our brave sailors. We took our departure after the memorable 17th of April, the date on which, by one of the favors of our adored sovereign, corporal punishments were abolished, and, in those difficult moments which one experiences more or less at sea, the idea alone that I commanded men whose dignity had been elevated always sustained me. I close with that toast which my honorable chief, the admiral who directs the Ministry of the Navy, has proposed: To the Emperor, the author of our happiness and of our glory!" ("Bravo! Hurrah!")

"Thus this banquet," says a St. Petersburg journal, "of a character eminently Russian, given in honor of our American guests, began and ended with the enthusiastic expression of a respectful love for the father of the people, the sovereign liberator. Our guests are convinced once more that the ardent and boundless love of Russians for their country, personified in the sovereign father of his people, guides all our thoughts. They have had proof that, in manifesting their sentiments to our venerated and cherished monarch, they have gone right to the heart of the Russian nation. The demonstrations of which they have been the object are evidence enough of this."

On the same evening of the banquet, Mr. Oscar G. Sawyer, correspondent of the *New-York Herald*, telegraphed to that journal the entire speech of Prince Gortchakoff, at a cost of seven thousand dollars.

CHAPTER XXV.

IMPERIAL PRESENTS—MR. JUKOFF'S FÊTE—FAREWELL TO THE EMPEROR—PRINCE GORTCHAKOFF'S DINNER—ALEXANDER NEVSKY—THE ALEXANDER INSTITUTE—THE BEAUHARNAIS PALACE.

SEPTEMBER 9th (*August* 28th).—On Sunday, at one o'clock P. M., Mr. Fox met Prince Gortchakoff, by appointment, at the Foreign Office. The Prince, after various complimentary allusions to the manner in which he had performed the delicate duties intrusted to him by his government, presented to him, in the name of the Emperor, a snuffbox set with diamonds, and the card-photographs of the Emperor and the Empress, with their autographs on them, the latter for Mrs. Fox.

The snuffbox, which is of gold, exquisitely chased, has the Emperor's miniature[1] on the centre of the lid, surrounded by twenty-six diamonds. Six larger diamonds

---

[1] Snuffboxes are given by sovereigns, in lieu of decorations, to those who do not receive the latter. There are three grades: plain gold boxes, boxes with diamonds, and those having both diamonds and the sovereign's signature. The latter are given only to persons of the highest distinction.

are set, three on each side, at equal distances from th[e] inner circle. The Emperor is represented in full militar[y] uniform, with various orders upon his breast.

His Excellency handed also to Mr. Fox a ring fo[r] Captain Murray and a similar one for Commander Beau[-]mont, each bearing the monogram "A. II." set with sma[ll] diamonds.

A small album, containing photographic *cartes* *[de] visite* of the Czars and Emperors of Russia, was pr[e]sented afterward, through Admiral Lessovsky, to eac[h] officer in the squadron.

Mr. Fox gave to Prince Gortchakoff, at his reques[t] copies of all the photographs of himself, taken in St. P[e]tersburg, for the Emperor and imperial family.

At seven o'clock Mr. Fox and other of the America[ns] dined with Mr. Jukoff at his residence on the banks [of] the river, four miles below St. Petersburg. About fif[ty] guests were present. Later in the evening a splend[id] *fête* was given in the gardens of the villa, which we[re] thronged with the beauty and fashion of the capital. T[he] grounds were magnificently illuminated, and every tr[ee] blazed with variegated fires. From the top of the hou[se,] all parts of which were aglow with lights, shone a st[ar] whose rays were reflected in the waters of the Ne[va.] The river was covered with boats, and the opposite ba[nk] was lined with spectators. Among the entertainme[nts] were national dances and singing by peasants in flat-bo[ats] on the water. The evening was beautiful, and the par[ty,] which was much enjoyed by all, did not break up un[til] long after midnight.

September 10th (August 29th). — Monday morning opened with rain, the first interruption of the pleasant weather for a number of weeks. At ten o'clock A. M., Mr. Fox went to Czarskoë-Selo, to take leave of the Emperor and the Empress. He was accompanied by Captain Murray, Commander Beaumont, and Mr. Loubat.

At noon the party were received by their Imperial Majesties very cordially and without ceremony. Both shook hands with Mr. Fox, the Emperor repeatedly. His Majesty asked him how he was pleased with Russia. Mr. Fox replied that it would be impossible to convey to his countrymen, in fitting language, the feeling of sympathy for the United States which he had found everywhere. The Emperor said that he wished the President and the American people to know how deeply the sending of the mission had affected him. He saw in the Resolution of Congress the friendship of two great nations, and it was his desire to perpetuate it. He hoped that Mr. Fox would testify to the American people the feelings of friendship which he had found to exist among the Russians, and that he personally would carry away with him pleasing recollections of the country. The Empress regretted that Mrs. Fox had not accompanied her husband to Russia.

During the interview, which lasted about twenty minutes, the Emperor spoke in French, Mr. Loubat translating his words into English.

At half-past five o'clock Messrs. Fox, Clay, Loubat, and Curtin, Captain Murray, Commander Beaumont, and Mr. Sawyer, dined with Prince Gortchakoff. About forty were present. Mr. Clay sat on the Prince's right and Mr. Fox on his left. There were no toasts nor speeches. The *menu*, which was printed in black on glazed board, was as follows:

>MENU DE SON EXCELLENCE.
>
>Potage Gremardot.
>Consommé aux quenelles.
>Petits pâtés et croquettes.
>Mayonnaise de gélinottes.
>Rosbif garni.
>Truites de Gatchina.
>Poulardes aux truffes.
>Fonds d'artichauts.
>Punch à la Romaine.
>Rôts divers.
>Salade.
>Gâteau Napolitain.
>Plombière d'ananas.
>Le 29 *Août*, 1866.

Alexander Michaïlovitch, Prince Gortchakoff—of one of the few princely families of Russia that descend from Rurik—was born in the year 1798. He was graduated at the Czarskoü-Selo College, and, having chosen the diplomatic career, first entered into the public service as secretary of the Russian embassy in London, in 1824. In 1830 he was *chargé d'affaires* in Florence, and the following year he was connected with the embassy at Vienna. In 1841 he was envoy extraordinary and minister plenipotentiary at the court of Württemberg. While acting in that capacity, he was instrumental in bringing about the marriage of the Grand-duchess Olga Nicholaevna with the Crown-Prince Carl, now King of Württemberg.

In 1850 Prince Gortchakoff was envoy extraordinary and minister plenipotentiary at the German Diet in Frankfort-on-the-Main; and in 1854, during the Crimean War, he succeeded Baron von Meyendorf as Russian ambassador at the court of Vienna, and it was owing chiefly to his influence that Austria maintained her neutrality during that terrible conflict.

In 1856 he replaced Count von Nesselrode as Minister of Foreign Affairs; and, a few years later, in one of his circulars concerning Neapolitan matters, he wrote that celebrated phrase, "*La Russie ne boude pas, elle se recueille.*" In 1862 he refused to accede to the proposition of M. Drouyn de l'Huys, Minister of Foreign Affairs of France, to join that country and England in an intervention in the internal affairs of the United States.

In 1862 he was appointed vice-chancellor, and received the grand cross of St. Andrew in diamonds, the highest decoration in the gift of his sovereign. The following year he prevented France and England from interfering in Polish affairs, and soon afterward became chancellor of the empire. In January, 1871, he denounced the Treaty of Paris, as far as it related to the neutralization of the Black Sea. His demands were acceded to by the contracting powers on the 13th of March of the same year, and the Emperor conferred on him for this eminent service the rank and title of serene highness.

Prince Gortchakoff still holds the position of Minister of Foreign Affairs, and attends to all its onerous duties, although now in his seventy-fifth year. Every American will join in the wish that he may live long to enjoy his honors, and to uphold the dignity of his country.

One of his sons, Prince Michael Alexandrovitch Gortchakoff, is also in the diplomatic service. He is now minister of Russia to Switzerland.

On the evening of this day, Mr. Loubat received intelligence of the sudden death of his father, near Paris. He therefore closed his connection with the mission at this point, and returned at once to France.

September 11*th* (*August* 30*th*).—On Tuesday took place the solemn and interesting service observed yearly in the Cathedral of St. Alexander Nevsky, in memory of the Grand-duke Alexander, in whose honor the monastery was founded by Peter the Great.

Mr. Fox had taken leave of the Emperor and of the imperial family, and was already preparing to bring his mission to a close by declining all further engagements; but the importance attached to these commemorative services induced him to attend them. He was accompanied by Captain Murray and Commander Beaumont.

The Emperor usually attends this mass, and the present occasion was no exception to the rule. He stood, attended by the Cezarevitch and other members of the imperial family, in one of the transepts, beside the silver shrine where repose the remains of St. Alexander Nevsky. Opposite were the foreign ambassadors, ministers, and envoys, and the nave was occupied by the great officers of the empire, and by such officials as had the *entrée*. All were in court costume, and orders shone on every breast.

Among this brilliant throng Mr. Fox was conspicuous for being the only one in citizen's dress, wearing, as he always did on such occasions, an evening suit of black. Our naval officers were remarkable for the simplicity of their uniforms; the absence of cocked-hats, epaulets, and aiguillettes from their dress receiving favorable commendation from the Russians.

In the Greek Church all stand, not excepting even the Emperor, during the service. No instrumental music is used in the ceremonies, nor are female voices allowed in the choirs, the soprano parts being taken by boys. Most of the prayers are intoned, and there are many recitative passages in the service which are sung by deep bass voices in a very impressive manner.

On the present occasion, the brilliant assemblage that filled the cathedral added to the magnificence and impressiveness of the ceremonial; and when the procession of priests and church dignitaries, clad in their splendid vestments, came from the chancel through the holy door of the ikonastas, bringing with it the perfume of swinging censers, and the music from concealed voices undulated through the sanctuary, now loud and sonorous, now dying away in the dim vault above, it was not difficult to believe in the sincerity of the messengers of Vladimir, who told him that at the service which they attended in St. Sophia's, in Constantinople, the angels of heaven mingled their voices with those of the choristers.[1]

---

[1] When Vladimir the Great had concluded to adopt a religion for Russia, which was then idolatrous, he sent out ten of his boyars to examine the different religions in the countries where they existed. On their return they

When the priests had withdrawn, and the last note of the music still vibrated in each heart, the Emperor, followed by the Czarevitch and the other members of the imperial family, passed down the nave through the expectant congregation. Every eye was upon them, for two men of nobler mien and form, and of greater physical beauty, have been rarely seen. His Majesty made a last gracious acknowledgment of the compliment which the Congress of the United States had paid him by recognizing Mr. Fox as he passed. The Czarevitch did the same, and the Emperor and the mission met no more.

At eight o'clock in the evening, Mr. Fox, accompanied by Captain Murray, Commander Beaumont, and other officers, visited the Alexander Institute, a government school for young ladies, where the daughters of those serving the state, from the rank of colonel upward, are educated. This institution is the pride of St. Petersburg, and deservedly so. The buildings are large and capacious and well adapted to their purpose, the teachers are the most capable in their respective branches that

---

reported concerning the Mohammedan, the Jewish, the Roman Catholic, and the Greek faiths. Vladimir was pleased with the voluptuous paradise and lovely houris of Mohammed, but could not overcome his repugnance to circumcision and the interdiction of wine. He rejected Judaism because he thought it neither rational to take advice from wanderers under the ban of Heaven, nor desirable to share their punishment. Roman Catholicism, too, he refused, because the Pope appeared to him to be an earthly deity, which he considered monstrous. But, when the messengers told how they had witnessed with rapturous admiration the solemnities of the Greek Church, and had heard the heavenly music in magnificent St. Sophia, it made a strong impression upon him, and in the year 989 he introduced that faith into his empire, and cast down all the idols.

can be obtained, and the greatest care is taken to render the course of instruction, moral, mental, and physical, as thorough as possible. The hygienic treatment of the pupils, who number usually about eight hundred, must be as near perfection as can be attained, judging from the appearance of those who were seen. They were all healthy, and rosy in complexion, with plump necks and arms. The graduating class wore the Russian costume, the remainder calico dresses, with low necks and bare arms, and neat white aprons.

Mr. Fox was received by all the officials, and by about three hundred of the girls, from six to sixteen years of age, and was presented with a large silver medal of the institute and a beautiful silk sofa-cushion representing our national colors, the latter the work of the young ladies.

While some of the younger officers were enjoying a dance, his Imperial Highness, the Prince of Oldenburg, director-general of the institute, invited Mr. Fox to accompany him to the other wing of the building. After a walk through a long arched corridor, they entered a room where another large body of the girls welcomed him with "Hail Columbia," singing it in English. When the song was done, two little children, each scarcely more than five years of age, came forward, bearing between them a bouquet so large as nearly to hide them. They recited a few lines of poetry and then presented their floral offering with a grace that would have done credit to maturer years. Four young girls followed with an album and portfolio of photographic views. Mr

Fox gave his card-photograph to them in return. When about to retire, he found himself suddenly surrounded by about two hundred of the budding beauties, all eagerly requesting a similar memento. Though flattered and amused by their importunities, Mr. Fox found the compliment too extensive to admit of the gratification of all their wishes. The few photographs he had were placed in the hands of the Prince, who with difficulty protected himself from the rush that was made upon him.

This interesting visit, made more notable by the novelty of dancing in an institution from which gentlemen are ordinarily excluded, was much enjoyed by all who had the pleasure of participating in it.

On taking leave, the directress announced to Mr. Fox that on the day of his departure the school would be assembled in the chapel and prayers would be offered to God for his safety. She also gave him a copy of the prayer of the Greek Church, in both Russian and English, which would be used on the occasion. It is as follows:

"FROM THE RITE OF BLESSINGS ON TRAVELS.

Let us pray to God in peace.

Lord, be merciful to travellers, Thy servants, by land and sea, forgive them all their trespasses, whether conscious or unconscious, and bless their travelling.

Let us pray.

Lord, send them an angel of peace to be their companion, their guide, to protect, secure, and keep them always out of harm's way.

Let us pray.

Lord, shield them from any mischief, or inimical design, and bring them home without encountering any evil.

Let us pray.

Lord, grant them a harmless, peaceful travelling, and a healthful return, in all godliness and honesty.

Let us pray.

Lord, keep them unhurt, and unsubdued by their enemies, whether visible or invisible; protect them from the malice of wicked men.

Let us pray.

Lord, bless their good intentions, and by Thy grace render these their intentions profitable to their souls and bodies.

Let us pray.

Lord, protect, save, pardon, and keep us by Thy grace. For Thine is the glory, the honor, and the adoration."

This touching episode deeply affected our envoy. He thanked the lady directress for her kindness, and told her that he should think of her and her charge when the hour of departure came, and should carry the remembrance of their prayer to his home.

September 12*th* (*August* 31*st*).—At ten o'clock, Mr. Fox, Captain Murray, and Commander Beaumont, were received by his Imperial Highness the Prince of Oldenburg, at his palace in the city.

Peter, Prince of Oldenburg, is the son of the late Prince Peter of Oldenburg, and of Catharine Paulovna, daughter of the Emperor Paul. He is, therefore, the cousin of the present Emperor. He is a general of infantry, and has the charge (under the direction of her Majesty the Empress) of the charitable and educational institutions of the empire.

At eleven o'clock the Topographical Bureau of the War Department was visited. The maps and plans of the chief public works of the empire were shown, and briefly explained to Mr. Fox. Of especial interest was the contemplated canal of Peter the Great, to connect the Volga, which empties into the Caspian, with the Don, which flows into the Black Sea. At one point these rivers approach each other within about one hundred and twenty-five miles. The Caspian Sea is eighty-two feet below the Mediterreanan, and receives the flow of other streams than the Volga, but the waters disappear by enormous evaporation.

One of the most beautiful palaces in this city of superb structures is that occupied by her Imperial Highness the Grand-duchess Marie, whose first husband was Maxinilian, Duke of Leuchtenberg, the son of Eugene de Beauharnais.

It is especially noted for its fine collection of paintings by Greuze, and a room where are preserved numerous memorials of the first Napoleon, and a few which belonged to Prince Eugene. The tent which the Emperor used in Egypt, the cimeter he wore at Marengo, and the cross of the Legion of Honor, which was on his breast when he died, are among the relics. One of the most touching *souvenirs* of the days that aroused France to military glory is the sword which belonged to General Alexander de Beauharnais, of which he was deprived at the disarming of the sections in Paris, subsequent to the Thirteenth Vendémiaire, and which Bonaparte restored to his son Eugene, then a lad of fourteen. The impression made upon the heart of the young commander of Paris by Madame de Beauharnais, when she called to thank him for his kindness, resulted in their marriage a few months later, on the eve of his departure to take command of the army of Italy.

The Grand-duchess Marie had departed for Germany at the time of Mr. Fox's visit, but she ordered the palace to be shown to him, and sent her young son to point out all the objects of interest. Before his departure, the envoy of Congress was requested to leave his photograph, which was placed among the other relics in the Napoleon room.

CHAPTER XXVI.

RIFLED GUNS AND TARGETS—THE COMMEMORATIVE CHAPEL—CRONSTADT CITIZENSHIP—FAREWELL BREAKFAST—PEASANT DEPUTATION—THE EMANCIPATION MEDAL—THE DEPARTURE.

SEPTEMBER 13*th* (1*st*).—Thursday opened with fine weather. In the morning Mr. Fox and a number of the officers visited the practice-ground of the army and navy, examined the targets, the rifled steel guns, and the models, and witnessed firing from an eight-inch breech-loading rifle.

Four-and-a-half-inch iron plates were shown that were penetrated by shot from this gun at seventeen hundred yards; and at eight hundred yards five one-inch plates were pierced, and a nine-inch plate behind them was broken. The guns are rifled on the Prussian system, and the shot, chilled-pointed, are coated with lead. Large honey-combed cakes of powder equal to a charge, and placed in a cartridge, are used, an initial velocity of thirteen hundred yards being insisted on.

The following table will show the size and weight of

the different breech-loaders in use, and the weight of the several charges of large powder and of the shot:

Calibre in inches.	Weight in poods.	Weight in pounds.	Powder, lbs.	Solid shot, lbs.
9	760	27,360	35	300
8	488	17,568	31.5	200
6	235	3,420	16	95
For boats, 3.42	18	648	1.5	14

The grounds are well adapted for experimental use. They admit of an extreme range of four miles.

In the afternoon, his Imperial Highness the Prince of Oldenburg called on the envoy of Congress at the Hôtel de France.

Mr. Fox had been invited to dine with the Grand-duchess Catherine, but, her presence being required at the laying of the corner-stone of the chapel, to be built on the spot where the attempt on the Emperor's life was made, the party had to be given up.

The *Invalide Russe*, of the same date, gave the following account of the ceremony of the founding of this chapel, dedicated to St. Alexander Nevsky, the Emperor's namesake:

"On the 1st of September, at four o'clock in the afternoon, an immense crowd assembled at the Summer Garden, filling all the space around, to witness the laying of the corner-stone of the chapel, on the very spot where the life of the great sovereign liberator was, by the will of Providence, saved by the hand of an enfranchised peasant. It is well known how much the Russian people have ever been devoted to their sovereigns; it is well known how much Russia has always honored and profoundly loved her noble Emperor; but, after the odious attempt of the 4th of April, this love and this devotion have increased, if that is possible. All the inhabitants of the capital wished to aid in the laying of the corner-stone of the chapel of the Summer Garden, and the garden itself and all the neighboring places were filled.

"The Emperor had assisted on the same day at the inauguration of the canal from Ladoga to Schlusselbourg, and this is the reason why the ceremony was postponed from four o'clock to half-past four of the afternoon. Around the place marked for the construction of the chapel, seats had been aranged for the public, but those who could not find place there had mounted, for the purpose of seeing, the trees, the parapet of the Neva, everywhere, in a word, where there was any possibility of hoisting themselves. The space which separates the Summer Garden from the steamboat-landing, decorated with flowers and evergreens, was reserved for the suite of the Emperor and for the dignitaries who were to take part in the ceremony. At half-past four precisely the Emperor arrived in a cutter at the landing, and went immediately to the tent, where his Eminence the Metropolitan Isidore awaited him with the clergy.

"After the *Te Deum* and the prayer for long life for the Emperor, his Majesty laid the first stone, and after him the other members of the imperial family laid some bricks. Mr. Komissaroff-Kostromsky assisted at the ceremony, and every one remarked the fervor with which this man prayed, on whom fell the lot to perform so grand a deed. During the whole continuance of the ceremony, the immense crowd which witnessed it preserved a religious silence; every one felt the importance of the event of which the monument to be erected will perpetuate the memory. But when, the ceremony ended, the Emperor went to his carriage, the people saluted him with loud and long hurrahs."

At four o'clock P. M. Mr. Fox left St. Petersburg and went on board the Augusta, at Cronstadt. At night a ball was given by Admiral Novossilsky, in the Cronstadt City Hall. It was a brilliant affair, and much enjoyed by all who attended. The guests were almost entirely officers of the navy, and their families. Dancing was kept up until one o'clock, when there was a supper, with speeches and toasts. Admiral Novossilsky toasted the Americans, and Mr. Fox returned the compliment. After supper, dancing was resumed, and continued until four o'clock, when the assembly broke up.

September 14*th* (2*d*).—An unpleasant, rainy day. Mr. Fox went up to St. Petersburg to make some final arrangements for leaving. As the official departure had already taken place, there were no calls, excepting a few on special business. Many books and other presents were sent to the hotel.

Notwithstanding the bad weather, the excursion-steamers, which had been running to the Miantonomoh almost daily since her arrival, still went down filled with people. A number of Americans from Moscow, and other places in the interior, also went aboard and made themselves happy under the stars and stripes.

In the afternoon, a deputation from the city government of Cronstadt waited on Mr. Fox, on board of the Augusta, and announced that his Majesty the Emperor had accorded his assent to the petition of the Merchants' Association of Cronstadt, that the title of honorary citizen should be conferred on him. They then presented to him the diploma, handsomely engrossed, within an ornamental border, on heavy Bristol board, twenty-four by nineteen inches in size, and enclosed in a rich portfolio of Russia leather. In the centre of the border, at the top, is a representation of the statue of Peter the Great at the Petrovsky landing in Cronstadt; on the left is a bust of Peter the Great, with commercial maritime emblems beneath it, and at the bottom a view in the city—the City Hall and public square; on the right is a bust of Alexander II., with naval emblems under it, and below a view of Fort St. Paul. In the centre, at the bottom, are the arms of the city of Cronstadt.

The inscription is in Russian. It reads, in English, as follows:

"The Corporation of the Town and Port of Cronstadt, with the sanction of his Imperial Majesty, have conferred on the Honorable G. V. Fox, Envoy Extraordinary of the Congress of the United States of America, and Member of the Washington Cabinet, the Honorary Citizenship of the Town and Port of Cronstadt, as a mark of the high esteem of one of the Towns of Russia for the great American Nation, which has empowered its Envoy to express to our great Emperor the sympathy of all the American people.

  (Signed) F. Stephanoff, *Mayor.*
        W. Kudriavzoff, ⎫
        W. Nikitine,   ⎬ *Members*
        M. Semgin,   ⎬ *of the*
        P. Ershoff,   ⎭ *Town Council.*
        P. Schakoff, *Secretary.*

September 15th (3d).—Saturday morning was cloudy, with light rain. At nine o'clock in the morning Mr. Fox took his final departure from St. Petersburg, and went down to the squadron in a steam-yacht.

At eleven o'clock a farewell breakfast was given to the mission by Admiral Crabbe, on his yacht Rurik. Besides Mr. Fox, there were present, of the Americans, Captain Murray, Commander Beaumont, and Mr. Curtin, the latter having come down from St. Petersburg to see the ships off. Among the Russian guests were Admiral Novossilsky, Lieutenant-General Greig, Prince Galitzine, and Rear-Admirals Baron Taube, Popoff, Izilmentieff, and Lessovsky, and the most of the gentlemen who took part directly in the reception of the Americans.

Fortunately, the weather cleared, and the sun came out bright about eleven o'clock. At this time the harbor presented almost as animated an appearance as on the day of the squadron's arrival. The waters were covered with sailing-yachts and other light craft, and the Rurik and the American ships were surrounded by steamboats loaded with people, who had come down to witness the departure.

The Rurik was gayly decked with the flags of both nations. The tables were set on the poop-deck, which was covered with an awning hung with the Russian and the American colors. Flowers were in profusion everywhere, and a band played the national airs.

The company sat down at noon. As soon as the champagne came on, Admiral Crabbe arose and said:

"You remember, gentlemen, with what attention and enthusiasm we followed the news of the reception in America of Admirals Lessovsky and Popoff. At last Heaven has allowed us to thank our dear guests personally for their hospitality. I deem it superfluous to speak of the friendship and the sympathy of the two great nations, for my words would be like drops added to an overflowing cup.

"We had the good fortune to be the first to receive our dear guests, to shake their hands, and to thank them for their visit. True feelings have no need of many words, and therefore I limit myself to wishing for the great country of our dear guests happiness and success in its social development, as well as a continued triumph over its enemies at home and abroad. Let us wish them a happy voyage, and ask them not to forget that our nation knows how to esteem all that is truly great and elevated.

"I shall close by proposing a toast that will answer all our wishes—to the health of our sincere friend, the Honorable G. V. Fox, to the health of those true sons of the sea, Captain Murray and Commander Beaumont, and to all their brave companions who leave us to-day. Let us give, gentlemen, a hearty Russian cheer in honor of our dear guests."

The whole company arose, and, crowding around the Americans, touched glasses with them, and gave them a round of hearty cheers. When order was again restored, Admiral Crabbe continued:

"The reception of our dear guests has been put into good and worthy hands. I propose a toast to Admiral Novossilsky."

Admiral Lessovsky reminded Mr. Fox that now, one o'clock, prayers for the safety of the Americans on their voyage home were chanting in the Alexander Institute, at which our envoy was visibly affected. Of all the evidences of sympathy and of good-will received during the sojourn of the embassy in Russia, this act of the young ladies of this noble school was one of the most touching.

After toasts to Admiral Crabbe and to Admiral Lessovsky, and the gentlemen who aided in the reception and entertainment of the Americans, Mr. Fox arose and said:

"Until this moment I thought that my heart was as firm as the ice that in winter covers the waters of the Neva, and, like that, reflected the warmth that fell upon it. But now, in these last moments, the affectionate esteem of my Russian friends overcomes me. Words fail to reach my lips. The kindness which surrounds me dissolves my heart. To Russia and our Russian friends! Farewell!"

Out of respect to the depth of feeling which inspired this sentiment, the company drank in silence.

At this moment a boat came alongside, bringing a deputation of peasants from the city of Tcherepovets, in the government of Novgorod, situated more than four hundred miles beyond the railroad. They presented Mr. Fox with bread and salt in basins of ornamented wood, and a bouquet of flowers, and tendered him the congratulations of their fellow-citizens. The leader of the deputation made a brief address, in which he said that Tcherepovets, a small city of Great Russia, thanked Mr. Fox for the words of sympathy and respect which he offered to Russia's sovereign and benefactor, from the great Republic on the other side of the ocean.

Mr. Fox answered: "Gentlemen, that ocean was formed by the aggregation of drops, like this vast empire which has arisen from the consolidation of communities, whose peasant representatives are now before me. As the sun stands in the centre of the universe, the concentration of force and the source of light and of warmth, so is the sovereign benefactor of Russia to the millions whom he has lifted from serfdom to manhood."

Mr. Fox's remarks were received with cheers, and, although no toast was given, the whole company drank to the Emperor's health.

In presenting the bread to Mr. Fox, the deputation remarked that it was baked in Tcherepovets, and called his attention to its singular elasticity, it resuming its proper form at once when pressed down.

"This bread," remarked Mr. Fox, "like liberty, may

sink for a moment under pressure, but immediately rises again."

Captain Murray then gave a toast to the Grand-Admiral of the Russian Navy, the Grand-duke Constantine Nicholaevitch; and Commander Beaumont followed with one to the health of her Imperial Highness the Grand-duchess Alexandra Josefovna. A telegraphic dispatch was at once sent to the Grand-duke, who was at Odessa, apprising him of the toast.

At the close of the breakfast, Lieutenant-General Greig presented, with appropriate remarks, to Mr. Fox and to Captain Murray and Commander Beaumont, copies of the medal struck to commemorate the emancipation edict.

General Greig spoke as follows, in the English language:

"Less happy than the most of the gentlemen here present, I have not had the opportunity of meeting often with the eminent statesman and good man *par excellence*, the envoy of the American Congress, with his worthy companions here who accompanied him in his mission unprecedented in history, nor with our other American guests; but what I have seen of them makes me sincerely regret that I have not met them oftener, and known them better.

"But, if I was not among the first who received them on their arrival in Russia, I can congratulate myself at least that I am among the number of the last, met to-day, to wish them a happy return to their distant country. For that I have used all my efforts, yet I do not take to myself any praise for it, for, though occupied as I am, the sun that gives light and life to the universe is incomparably busier than I am; however, the sun himself, our Russian sun, has pierced the fog, has driven away the rain, and has shown himself in all his brightness to send a compliment and a smile of adieu to our friends who are going far away from us.

"I have said that I have seen little of our guests, but I have heard them much spoken of, which, having ears, I could not help, for the names of Fox, Murray, and Beaumont, are pronounced by millions and millions of people, from our rich capitals to the utmost corners of our vast territory. Their remembrance, for a long time, a very long time, should live among us. I hope and desire that they also will remember all they have seen, all they have heard, and all they have thought, during their stay in Russia, in looking at our life at home. They will take away many solid tokens of remembrance which will recall Russia to their minds; but I wish to add another token yet, the last in point of time, but not the last in its significance.

"The friendship of the two nations, and the feelings that they have toward each other, astonish the world, which, reflecting, seeks the reason of this incomprehensible phenomenon. The name of this reason is legion. But it cannot be questioned that, among the causes to which is due this mutual spirit, is the great event which has been accomplished almost simultaneously in the two countries—there by a sanguinary struggle, here by the path of peace. The token I have presented to Mr. Fox is the medal struck in memory of the enfranchisement of the peasants. In my official position I should have presented it sooner if he had visited the Mint. But I am happy that Fortune has willed that I should present this medal at the last moments of his stay in Russia. He will see on it the likeness of our blessed sovereign, and the effigy of a nobleman and of a peasant. Always friends, the sovereign, the nobility, and the people, have equally and unanimously expressed the feelings which Russia sincerely and cordially entertains for you.

"*United*—a word that forms a part of the name by which you are known among the nations of the world—will always be your glory and your strength, because strength lies in union. May the union of your States and the union of the great Republic of the West and the great Empire of the East be strong and eternal!"

This was the last of the many complimentary addresses delivered to the mission while in Russia, and this breakfast terminated the long series of demonstrations of which both parties will retain a lasting remembrance.

The commemorative medal presented to Mr. Fox was of gold, of the weight of three-quarters of a pound. Those given to Captain Murray and Commander Beaumont were of silver, of the same size and design.

Mr. Fox went on board of the Augusta shortly after four o'clock. As he left the Rurik, that vessel saluted him with seventeen guns, to which the Augusta replied. The squadron got under way at once, and left the port under escort of a number of Russian ships in the following order: the monitor Perun, the double-cupola ironclad Smertch, the steam-frigate Khrabry, the steam-yacht Rurik, the frigate Svietlana, and last the Augusta and the Miantonomoh. Steamboats, with passengers and bands of music, and many sailing-craft, accompanied them out of the roadstead. National salutes thundered from the forts, our vessels replied, the flags were cheered, and, accompanied by music and parting hurrahs, the squadron steamed out into the Gulf of Finland.

At seven o'clock in the evening, after a display of fireworks on the Russian ships, which was answered by the Augusta, Admiral Crabbe bade farewell, and, ordering the Svietlana and the Khrabry to see the Americans safely out of the Gulf of Finland, took his departure in the Rurik.

Mr. Fox found on board of the Augusta a note from Admiral Novossilsky, and a picture of our Saviour, presented, as the admiral wrote, by a peasant named Michael Insieff, who had bought it from the savings of his daily labor, and who desired to have it sent to the American envoy as an expression of his feelings toward the nation that had sympathized with his Emperor.

This chapter cannot conclude better than in the words of Mr. Fox himself, who, in a dispatch to Secretary Welles, thus summed up the results of his mission:

"Rear-Admiral Lessovsky and the officers associated with him were unremitting in their attentions, and faithfully observed the instructions of the Emperor to see that we received a 'Russian welcome.' But the striking feature of our visit was the spontaneous reception everywhere accorded to us by the people themselves. From the most remote parts of the empire, telegrams were sent welcoming us, and expressing the most grateful feelings toward the people of the United States.

"The first toast at entertainments was to the President of the United States, Mr. Johnson, and his picture, with Washington's and Lincoln's, usually graced every assembly.

"The speeches were friendly, appropriate, and full of feeling. The flag of the United States has been shown, and honored, for a thousand miles in the interior of Russia, and our national airs have become familiar to her people.

"The Emperor reviewed his troops, alternating the music of the two empires as the cloud of Cossacks swept past in a charge.

"If nations require friends, and must lean toward each other like individuals, here are eighty millions of people; one race, one language, and a unit in their feelings of friendship for the United States.

"The present Emperor has conferred upon them emancipation, liberty of the press, abolishment of the knout local self-government, and trial by jury. Under these wise measures, the empire begins to feel that conscious strength which springs from national unity resting upon the diffusion of light and power to all classes.

"The unprecedented distinction conferred upon a foreigner, in electing him an honorary citizen, by permission of the Emperor, of St. Petersburg, Cronstadt, Moscow Kortcheva, and Kostroma; the unanimous welcome given to us by all classes, and the unusual reception extended to the officers and crew, by making the former without preference guests of the government, are due chiefly to the friendly action of Congress in passing the resolution of sympathy, and to the government in sending an official to Russia in a squadron of armed ships to deliver it."

CHAPTER XXVII.

IN THE BALTIC—THE APPROACH TO STOCKHOLM—OFFICIAL COURTESIES—GUSTAVUS III.—SKOKLOSTER—JEFFERSON—PRESENTATION AT COURT—ROYAL VISIT TO THE SHIPS—THE DJURGÅRD.

SEPTEMBER 16*th* (4*th*).—Sunday morning opened with light southerly winds, and fine weather. The two Russian men-of-war were still in company with the squadron. At noon the ships were off Kall Baden light, which was distant about six miles. The day ended with fresh breezes from the west-southwest, and with a drizzling rain.

September 17*th* (5*th*).—Fresh breezes from the west-southwest continued, with rain and a rough sea. At seven o'clock A. M. the Svietlana and the Khrabry each fired a national salute of twenty-one guns, and afterward a personal salute of seventeen guns, which were answered by the Augusta. They then cheered our ships, and parted company with them.

At a quarter before seven o'clock in the evening, the

Augusta and Miantonomoh entered the Sandham Passage to Stockholm, and anchored for the night.

September 18th.—The approach to Stockholm from the Baltic is very striking and beautiful, unexcelled probably by any similar view in the world. The city is situated at the end of a magnificent fjord or arm of the sea, thirty-six miles from the open water, following the channels, or twenty-four miles in an air-line. The Skærgard, as the fjord is called, is more properly an archipelago indented into the land. Its course from the Baltic up is dotted with islands, among which the channel winds, revealing new beauties at every turn. Main-land and islands frown with rugged cliffs of granite and porphyry, against a background of oaks and pines. Sometimes crags and forests extend for miles with no signs of habitation save an occasional fisherman's hut, and then come grassy slopes, and beautiful villas, with gardens stretching to the water's edge.

As the ships steamed through the archipelago, new surprises met the eye in every direction. Crags and forest, green knolls and deep-cleft glens, alternated with endless variety, framed with the blue waters of the fjord. Now and then, heavy luggers, fishing-smacks, and hay-boats, passed, and pretty sail-boats, filled with ladies and gentlemen, flitted in and out among the islands. Nearer the city, the water appeared alive with sails and steamers, and soon, from the cloud of smoke which overhung the horizon, steeples and towers, and the great palace, broke in shadowy outline, and then Stockholm burst into view, with its splendid natural surroundings, its terraced heights, its hills crowned with trees, its gardens sloping to the Mülar, and all the moving panorama on the intersecting waters.

Stockholm has been called the Venice of the North; and there is much about it to suggest a resemblance. The city, built at the junction of the Mülar Lake with the Skœngard, is a maze of island, bridge, and water. The central island, which is the commercial quarter, is the site of the ancient city. The others are offshoots over which the growing town gradually extended, and became connected by bridges.

Stockholm (Pile Island) derives its name from the fact that a portion of the old city is built upon a foundation of piles. It has three principal divisions: the Stad, or original city; the Norrmalm, or northern suburb; and the Södermalm, or southern suburb. In the Stad, which is the commercial quarter, the streets are mostly narrow and crooked. The Norrmalm is the fashionable quarter; in it are the residences of the nobility, and the wealthy classes, and its streets are laid out with modern symmetry and elegance. The Södermalm rises from the water in a series of rocky terraces upon a high cliff, overlooking the harbor. It also is modern built, and it is the site of many large manufactories, principally of woollen, linen, cotton, and silk fabrics. Opposite the palace is the navy-yard, on an island called Skeppsholm (Ship Island). A squadron of gunboats is usually stationed here. On the landward side, Stockholm is undefended, but it is supposed to be impregnable on th seaward side, its approaches being covered by the strong fortress of Waxholm.

The Augusta and the Miantomonoh anchored off the city early in the morning. Their arrival created as much interest as it had done elsewhere, and the monitor was soon surrounded by numbers of boats.

Mr. Fox at once paid his respects to the United States minister at the court of Sweden, the Honorable James H. Campbell; and afterward called upon Rear-Admiral Lillichöök; upon the Minister of Foreign Affairs, Count Manderström; and upon the Russian minister at the court of Sweden, the Privy-Councillor Daschkoff.

The remainder of the day was spent in visiting various objects of interest in the city, among which was the "Exposition of Scandinavian Products," an exhibition illustrative of the agricultural and mechanical industry of Denmark, Sweden, Norway, and Finland.

September 19th.—Wednesday opened bright and clear. In the morning the Russian minister and his family, and the family of Count Manderström, visited the Miantonomoh, in company with Mr. Fox.

The evening was spent at the opera-house, where "Il Trovatore" was sung. This is the oldest opera-house in Europe, having been built by Gustavus III., in 1782, and is the same building in which he was assassinated ten years later, by Ankarström, the instrument of a conspiracy of disaffected nobles.

The King received notice of the designs of his enemies, but paid no heed to it. On the evening of the 16th of March, 1792, while his hair-dresser was arranging his coiffure, preparatory to going to a *bal-masqué*, to be held that night at the opera-house, he received a letter of warning. Gustavus read it, and handed it to his secretary, Baron Bjelke, asking him what he thought of it. Bjelke, who was in the conspiracy, replied:

"Sire, this letter has been written to frighten you."

"Frighten me!" cried the King, springing up. "I would like to see the man who can do that."

Regardless of the letter, he went to the ball. As soon as the conspirators saw their opportunity, they crowded around him, and separated him from his attendants, when Ankarström stepped up and touched him on the shoulder. As the King turned to see who had accosted him, the assassin discharged an air-pistol into his side.[1]

They carried him bleeding to a little room on the first floor, whence he was borne to the palace, where he lay in agony for thirteen days before death came to his relief. In the Klädskammar, the museum where are preserved the relics of Sweden's royalties, is shown the masquerade dress he wore that night, a suit of gray silk, a black-silk domino, and a black beaver with white plume; and with it is the shirt, stained with blood, just as it was taken from his body.

Gustavus III. was the first European monarch to volunteer the recognition of the independence of the American colonies.

[1] Verdi's opera, "Un Ballo in Maschera," is founded on this theme.

September 20th.—Rain fell on Thursday morning, and continued at intervals through the day. At ten o'clock, by invitation of the naval officials, Mr. Fox and several officers went by steamboat up the Mälar Lake, about thirty-six miles, to visit Skokloster, the château built by the celebrated Count Carl Gustaf von Wrangel, now belonging to the Brahe family, lineal descendants of Tycho Brahe, the great astronomer. It fell to them by marriage with the Wrangels. It is a quadrangular structure, with high octagonal towers at each corner, on a most romantic site, amid a grove of pine, on the shores of the lake, the placid waters of which it overlooks. The original building, founded in the last of the thirteenth century, was a convent, presided over by an abbess. It was burned about two hundred years after. The present structure is comparatively modern, dating from the early part of the seventeenth century.

Several hours were spent in examining the collection of arms and armor, and other curiosities, which are of great historical interest. There are many portraits of celebrated Swedes and of members of the family, among the latter one of Tycho Brahe. The library contains about twenty-five thousand volumes and many rare manuscripts.

On the return, dinner was served on the steamer, and speeches and friendly sentiments made the afternoon pass rapidly. Toward evening the weather partially cleared. As the boat passed the residence of Mr. Frestadius, the American consul at Stockholm, situated on a point of and projecting into the lake, the grounds were illuminated. The effect of the many-colored lights among the trees was very beautiful.

Among the Swedish officers who accompanied the Americans to Skokloster, was Commodore Adlersparre, Assistant-Minister of the Navy and member of the Chamber of Nobles. In his youth he served in the United States Navy, and he was a shipmate of Mr. Fox's on the corvette Cyane in 1838, '39, and '40. To him Mr. Fox and the American officers were indebted for many polite attentions during their stay in Stockholm.

September 21st.—Friday brought more rain. Another visit was made to the Exposition, where, among many other interesting objects, a singular breech-loading gun attracted the attention of our officers.

Mr. Fox and several other gentlemen lunched with the American consul. About thirty persons were present. The occasion was enlivened by speeches and toasts.

At five o'clock Mr. Fox dined with the Russian minister at the court of Sweden, Mr. Daschkoff. The dinner was elegant in all its appointments, the table-service being of silver gilt.

The envoy of Congress had the honor of handing in to the dining-room the mother of Mr. Daschkoff, who remarked, as she took Mr. Fox's arm, "I was the wife of the Russian minister to your country in the days of Jefferson." It was to this minister that Mr. Jefferson wrote a letter, of which the following is an extract:

"Monticello, *August* 12, 1809.

"Sir: Your favor of July 5th has been duly received, and, in it, that of my friend Mr. Short. I congratulate you on your safe arrival in the American hemisphere, after a voyage which must have been lengthy in time as it was in space. I hope you may experience no unfavorable change in your health in so great a change of climate, and that our fervid sun may be found as innocent as our cloudless skies must be agreeable. I hail you with particular pleasure, as the first harbinger of those friendly relations with your country, so desirable to us. Both nations being in character and practice essentially pacific, a common interest in the rights of peaceable nations gives us a common cause in their maintenance."

Mr. Daschkoff was minister from Russia to the United States from 1809 to 1819.

September 22*d.*—Saturday was cloudy, but no rain fell. In the morning, Mr. Fox, Captain Murray, and Commander Beaumont, had the honor of a formal presentation to the King, at the Royal Palace in the city, through the American minister, Mr. Campbell. His Majesty wore a gray morning-suit, with a frock-coat, having just come in from the country.

Charles XV., Louis Eugène, King of Sweden and Norway, of the Goths and the Wends, born May 3, 1826, succeeded his father, King Oscar I., July 8, 1859. He was married, June 19, 1850, to Wilhelmine Frederique Alexandrine Anne Louise, Princess of Orauge, born Au-

gust 5, 1828, the daughter of William Frederick, Prince of the Netherlands. She died March 30, 1871; and he died September 18, 1872. The sole issue of this marriage was the Princess Louise Josephine Eugénie, born October 31, 1851; married, July 28, 1869, to Christian Frederick William Charles, Prince Royal of Denmark.

Jean Baptiste Jules Bernadotte, Marshal of the French Empire, Prince of Ponte Corvo, the founder of the present royal family of Sweden, was born January 26, 1764, at Pau, in Southern France. He married, in 1798, Eugénie Bernhardine Désirée Clary, daughter of a wealthy merchant of Marseilles, and sister of Madame Joseph Bonaparte. By this marriage he had one son only, Joseph François Oscar, born in Paris, July 4, 1799. His name, Oscar, was chosen as a compliment to Napoleon, who became his godfather on his return from Egypt, from one of the heroes of his favorite Ossian.

Bernadotte was elected Crown-Prince of Sweden and Norway, August 21, 1810. Charles XIII., the last of the line of Vasa, died February 5, 1818, and Bernadotte was crowned on the 11th of May following, under the title of Charles XIV. John.

After a wise administration of twenty-six years, during which the public and private credit of his adopted country was restored, he died, and was succeeded by his son, March 8, 1844.

Oscar I. married, June 19, 1823, Josephine Maximilienne Eugénie Napoléone, daughter of Prince Eugène Beauharnais and of his wife, the Princess Augusta Amelia, daughter of Maximilian I., King of Bavaria.

They had the following children:

1. Charles Louis Eugène, born May 3, 1826; King of Sweden at the time of Mr. Fox's visit.

2. François Gustave Oscar, born June 18, 1827; died young.

3. Oscar Frédéric, born January 21, 1829; married, June 6, 1857, Sophia Wilhelmine Marianne Henrietta, daughter of William, Duke of Nassau. His brother, Charles XV., dying without male issue, he succeeded him as Oscar II. He has four sons.

4. Charlotte Eugénie Augusta Amelia Albertine, born April 24, 1830.

5. Nicholas Augustus, born August 24, 1831; married, April 16, 1864, Theresa Amelia Caroline Josephine Antoinette, Duchess of Saxe, daughter of the late Edward, Prince of Saxe-Altenburg.

In the interview with Mr. Fox, his Majesty spoke of the great revenues of the United States Government, which had increased so enormously within a comparatively short period. Mr. Fox replied that he looked upon the fact as a national calamity.

"Why so?" asked the King.

"Because," replied Mr. Fox, "we have every reason to fear that our government will become extravagant in consequence, to be followed by corruption and a decline of public morals."

"My country will never suffer in that way," rejoined his Majesty, with a smile.

The great palace, where the presentation took place,

stands upon an eminence in the central island of the city. Its massive walls, which rise above all the surrounding buildings, are among the first objects to catch the eye on approaching Stockholm from the Baltic. It is in the Italian style, and forms a regular quadrangle flanked by handsome wings on the east and west. The lower story is of granite, the rest of brick faced with sandstone. It was built about the middle of the last century by the younger Tessin, from designs by his father.

On the east side the palace-hill slopes down to the water, forming a broad, open space, where the troops parade. At the top is a granite obelisk one hundred feet high, and at the foot of the incline on the quay stands the splendid bronze statue of Gustavus III. by Sergel.

Prince Oscar resided at the time in the palace of the heir-apparent, a short distance from the Royal Palace, on the Square of Gustavus Adolphus, in the centre of which stands Sergel's equestrian statue of the great soldier. He is represented as a victor crowned with laurels.

At three o'clock in the afternoon, his Majesty the King and his Royal Highness Prince Oscar, accompanied by the chief of the Navy Department, Rear-Admiral Count Platen, visited the ships informally. Mr. Fox received them on the Miantonomoh with the customary honors. His Majesty examined all parts of the monitor, and appeared to take great interest in every thing connected with her.

At five o'clock Mr. Fox and several of the officers dined with Mr. Campbell at Hasselbacken (Hazel Mount), a fashionable resort in the Djurgård, or Deer Park.

The Djurgård, the favorite summer resort of Stockholm, is unexcelled for natural beauty by any park in the world. Its beech-trees are unrivalled, and its oaks are scarcely less remarkable. Broad carriage-drives and sylvan paths lead through it in every direction, revealing at each turn some new variety of scenery. Beautiful lawns, sloping hills, open woods and tangled forests, desolate crags, rocks overgrown with moss and lichen, charming intermixtures of land and water, sterility and verdure, greet the eye on every side.

In ancient times it was a dependency of the Cloister of Clara, and under Charles IX. it became a royal menagerie. It is now a place of recreation, and is filled with beautiful villas, in the Swiss and Italian style, *cafés* and restaurants, tivolis and alhambras. There are also a circus and a small theatre. The garden has throngs of visitors, particularly on pleasant evenings, when the bands play and the buildings and walks glow with innumerable lights. The people sitting at the marble tables, eating ices and drinking *liqueurs* and Swedish punch, new-comers passing from group to group, and the waiters flitting to and fro, make a lively and cheerful scene.

The Swedes, while unlimited in the use of distilled spirits, are remarkable for their general sobriety. Their good temper is proverbial, and brawls and quarrels are almost unknown in their places of public resort. The courtesy of all classes of people toward each other is very noticeable to one accustomed to the manners of more excitable nations.

Hasselbacken is the principal restaurant of the Djurgård, a veritable culinary palace, where, surrounded by all that is beautiful in nature and exquisite in art, the *bons vivants* of Stockholm go to enjoy the pleasures of the table.

About fifty gentlemen were present at the dinner given by the American minister, among whom were the chief officials of the Government and the foreign diplomatic corps. Count Manderström spoke in very complimentary terms of the United States, to which Mr. Fox replied, thanking his Excellency for calling to mind the early proffer of Sweden to form a treaty of amity with the United States, then struggling for independence. He said that he anchored an American monitor at Stockholm as an acknowledgment of the services which John Ericsson had rendered to his adopted country in her dire necessity, by creating this type of vessel. He expressed also the satisfaction of his government at the immigration from Sweden, composed of honest, industrious, and sober people; and added that the diminution of the boundaries of Scandinavia, since the seventeenth century, had not lessened the influence of this liberty-loving race, whose enterprising spirit and martial character had identified it permanently with the civilization of Europe, and foreshadowed an equal destiny in the New World, which it was the first to visit.

CHAPTER XXVIII.

RIDDARHOLM—BIRGER JARL—THE MOSEBACKEN—ULRIKSDAL—THE ROYAL DINNER—HAGA—ROSENDAL—DROTTNINGHOLM—QUEEN-DOWAGER JOSEPHINE—DEPARTURE—KIEL—PRINCE ADALBERT OF PRUSSIA—PARTING SALUTES.

SEPTEMBER 23*d*.—Sunday opened with fine weather.

In the morning, Mr. Fox, accompanied by Mr. Campbell and the principal officers in the squadron, visited the celebrated Riddarholm (Knight's Island) Church, where Sweden's kings, nobles, and knights of the Seraphim Order, are buried.

Riddarholm is one of the three original islands on which the old city was built. The church is a red-brick edifice, with a tall iron spire. The original building, which was a convent of Gray Friars, was erected by King Magnus Ladulås in 1286. It is now the special mausoleum of the knights of the Order of the Seraphim, said to have been founded by the same sovereign in 1285. In one of its towers hangs a bell, which is never used excepting to toll the death of a brother, when his shield is borne to the church, to be hung upon the walls among the arms of those who have gone before. In front of the high altar are the monuments of Kings Magnus Ladulås and Carl Knutson, with their effigies upon them, arrayed in royal robes and crowned.

Gustavus Adolphus lies in one of the chapels, among others of his race, in a tomb prepared by himself in 1629, three years before he met his fate at Lützen. His remains are in a sarcophagus of Italian marble, surrounded by the trophies of his victories, banners dusty and torn, arms and military trappings, and the rusty keys of towns and fortresses. In the marble is chiselled the appropriate motto, "Moriens Triumphavit." Opposite is the chapel devoted to the Charleses, where reposes all that is earthly of many of the name. Here lies Charles XII., in a white sarcophagus on a pedestal of green marble, his tomb surrounded, like that of Gustavus, with the relics of his eventful life, drums, muskets, tattered ensigns, and other paraphernalia of war, reminding one of the inexorable lot which consigns all, prince and peasant, to a common dust.

In still another chapel is the sarcophagus of Bernadotte, hewn from a block of Elfdal porphyry. It is copied from that of Agrippa at Rome. Near it is the tomb of Oscar I., second of his line, and that of the lamented Prince Gustavus, his son, who, had he lived, would now be king.

No other place in Europe is more likely to suggest to the reflective mind more interesting reminiscences or sadder thoughts than this old church of Riddarholm. In its crypts sleep the great ones of earth, kings and warriors, who made indelible marks on the world's history, in the midst of the mouldering implements of their ambition, while without the busy world moves on within sight and sound of their tombs. Public buildings surround its chapels, and a girdle of shipping about the island brings commerce within reach of its ancient towers.

Not far from the church is an open place, in the centre of which is the bronze statue, by Fogelberg, of Birger Jarl (Earl Birger), the father of King Waldemar of Sweden, and founder of Stockholm, in 1260. The grim warrior is clad in a full suit of scale-armor, and stands, most inappropriately, upon a marble pedestal.

Across a granite bridge, connecting the Riddarholm with the main island, is the Riddarhus, or House of Assembly of the Nobles, standing on a square of the same name. In its hall are the shields of more than three thousand Swedish nobles. It is an old building, and has been the scene of many important events in Swedish history. In its front is the bronze statue of Gustavus Vasa, crowned with laurel.

The party next visited the Mosebacken (Moses Hill), whence is obtained a splendid view of the city and surounding country. A fine square, with a theatre, the School of Navigation, and other public buildings, occupies its summit. It opens into a garden of beautiful walks and terraces, where a band plays, and where people come, pleasant afternoons and evenings, to drink coffee and to enjoy the view.

At three o'clock Mr. Fox, Mr. Campbell, Captain Murray, Commander Beaumont, and six other officers of the squadron, started for Ulriksdal, a favorite summer resort of the reigning family, where they were invited to dine with their Majesties, the King and Queen, at half-past four o'clock.

Ulriksdal is a large château, pleasantly situated on the lake-shore. It has been a dependency of the crown since the seventeenth century. It was built by the celebrated Jacob Pontusson de la Gardie, who named it Jakobsdal. It passed to his son, Magnus Gabriel de la Gardie, the favorite of Queen Christina, and it was from under its roof that the erratic daughter of Gustavus Adolphus set out for her coronation at Stockholm. The family of De la Gardie sold it to Queen Hedwiga Eleonora, who gave it to her grandson, Prince Ulrik, who lived long enough only to rename it Ulriksdal. At his death it passed to the crown.

Charles XIV. (Bernadotte) made it an asylum for invalid soldiers. Oscar I. gave it to his son, Prince Charles, who took it again into favor, and made it his summer residence. Its plain exterior suited his simple tastes, and after he became king it continued to be his favorite place of resort. Its interior is a splendid museum of articles of virtu, ancient bronzes, cabinets, armor and arms, Sèvres ware, and ancient Chinese and Japanese curiosities, collected mostly by his Majesty.

At the dinner, there were present Prince Oscar (now King Oscar II.), brother of the King, Princess Louise, the only child of their Majesties, and now wife of the Prince Royal of Denmark, several members of the cabinet, and a number of the ladies of the court. Mr. Fox had the honor of a seat beside the Queen.

The *menu*, written on plain paper within a printed border of fruits and flowers, surmounted by the Swedish crown, was as follows:

DÎNER
du 23 *Septembre*, 1866.

Potage aux queues de bœuf.
Brochets au gratin, sauce gratin, pommes de terre.
Selle de venaison, sauce venaison, croquettes de pommes de terre.
Bordure de foies gras à la Toulouse.
Perdreaux bardés rôtis, salade.
Chouxfleurs, sauce au beurre.
Fondue au Parmesan.
Gâteau de mille feuilles garni de glace.

During the dinner his Majesty frequently addressed questions across the table to his guests. Before leaving the table he took a card-photograph of himself from his case, and, writing his name on it, handed it to Mr. Fox.

After dinner, he invited the officers into his smoking-room, and, closing the door on the formalities of the court, joined his democratic friends in a cigar, and the most animated conversation. He inquired particularly for Frederick Rosencrantz, who was serving in our volunteer army, but formerly had been an aide-de-camp of his Majesty; and writing his own name on one of his card-photographs, he requested Mr. Fox to have it delivered to him on his return to the United States. Mr. Fox afterward sent the picture through Major-General Meade, on whose staff Lieutenant-Colonel Rosencrantz (now of the Sixteenth Regiment of Infantry) was then serving.

When our envoy was about to take leave of his Majesty, the next day being appointed for the sailing of the squadron, the King requested him to remain two days longer, that he might present him to the Queen-Dowager Josephine, his mother, daughter of Prince Eugene Beauharnais.

September 24*th*.—Monday opened with fine weather. In the morning a second visit was made to Mosebacken, and to the Catherine Church on its summit. The party ascended to the dome of the church, which overlooks Stockholm, and commands a view of Haga and Bellevue, royal parks. In the distance the Mälar stretches its rocky shores, crowned with birch-woods, and on the left a narrowing expanse of water, dotted with moving sails, leads to the Baltic. From this point Skeppsholm and Castellholm (Castle Island) appear to form a kind of promontory extending into the Skærengard. The two islands are connected by a wooden bridge. The latter derives its name from a strongly-fortified brick tower on it, which commands the harbor.

At five o'clock Mr. Fox, Mr. Campbell, Captain Murray, Commander Beaumont, and several other officers of the squadron, dined with Count Platen, the Minister of the Navy. About seventy persons were present.

The Countess Platen presented Mr. Fox with two photographs of portraits of Gustavus Vasa.

September 25*th*.—On Tuesday morning, which was foggy, Mr. Fox and several of the officers drove to Haga, one of the largest and most beautiful of the royal parks of Europe. It was created by Gustavus III., who bought a farm named Haga on the site, in 1771, and, a few years after, built the residence still standing. It was from this little palace that the King went to the opera-house on the fatal 16th of March, 1792.

Not far from Haga is the Church of Solna, believed by antiquaries to be one of the most ancient buildings in Sweden. It is circular in form, and is built of round stones. It was once a pagan temple, but became a Christian church in the earliest days of Christianity in Sweden. In its yard is buried Berzelius, the great chemist.

The party went thence to Rosendal, a summer residence connecting with the Djurgård, built by King Charles XIV. In its garden stands the great porphyry vase from Elfdal, in Dalecarlia.

At half-past two o'clock, Mr. Fox, Mr. Campbell, and the other invited gentlemen, went, in company with the King and Prince Oscar, on a little steamer to Drottningholm, the summer residence of the Queen-Dowager Josephine, situated on Lofön, a beautiful island of Lake Mäar. An hour was occupied in the trip. On arrival, his Majesty showed his guests through the palace and pointed out to them the many objects of interest in and around it.

Drottningholm is the most stately country-palace in the land, and merits the name of the Versailles of Sweden. Its foundations were laid by Queen Hedwiga Eleonora on the site of a château which had been burned in 1661, the same year in which Louis XIV. began the alerations and additions which converted the hunting-lodge of Louis XIII. into one of the most remarkable royal residences in Europe. The architect of Drottningholm was Tessin the elder, but the grand staircase was the work of Tessin the younger, who designed also the park and magnificent gardens. The palace has splendid galleries of paintings and sculpture, and rare collections of precious marbles and of old Gobelin tapestries. One gallery, devoted to pictures of the contemporaries of Charles XV., contains a fine portrait of the Empress of Austria, one of the most beautiful women of the age. The gardens are profusely ornamented with vases and statuary, fountains, miniature lakes, and pretty islets. Among the buildings is the China Palace, a pavilion in the Chinese style, which was built at Stockholm by King Adolphus Frederick, brought by water and set up at Drottningholm as a surprise to his queen, Louisa Ulrica, on her birthday. It is now a museum of Chinese and Japanese curiosities.

Mr. Fox and the gentlemen accompanying him were presented to the Queen Dowager by his Majesty the King. The Queen, her daughter, and several maids of honor, were present at the ceremony.

Queen Josephine, the eldest child of Prince Eugene Beauharnais, was born March 14, 1807. She is now (1873) the only living grandchild of the Empress Josephine.

At four o'clock lunch was served. The ladies sat at table by themselves. The King, Prince Oscar, and the Americans, ate standing.

The *menu* was written within an ornamental borde

printed in black, with the crown surrounded by rays at the top:

DÉJEUNER DINATOIRE

de 25 *Septembre*, 1866.

Potage à la Windsor.
Saumons frais, garnis d'huitres.
Roast-beef à l'Anglaise.
Poulets santés aux champignons.
Coqs de bruyère garnis de gélinottes.
Salade de laitue.
Petits pois à la Française.
Glace au marasquin et petits gâteaux.
Dessert.

After lunch, photographs were exchanged, and the gentlemen were invited to record their names in a book. The King then took leave of the party, putting them in charge of Prince Oscar, who, at the request of Queen Josephine, drove them about the park, and showed the different points of interest.

At evening they reëmbarked for Stockholm on the same little steamer which had brought them to Drottningholm.

On their arrival in the city Mr. Fox and his companions bade adieu to their friends, and went on board the ships, expecting to sail early in the morning.

September 26th.—Wednesday opened with thick fog, which lasted all day, preventing the departure of the squadron. In the evening some of the officers attended the opera of the "Prophet," in which the American skater, J. Haines, performed on parlor-skates.

September 27th.—At nine A. M., Thursday morning, the fog lifted, and the ships got under way. Count Platen sent a Swedish gunboat to accompany them down the Skrengard, and to see them safely into clear water. The United States minister went a part of the way down with Mr. Fox, and was cheered at his departure. The squadron went out by the Landseer Passage. The gunboat continued with them until seven o'clock P. M., when she exchanged cheers with our vessels, and returned to Stockholm.

September 28th.—Friday opened with fine, clear weather, with the wind from the south and a smooth sea. Early in the morning Gottland Island was passed, and in the afternoon Bornholm was seen on the east. The former belongs to Sweden, the latter to Denmark. Bornholm has a rocky coast, with high, precipitous cliffs.

September 29th.—Light southerly wind and a smooth sea; the weather still fine and clear. The ships passed between Laaland and Falster Islands and the main-land of Mecklenburg, heading for Kiel Bay. Laaland, Falster, and several other small islands in the same group, constitute the district of Laaland, in Denmark. The larger island is about sixty miles long, and is low, level, and mostly marshy. It has a lake in its centre, about five miles in length.

About six o'clock P. M. the squadron passed through the Fehmern Strait, and at eleven o'clock both ships came to anchor off the town of Kiel. An officer came on board at once, in the name of the admiral commanding, to offer official greetings, and to extend the usual courtesies.

Kiel, previous to the Sleswig-Holstein War in 1866, was a province of Denmark, but it now belongs to Prussia. It is situated on the Kielerfiord, a deep bay of the Baltic, which has finely-wooded banks and all the appearance of a lake. It is a well-built, walled town, with straight, well-paved streets, and contains about twenty thousand inhabitants. Its market-place, which is large and picturesque, contains several fine buildings, among them the Church of St. Nicholas, which has a lofty tower. At the east end of the town is the castle, the residence of the Duke of Holstein-Glücksburg. It is a modern structure, having been rebuilt since 1838. The university, founded in 1665, has a library of eighty thousand volumes, and usually about three hundred students. The environs of the town are very beautiful, with pleasant walks amid shady groves, and fine views of the Baltic and of the surrounding country.

Kiel, as the principal fortified naval port of Prussia, is rapidly growing into importance. It is the best harbor on the south of the Baltic, having plenty of water, and its spacious quays admitting vessels drawing sixteen feet. It is also admirably situated for trade, it being the terminus of the Holstein Canal, which connects the Baltic with the German Ocean.

September 30th.—Sunday opened with clear, warm weather. Mr. Fox and Captain Murray went on shore in the morning, and made an official call on Rear-Admiral

Jackman, commanding the district. Mr. Fox then telegraphed to the United States minister at Berlin, the Honorable Joseph A. Wright, informing him of the arrival of the squadron in Prussian waters. Mr. Wright answered that he would go to Kiel on the morrow (Monday), in company with Prince Adalbert, the commander-in-chief of the navy, to visit the monitor.

At half-past seven o'clock, Mr. Fox, Captain Murray, and Commander Beaumont, and a number of other officers of the squadron, supped with Admiral Jackman. Forty or fifty guests were present, and the evening passed in the most agreeable manner.

October 1st.—The pleasant weather continued. At nine o'clock the Augusta saluted the Prussian flag with twenty-one guns, and afterward the admiral with thirteen guns. The national salute was returned, and a salute of fifteen guns was given to Mr. Fox as Assistant Secretary of the Navy.

At ten o'clock, the United States minister, Mr. Wright, arrived. At eleven o'clock, his Royal Highness, Prince Adalbert, admiral and commander-in-chief of the Prussian Navy, came on board of the Augusta. He was saluted, as admiral, with seventeen guns, and was received with all the honors due his rank and position. He went thence on board of the Miantonomoh, accompanied by Mr. Fox, Mr. Wright, and the principal officers. The Prince remained two hours on the ship, and examined her in all her parts with minute care.

Prince Henry William Adalbert, born October 29, 1811, is the son of Prince Frederick Louis Charles, who was the son of King Frederick William II. of Prussia. He is, therefore, first cousin to the present King, now Emperor of Germany.

At six o'clock, Mr. Fox, Captain Murray, and Commander Beaumont, had the honor of dining with his Royal Highness in the town. About fifty officials and naval officers were present. The United States minister sat on the Prince's right, and Mr. Fox on his left. The Prince toasted the American Navy, to which Captain Murray replied happily. Speeches were made by Mr. Wright, Mr. Fox, and others, the customary toasts were drunk, and the dinner passed of in the most sociable manner.

On this day Mr. Fox indorsed on Captain Murray's orders that he had no further need of the ships, and they made ready to sail in accordance with previous instrucions.

October 2d.—On Tuesday morning Mr. Fox took leave of the ships. As he departed, the American flag was hauled down at the main, and he was saluted with fifteen guns. He left on the evening train for Hamburg.

CHAPTER XXIX.

OFFICIAL CORRESPONDENCE.

THE following correspondence needs no explanation:

[MR. FOX TO MR. SEWARD.]

PORTSMOUTH, NEW HAMPSHIRE,
December 17, 1866.

SIR: Having returned from my visit to Russia on the 13th instant, I discharge a duty by enclosing to you herewith the following papers introductory—a memorandum of papers in Russian:

1. Autograph letter of Peter the Great.
2. A poem by Derschavin, a lyric poet of the time of Catherine II., with autographic corrections and remarks.
3. An autographic poem by Puschkin.
4. A letter of Schukowsky, governor of Alexander II.
5. A fragment, autographic, of Gogol.
6. "The First Snow," a poem by Countess Rostopchine (autographic).
7. A *fac-simile* from the Russian history of Karamzin; and—
8. An autographic remark by Schafarik.

I received these, last August, from Mr. Pogodin, a distinguished citizen of Moscow, who requested me to present them to some national institute or museum in

Washington. I ask you to acknowledge their receipt, and to give such direction to them as in your judgment shall best fulfil the wishes of the donor.

I have the honor to be your obedient servant,

G. V. Fox,
Late Assistant Secretary of the Navy.

Hon. William H. Seward,
Secretary of State, Washington, D. C.

[MR. SEWARD TO MR. FOX.]

Department of State, Washington,
December 20, 1866.

Sir: I have received your communication of the 17th instant, and its accompaniments, which Mr. Pogodin requested you to present to some national institute or museum in this city. I have placed them among the archives of the department, and I beg that you will accept my thanks for your kindness in allowing me the privilege of disposing of these interesting autographs.

I am, sir, your obedient servant,

William H. Seward.

G. V. Fox, Esq.,
Portsmouth, New Hampshire.

[MR. FOX TO MR. SEWARD.]

Washington, D. C., *February* 25, 1867.

Sir: On the 30th of September last I submitted to you a hasty narrative of the reception which I met with in Russia while executing your instructions in delivering personally to the sovereign of that country the resolution of Congress expressive of the feelings of the people of the United States in reference to his providential escape from the hand of an assassin. I have recorded in that narrative the remarks of the Emperor, and the various demonstrations of the people, which manifested their gratification at the sympathy felt for them by the American people. I have endeavored in this way to comply with the wish often repeated to me by his Majesty, to make known to the Government and my countrymen the feelings of friendship which existed in Russia toward America. But all that I have written myself and all that was written for the press, by persons far more capable than I feel myself to be to describe the manifestations of these feelings, fail to convey any adequate idea of the enthusiasm which pervades the people of Russia toward the United States, and their sincere wishes for the continued prosperity and power of our country.

The expression of the sympathy felt by the Emperor for this country in its great struggle for national unity made by Prince Gortchakoff, in 1861, when several of the great powers of Europe were coöperating in the effort to destroy it, and taking measures to profit by its destruction, was gratefully appreciated by the Government and people of the United States as a timely and effective demonstration in our behalf. But it was not until I had traversed so great a part of the Russian Empire, and witnessed how cordial and wide-spread among all classes in that powerful country was the friendship for America, that I appreciated the practical importance of the Emperor's sympathy in its bearings upon the course of our great contest, and in its influence upon the conduct of other nations toward us.

The crowds that gathered around us at every social meeting, singing the plaintive national songs, the flowers presented by the hands of beauty and innocence, the numerous presents offered upon all suitable occasions, the imperial honor granted at Kostroma of casting down their garments for us to walk upon, the deep feeling which the great mass of the people evinced whenever the name of our country was mentioned, and the many touching incidents which such sympathies evoked, were not produced by curiosity or instigated by officials. The Russians have been familiar with royal embassies from powerful and magnificent courts for many centuries. It was a heart-impulse of the people in favor of our country which occasioned these extraordinary demonstrations toward the messenger of good-will, founded on their instinctive knowledge that, while our countries were widely separated from each other on the globe and in forms of government, there was yet a community of interest on great points which identified the friendships of the people with patriotism itself.

It may serve to illustrate the prevailing feeling respecting the relations of the two countries to state that I saw at the residence of Prince Gortchakoff, in St. Petersburg, a beautiful model, in steel, of one of Ericsson's monitors, a form of vessel now associated in the popular mind with American genius and power, which had been presented to the prince as a grateful recognition of the part he had borne as his Majesty's Minister of Foreign Affairs.

With great respect, your obedient servant,

G. V. Fox.

Hon. William H. Seward, *Secretary of State.*

[MR. SEWARD TO MR. FOX.]

Department of State,
Washington, *February* 25, 1867.

Sir: I have received your interesting letter of this date, giving an account of the manner in which you have executed the instructions of this Department with reference to the presentation to the Emperor of Russia of the resolution of Congress congratulating him upon his escape from an attempted assassination.

In reply, I have to inform you that your proceedings upon the occasion referred to are entirely approved.

I am, sir, your obedient servant,

William H. Seward.

G. V. Fox, Esq., *Washington.*

[MR. FOX TO MR. SEWARD.]

Washington, D. C., *February* 25, 1867.

Sir: I have reported the gifts and distinctions bestowed upon the officers and myself while in Europe last summer.

Article I., Sec. 9, of the Constitution of the United States declares that—

"No title of nobility shall be granted by the United States; and no person holding any office of profit o trust under them shall, without the consent of Congress, accept of any present, emolument, office, or title, of any kind whatever, from any king, prince, or foreign state."

Agreeable to the spirit of this prohibition, and in behalf of all recipients, I briefly enumerate the honors and presents which come under this restriction, and such as are, in my opinion, doubtful.

At St. Petersburg the officers of the two vessels received from the Emperor a present of one or more books. Captain Murray, the senior officer, and Commander Beaumont were each presented with a diamond ring, in the name of his Majesty.

At an interview with Prince Gortchakoff, Minister of Foreign Affairs, previous to my departure, he was kind enough to speak favorably of my conduct of the mission intrusted to me, and he announced that the Emperor desired to bestow on me a souvenir of himself, as an expression of his personal satisfaction with me, and that he trusted it would be accepted and retained. He then handed me a magnificent enamelled gold snuffbox, which had upon its lid a miniature of the Emperor Alexander II., surrounded with large diamonds. He gave me a copy of his own address at the English Club dinner, a copy of the autograph letter of the Emperor to the President, both of which have been published, and a copy of his dispatch to the Russian Minister at Washington, Mr. Stoeckl, concerning my mission, dated at Peterhof, August $\frac{11}{23}$, 1866, not yet published.

I had the honor to have conferred on me the honorary citizenship of the cities of Cronstadt, St. Petersburg, Moscow, Kostroma, and Kortcheva, which required the authorization of the Emperor, and therefore may come within the limit of the prohibition in the Constitution.

I have a large number of books, received from institutions, individuals, and societies, which are now in the Boston Navy-Yard. They are mostly statistical, and, although personal gifts, I intend to distribute them where the information they contain will be made useful, by translation and publication. There were books, autographs, and other articles, sent to me with special requests, which have been allotted as the donors requested.

Before leaving Paris, on my way to the United States, the Emperor Napoleon III. sent me the cross of an officer of the Legion of Honor, and upon my return, after I had ceased to be an official of the United States, I received notice that the King of Denmark had sent me the cross of Commander of the Order of Dannebrog, and the King of Italy the cross of Commander of St. Maurice and St. Lazarus.

I believe it proper to refer these matters to Congress for its action, although I am no longer in the public service. Accordingly, I have the honor to request that you will give this communication that direction.

With great respect,
Your ob't servant,
G. V. Fox.

Hon. Wm. H. Seward, *Secretary of State.*

[MR. FOX TO MR. SEWARD.]

Portsmouth, New Hampshire, *July* 23, 1867.

Sir: In a letter which I had the honor to write on the 25th of February last, I reported to you that a large number of books had been presented to me in Russia, upon the occasion of my visit to that country as bearer of the resolution of Congress.

Through the kindness of Professor Henry, a correct catalogue of these books has been prepared, which is herewith transmitted.

Those which were presented to me by the Emperor of Russia I have retained, under authority given to me by joint resolution of Congress.

The remainder I present, through the State Department, to the library of the Smithsonian Institution, which now forms a part of the national library of our country.

With great respect, your obedient servant,

G. V. Fox.

Hon. William H. Seward,
Secretary of State.

[MR. SEWARD TO MR. FOX.]

Department of State, Washington,
September 20, 1867.

Sir: I have the honor to acknowledge the receipt of your letter of the 23d of July last, transmitting a catalogue of books presented to you by the Emperor of Russia upon the occasion of your visit to that country as the bearer of the resolution of Congress.

I have also to acknowledge the receipt of a large number of those valuable works which have been donated by you to the library of the Smithsonian Institution, which now forms a part of the Library of Congress, namely : 179 volumes finely bound, many in quarto, others in octavo major; 16 atlases and albums, illustrating accompanying books, texts, or descriptions, some eagle, others elephant size, all bound in cloth, morocco, etc. ; 72 maps, some bound in covers or cases, four city plans in cases and on cloth ; and 12 pamphlets : making in all 282 pieces, all of which have been placed in the library of the Smithsonian Institution, in accordance with your intentions.

In accepting, on behalf of the Government and people of the United States, so important and instructive an acquisition to the national library, I may safely assure you that they will be gratefully appreciated and carefully preserved.

I have the honor to be, sir, your obedient servant,

WILLIAM H. SEWARD.

G. V. Fox, Esq., *Washington.*

[FROM ADMIRAL CRABBE TO MR. FOX.]

St. Petersburg, Russia,
May 9 (21), 1869.

SIR: The Russian nation has a most retentive memory for the past attention and respect paid to their beloved Emperor. And the American embassy in the year 1866 is still fresh in the memory of the people. As proof of this fact, I have the pleasure, at the request of the brothers Milutine, merchants of Tcherepovetz, to for ward you a case containing the picture of a memorial which has been shown to the Emperor, and most graciously approved of by his Majesty.

I flatter myself with the idea that this picture will be a pleasing memento to you and yours of the lasting impression produced in Russia by the embassy sent by the American Congress, of which you were the worthy chief.

I avail myself of this opportunity to assure you of my high consideration, and remain,

        Sir, your obedient humble servant,
    (Signed)   CRABBE.

To the Honorable Gustavus V. Fox,
    Portsmouth, N. H., U. S. of America.

Description of the Ornamental Window forming the Frame of the Memorial sent to the Honorable GUSTAVUS V. Fox, *by the Brothers* MILUTINE, *Merchants of Tcherepovetz.*

The frame is carved in Russian wood of different qualities and tints, from a design by Colonel N. Mussard. The carving was done in twelve days by a Russian peasant, Leontieff.

The objects represented on the frame are as follows:

The Byzantine Cross.
The Chalice.
A star on each side.
A Russian salt-cellar.
The Bread.
A Russian towel on supporters.

The arms of the Government of Novgorod.

The Dove with an olive-branch.

The picture inside represents the memorial stand, with inscriptions.

On both sides of the ornamental window are ears of corn, the emblems of fertility.

The whole is executed in pure Russian style.

[FROM MR. FOX TO SECRETARY FISH.]

LOWELL, MASS., *Sept.* 21, 1869.

SIR: I have the honor to enclose herewith a copy of a letter from Vice-Admiral Crabbe, Minister of Marine at St. Petersburg, forwarded with the memorial picture, by the Consul-General of Russia at New York, a copy of whose letter is also enclosed.

The letter of the minister and the testimonial which accompanied it are expressive of the grateful remembrance which Russia cherishes for the sympathetic resolution of Congress, which I had the honor to present to the Emperor in 1866.

With great respect, your obedient servant,

G. V. Fox.

Hon. HAMILTON FISH, *Secretary of State, Washington, D. C.*

[MR. FISH TO MR. FOX.]

DEPARTMENT OF STATE, WASHINGTON, *October* 5, 1867.

SIR: I have to acknowledge the receipt of your letter of the 21st ultimo, and the papers which accompanied it in relation to an interesting memorial picture which ha been presented to you in commemoration of your mission to Russia.

That memento, and the correspondence by which it was accompanied, are gratifying manifestations of a friendly spirit which I am happy to believe is cordially reciprocated by the people of the United States.

I am, sir, your very obedient servant,

(Signed) HAMILTON FISH.

G. V. Fox, Esq., *Lowell, Massachusetts.*

APPENDIX.

A.

DISPATCH FROM PRINCE GORTCHAKOFF, VICE-CHANCELLOR AND MINISTER OF FOREIGN AFFAIRS OF THE EMPIRE OF RUSSIA, TO MR. DE STOECKL, RUSSIAN MINISTER AT WASHINGTON.

St. Petersburg, *July* 10, 1861.

Sir: From the beginning of the conflict which divides the United States of America you have been desired to make known to the Federal Government the deep interest with which our august master was observing the development of a crisis which puts in question the prosperity and even the existence of the Union.

The Emperor profoundly regrets to see that the hope of a peaceful solution is not realized, and that American citizens, already in arms against each other, are ready to let loose upon their country the most formidable of the scourges of political society—civil war.

For the more than eighty years that it has existed the American Union owes its independence, its towering rise, and its progress, to the concord of its members, consecrated, under the auspices of its illustrious founder, by institutions which have been able to reconcile union with liberty. This union has been fruitful. It has exhibited to the world the spectacle of a prosperity without example in the annals of history.

It would be deplorable that, after so conclusive an experience, the United States should be hurried into a breach of the solemn compact which up to this time has made their power.

In spite of the diversity of their constitutions and of their interests, and perhaps even *because* of this diversity, Providence seems to urge them to draw closer the traditional bond which is the basis and the very condition of their political existence. In any event, the sacrifices, which they might impose upon themselves to maintain it, are beyond comparison with those which dissolution would bring after it. United, they perfect themselves; isolated, they are paralyzed.

The struggle which unhappily has just arisen can neither be indefinitely prolonged, nor lead to the total destruction of one of the parties. Sooner or later it will be necessary to come to some settlement, whatsoever it may be, which may cause the divergent interests now actually in conflict to coexist.

The American nation would, then, give a proof of high political wisdom in seeking in common such a settlement before a useless effusion of blood, a barren squandering of strength and of public riches, and acts of violence and reciprocal reprisals, shall have come to deepen an abyss between the two parties to the confederation, to end definitely in their mutual exhaustion, and in the ruin, perhaps irreparable, of their commercial and political power.

Our august master cannot resign himself to admit such deplorable anticipations. His Imperial Majesty still places his confidence in that practical good sense of the citizens of the Union, who appreciate so judiciously their true interests. His Majesty is happy to believe that the members of the Federal Government and the influential men of the two parties will seize all occasions and will unite all their efforts to calm the effervescence of the passions. There are no interests so divergent that it may not be possible to reconcile them, by laboring to that end with zeal and perseverance, in a spirit of justice and moderation.

If, within the limits of your friendly relations, your language and your counsels may contribute to this result, you will respond, sir, to the intentions of His Majesty the Emperor, in devoting to this the personal influence which you may have been able to acquire during your long residence at Washington, and the consideration which belongs to your character, as the representative of a sovereign animated by the most friendly sentiments toward the American Union. This Union is not simply in our eyes an element essential to the universal *political* equilibrium. It constitutes, besides, a nation to which our august master and all Russia have pledged the most friendly interest; for the two countries, placed at the extremities of the two worlds, both in the ascending period of their development, appear called to a natural community of interests and of sympathies, of which they have already given mutual proofs to each other.

I do not wish here to approach any of the questions which divide the United States. We are not called upon to express ourselves in this contest. The preceding considerations have no other object than to attest the lively solicitude of the Emperor, in presence of the dangers which menace the American Union, and the sincere wishes which his Majesty entertains for the maintenance of that great work, so laboriously raised, which appeared so rich in its future.

It is in this sense, sir, that I desire you to express yourself, as well to the members of the General Government as to influential persons whom you may meet, giving them the assurance that in every event the American nation may count upon the most cordial sympathy on the part of our august master, during the important crisis which it is passing through at present.

Receive, sir, the expression of my very distinguished consideration.

(Signed) GORTCHAKOFF.

Mr. DE STOECKL, etc., etc., etc.

B.

THE NAMES OF UNITED STATES MEN-OF-WAR.

The original law regulating the nomenclature of the vessels of the United States was passed March 3, 1819, before the introduction of steamers. By its provisions, vessels of the first class, ships-of-the-line, were named after the States of the Union; of the second class, frigates, after the rivers; and of the third class, sloops, etc., after the cities and towns.

The introduction of steam having created a revolution in naval matters, a new act was passed by Congress, March 12, 1858, which provided that vessels of forty guns and upward should constitute the first class, and should be named from the States; vessels of from twenty to forty guns, second class, from cities, towns, and rivers; and vessels under twenty guns, third class, as the Secretary of the Navy, under the direction of the President, should determine.

The introduction of very large guns reduced nearly all modern vessels to a number below twenty guns; and the seven hundred ships of our civil war were named, accordingly, as the Secretary pleased. He followed, however, the traditions of the Navy by preserving the Indian names of the country, all of which have a local value, and many of which have been immortalized in song and story.

The rates of vessels are now designated by the Secretary of the Navy. They are classed as follows:

First-rates	3,000 tons and upward.
Second-rates	2,000 to 3,000 tons.
Third-rates	800 to 2,000 tons.
Fourth-rates	below 800 tons.

The tonnage is the cubic contents of the ship expressed in tons. In 1866 there were sixty-three iron-clads in our navy. Of these, forty-one were single-turret monitors and thirteen were two-turret monitors. The remainder were casemate vessels, with the exception of the Roanoke, which had three turrets. The following list shows the names, size of guns, and derivation of the names of the monitors of the same type as the Miantonomoh:

NAME.	BATTERY.	DERIVATION OF NAME.
Passaconaway	4 15-inch guns.	The chief Indian sachem of New Hampshire.
Quinsigamond	" "	A lake in Massachusetts, and the Indian name of Worcester, Mass.
Kalamazoo	" "	A river, county, and city, in Michigan.
Shakamaxon	" "	A river in Pennsylvania.
Agamenticus	" "	A mountain in Maine, near Portsmouth, New Hampshire; the highest land on the sea-coast between Portland and the Rio Grande.
Monadnock	" "	A mountain in New Hampshire.
Miantonomoh	" "	Chief of the Narragansett Indians, Rhode Island.
Tonawanda	" "	A small river in Western New York.
Puritan	2 20-inch "	
Onondaga	2 15, 2 11-in. guns.	An Indian tribe of Western New York.
Winnebago	4 11-inch guns.	An Indian tribe of Michigan and Wisconsin.
Chickasaw	" "	An Indian tribe of the Mississippi Valley
Kickapoo	" "	" " " " " "

C.
MIANTONOMOH GALOP.
FOR THE PIANO-FORTE.
Composed and respectfully dedicated to the Assistant Secretary of the Navy,
Hon. G. V. FOX,
By HEINRICH FURSTNOW, Musical Director at Pawtucket.

FOX'S MISSION TO RUSSIA.

APPENDIX. 435

D.

SPEECH OF PRINCE GORTCHAKOFF AT THE BANQUET OF THE ENGLISH CLUB AT ST. PETERSBURG, SEPTEMBER 8 (AUGUST 27), 1866.

Messieurs : Nos amis d'au-delà de l'Atlantique connaissent les sentiments que nous inspire leur présence parmi nous et l'objet de leur venue. Ces sentiments leur ont été exprimés à tous les degrés de l'échelle sociale, là où l'esprit orne la pensée, là où le cœur ne connaît qu'un langage primitif. Ils se sont fait entendre comme l'écho d'une seule voix ; la mienne ne saurait guère y ajouter.

L'acte exceptionnel, unique dans l'histoire, par lequel le Congrès a fait parvenir un message d'affection à notre Souverain, le choix de la personne qui en a été chargée et dont tous nous avons été à même d'apprécier la haute distinction, la dignité calme, unie à la chaleur du cœur,—l'habileté courageuse de ceux qui ont dirigé la traversée, en résolvant un problème qui jusqu'ici avait échappé à la science moderne, enfin le fait que parmi nous se trouve un représentant de cette nation qui durant une série d'années et dans toutes les circonstances nous a donné une preuve de son meilleur vouloir pour entretenir la bonne intelligence entre les deux pays—tout cela, messieurs, constitue une œuvre complète d'harmonie sans dissonances.

Je me réjouis de la présence de ces messieurs au milieu de nous, car je crois que la Russie ne perd pas à être vue de près. La distance arrondit les lignes d'un horizon éloigné, mais elle empêche de connaître à fond les détails du site.

Je m'applaudis, que des esprits pratiques étrangers à toute prévention soient venus nous juger tel que nous sommes. Ils auront été à même d'apprécier et le Souverain qui est la plus grande gloire du pays et la nation qui en est la force.

On dit que les bons règnes constituent les pages blanches de l'histoire. Ce dicton n'est point d'une vérité absolue. S'il y a un règne dont toutes les pages sont fécondes de réformes d'une haute portée dans l'intérêt de l'organisation intérieure ; s'il est un règne voué à la sollicitude du présent, en vue d'un grand avenir—c'est celui qui réunit aujourd'hui tous les sentiments affectueux et dévoués du pays ; parce que tous nous avons l'intime conviction que tous les instants de cette noble existence sont consacrés avec une abnégation sans limites au bien-être de notre pays.

Je ne citerai parmi ces œuvres multiples que la plus grande de toutes,—celle de l'émancipation, et ici je demande à nos amis Américains la permission d'un élan de franchise. Le message du Congrès contient une erreur, qui ne peut s'expliquer que par la distance lorsqu'il fait mention d'un ennemi de l'émancipation. L'insensé auquel il fait allusion n'appartient à aucune nationalité. Il n'avait aucun enjeu personnel dans les destinées du pays, il ne représente que l'aveugle hasard de la naissance.

En Russie, messieurs, il n'existe pas un seul ennemi de l'émancipation. Les classes qui doivent à cet acte leur liberté l'ont acclamé avec le même enthousiasme que celle à laquelle cette mesure a imposé de lourds sacrifices. C'est un témoignage que notre Souverain a rendu le premier à Sa noblesse territoriale, et je crois, messieurs, que dans cette enceinte, qui réunit les intelligences et les intérêts, aucune voix ne s'élèvera pour contredire mes paroles.

Je n'ai pas besoin d'insister sur les manifestations de sympathie entre les deux pays. Elles éclatent au grand jour. C'est un fait des plus intéressants de notre époque,—un fait qui crée entre deux peuples,—je me permettrai de dire, entre deux continents,—des germes de bienveillance et d'amitié réciproque qui porteront fruit, qui créent des traditions et qui tendent à consolider entre eux des rapports basés sur un véritable esprit de civilisation chrétienne. Cette entente ne repose pas sur une proximité géographique. L'abîme de mers nous sépare. Elle ne repose pas non plus sur des parchemins —je n'en trouve aucune trace dans les archives du ministère qui m'est confié. Elle est instinctive ; dès lors j'ose me permettre de l'appeler providentielle. Je m'applaudis de cette entente. J'ai foi dans sa durée. Dans ma situation politique tous mes soins tendront à la consolider. Je dis soins, et non efforts, parce qu'il ne faut pas d'efforts quand il s'agit d'une attraction spontanée et réciproque.

Un autre motif qui me porte à proclamer hautement mon appréciation de cette entente,—c'est qu'elle n'est ni une menace, ni péril pour personne. Elle ne s'inspire d'aucune convoitise, d'aucune arrière-pensée. Le Seigneur a fait aux deux pays des conditions d'existence où leur grande vie intérieure peut leur suffire.

Les États-Unis d'Amérique sont invulnérables chez eux. Cet état de choses ne se fonde pas seulement sur le fait que le rempart de l'Océan les garantit des conflits Européens, mais sur l'esprit public qui y règne, sur le caractère personnel des citoyens. L'Amérique ne peut éprouver de mal que celui qu'elle se ferait elle-même. Nous avons couvert de crêpe les pages douloureuses de ces derniers temps. Nous avons vu avec un profond regret la lutte entre les frères du Nord et les frères du Sud, mais nous avons toujours eu foi dans le triomphe final de l'Union, et nous en espérons la consolidation durable des efforts du Président actuel, dont le système, s'inspirant à la fois de fermeté et de modération, a toutes nos sympathies.

Sous ce rapport, messieurs, je me permets de trouver aussi une certaine analogie entre les deux pays. La Russie, par sa position géographique, peut être entraînée dans les complications Européennes; les chances de la guerre peuvent nous faire subir des revers. Néanmoins je pense que la même invulnérabilité existe également pour la Russie et qu'elle se manifestera toutes les fois que la dignité et l'honneur du pays seraient sérieusement menacés, car alors, comme dans toutes les crises de notre histoire, la puissance véritable de la Russie se fera jour; elle ne repose pas uniquement sur son étendue territoriale, ou sur le chiffre de sa population; elle découle du lien intime et indissoluble qui unit le Souverain à la nation et qui remet entre Ses mains toutes les forces matérielles et intellectuelles du pays, comme elle concentre en Lui aujourd'hui tous les sentiments d'amour et de dévouement.

Je vous remercie, messieurs, de l'indulgence que vous avez accordée à mes paroles, tout en regrettant que les sentiments qui nous animent tous aient reçu une expression aussi imparfaite.

Avant de terminer je ne veux pas laisser subsister une lacune que nos amis d'Amérique seraient en droit de nous reprocher, si j'oubliais de consacrer des paroles de respect à la mémoire du Président Lincoln,—de ce grand citoyen qui a sacrifié sa vie dans l'accomplissement de ses devoirs.

Veuillez permettre que, revenant sur une santé que nous avons déjà portée, je propose un toast à la prospérité des États-Unis, au succès de l'œuvre de pacification du président actuel, à M. Fox auquel a été confié une tâche qui ne pouvait pas être remise en de meilleures mains, aux Capitaines Murray et Beaumont dont l'intrépide habileté a assuré la réussite de cette lointaine traversée, ainsi que collectivement à tous ceux qui y ont participé. Je ne commettrai pas l'ingratitude d'oublier le Représentant actuel des États-Unis au milieu de nous, qui nous a constamment donné des preuves de son affection pour la Russie.

Lorsque nos amis d'Amérique rentreront chez eux je désire qu'ils emportent et conservent les sentiments qu'ils nous lèguent; qu'ils disent à leurs compatriotes qu'une grande nation n'oubliera jamais la preuve de sympathie offerte à son Souverain, qu'elle n'oubliera jamais qu'il s'est trouvé dans l'histoire des deux pays un moment où nous et nos amis d'Amérique avons vécu de la même vie, où ils ont partagé nos angoisses, comme ils se sont associés à nos joies.

E.

RECEPTION OF HIS IMPERIAL HIGHNESS THE GRAND-DUKE ALEXIS, IN LOWELL.

[*From the Lowell Vox Populi, Dec. 18, 1871.*]

The pleasure which our citizens derived, on Saturday, from the visit of the third son of our good friend the Emperor Alexander II. of Russia, is due to the fact that our fellow-citizen, Honorable G. V. Fox, was sent to that country, in 1866, on a special mission, a full account of which, collated from the Russian papers, was published by order of the State Department, and can be found in the diplomatic correspondence of 1867–'69.

The Russian minister having sent word that the Grand-duke would "certainly visit his good friend Mr. Fox, at Lowell," an official invitation by his honor Mayor Sherman was sent to New York and accepted. A city committee was immediately appointed, consisting of Mayor Sherman, Aldermen Haggett, Battles, and Salmon, and Councilmen Perkins, Cummiskey, Sanborn, Blanchard, and Knapp. These gentlemen, in consultation with Captain Fox, made the arrangements, which have proved so agreeable to our distinguished visitors. Saturday, the 9th instant, at 9 A. M., having been designated as the hour to leave Boston, a committee of the city government, consisting of Aldermen Haggett and Salmon, and Councilman Perkins, proceeded to Boston Friday afternoon, to pay their respects and arrange for taking charge of the party at the Revere House. The Boston, Lowell & Nashua Railroad Company placed a special train at the service of the Lowell city government, one car of which was a superb "Pullman."

At 7.30, all the aldermen and councilmen proceeded to Boston. The Grand-duke, with his usual promptness, left the Revere House precisely at 8.50, under the escort of the city committee, and was received at the station by the aldermen and councilmen of Lowell, and at 9 o'clock they were under way. There was no important incident on the route; the usual introductions, the cordial fraternization of the two nationalities, and the inevitable cigarettes, consumed the time, and at 9.30 the train entered the Middlesex-Street station, where the Grand-duke was received by the Honorable G. V. Fox, and introduced to his Honor Mayor E. F. Sherman, who sincerely welcomed him to Lowell, and the party immediately took seats in carriages in the following order:

First carriage—His Imperial Highness the Grand-duke Alexis; his Excellency C. Catacazy, Russian Minister; his Honor the Mayor, E. F. Sherman; Honorable G. V. Fox.

Second carriage—Vice-Admiral Possiet, Russian Imperial Navy; Rear-Admiral C. Steedman, United States Navy; Alderman Battles, Councilman Perkins.

Third carriage—Count Olsonfieff, Alderman Salmon, Mr. Shirkoff, Secretary of the Russian Legation; Mayor Gaston, of Boston

Fourth carriage—W. D. Bodisco, Russian Consul-General at New York; Alderman Haggett, Councilman Cummiskey.

Fifth carriage—The Press, represented by Mr. Marden, Mr. Stone, Mr. Knapp, and Mr. Hills.

Several other carriages, containing distinguished gentlemen from Boston and New York, followed.

There was a large crowd at the station, and, though the Duke was troubled with a slight cold, arising from his determination to go bravely through all the greetings, so cordially extended to him, yet the cheers and the tremendous ringing of bells all over the city at once awakened his attention, and afforded him gratification. The visitors proceeded rapidly through Thorndike, Highland, Elm, Central, and Hurd Streets, to the Middlesex Mills, entering at the second gate and driving to No. 3 Mill, where the party alighted and ascended to the weave-room, examining carefully the beautiful shawls produced by the skill of the girls; thence to the twist-room, where the Russian flag, surrounded by all the products of this company, was arranged in the most tasteful manner. The works of the Middlesex Company being under the direction of Captain Fox, special efforts seem to have been made to please the ducal party. The Russian flag was hoisted at the largest mill, and the American flag at the office. When the Grand-duke rode through the yard on his way out, he found the bell ringing, and all the operatives assembled to cheer him, which he frequently acknowledged by gracefully lifting his hat.

The next mill visited was the Lowell Company's, Samuel Fay, agent. Here the finished carpets were first shown, and then a rapid survey of all the weaving. At the Merrimack Mills, J. G. Palfrey, superintendent of the cotton, and H. Burrows, superintendent of printing, a more extended examination was made. The Grand-duke most cheerfully consented to visit several weave-rooms, at the request of the girls, who sent a message to that effect. The printing of calicoes and the various processes shown by Mr. Burrows, were of special interest to the Russians; and at their departure they were shown the photograph of the print-mills at Moscow, given to Mr. Burrows by Mr. Fox on his return from Russia. It was at this mill, in 1866, that Mr. Fox obtained the patterns which he gave to the Pacific Mills, at Lawrence, and the Merrimack, at Lowell, whence came the very successful fabric called *robe de chambres*. Leaving these works, they drove to the Lawrence Company, Daniel Hussey, agent, and were taken through the hosiery and finishing department. Upon leaving, the Grand-duke expressed a desire to look at a boarding-house where the operatives lived. His request was immediately complied with; and, without any warning to the house-keeper, or any of the inmates, he and the Russian ministre walked into No. 37, on the Lawrence Corporation, followed by Mr. Hussey, the agent, and Captain Fox. They examined the kitchen, the food, the sitting-room, the bedrooms, and at each place the Grand-duke and Mr. Catacazy had a parley in their own language; and finally the Grand-duke said to Captain Fox, "I wish we had such places as this in Russia."

The period for the "zakuska" at Captain Fox's having nearly arrived, a drive to the Pawtucket Falls was made, thence down Merrimack Street to No. 355, the residence of our fellow-citizen. The Russian and American flags were displayed on staffs to the right and left of the entrance, the Russian occupying the post of honor, and adorned with a wreath of laurel-leaves fastened with blue and white ribbons, used at Mr. Fox's reception in St. Petersburg. A large crowd had assembled in front of the house, which cheered the Grand-duke lustily as he entered, followed by his suite, the Mayor, and City Committee. The ladies assembled to receive his Imperial Highness were: Mrs. G. V. Fox; Mrs. Levi Woodbury, of Portsmouth, N. H. (her mother); Miss Ellen de Quincy Woodbury (her sister); Miss Mary Clapp, of Portland, Me. (her cousin); and Miss Anna Fox, of

Lowell, a niece of Captain Fox. There were also present as relatives: Hon. A. W. H. Clapp, of Portland; Hon. Charles Levi Woodbury, of Boston; Mr. L. Woodbury Blair; and Mr. Woodbury Lowery, of Harvard College. Mr. Fox presented his wife and each of the ladies and his relatives to the Grand-duke, after which there were no more formal presentations. The display of flowers was very abundant, and exceedingly graceful, and seemed appropriate for one so young.

His Imperial Highness and suite became very much interested in the memorials of Captain Fox's mission to Russia, the gifts of the Emperor Alexander II., and the cities and public bodies of that country. The diamond snuff box, containing an exquisite portrait of the Emperor on ivory, surrounded by brilliants, was much admired by all. Next was a photograph of the Emperor, in a frame representing the window of a Swiss *chalet*; this hung ten years in the city-hall at Moscow. The casket of malachite and golden bronze, more than two feet square, containing the diploma of citizenship of St. Petersburg, was the most conspicuous object in the drawing-room. Near it was the portfolio of the Moscow citizenship, the leather and artistic mountings of which were only exceeded by the diploma itself. Upon the walls hung two other diplomas of citizenship, Kostroma and Cronstadt, elaborately executed; also, paintings of St. Petersburg, copied from those in the Winter Palace. At the extremity of the room hung the memorial picture, in a conspicuous Byzantine frame, representing, with other scenes, the last presentation of bread and salt to Captain Fox, on his departure from Cronstadt. The Grand-duke remarked that he saw this in Russia. Near it was a large case of rare minerals, presented by the School of Mines at St. Petersburg, the Coronation Book and volume of antiquities, gifts of the Emperor, and photographs of all the places visited by Captain Fox. The Grand-duke and party finished by looking at a malachite album, containing the *cartes* of the imperial family and the most eminent men of Russia, with their autographs.

His Imperial Highness then offered his arm to Mrs. Fox, and others following, conducted the ladies to the dining-room, where a choice and profuse repast was spread. This room was likewise adorned with flowers, the portraits of the Emperor and Empress being tastefully ornamented with sprays pending from a representation in flowers of the national crown of Russia. The portrait of the venerable Metropolitan Philaret occupied a conspicuous position. There was also the picture of the Grand-duke Constantine, Prince

Gortchakoff, and Vice-Admiral Crabbe, presented in Russia, with autographs; two pictures representing the banquets given to Captain Fox at St. Petersburg and Moscow; and, over the door, photographs of the Church of St. Isaac, the bronze equestrian statue of Peter the Great, and the monitor Miantonomoh, with accompanying squadron, on its way to Russia.

The Grand-duke finished his lunch by touching glasses with Captain Fox, and saying that he thanked him for his hospitality, and that his visit to Russia had left so good an impression that every one there wished him to return. The ladies then returned to the parlor, leaving the dining-room for the other guests, while the Duke and suite withdrew to the tea-room adjoining, where yellow tea was served in Russian fashion, with cigars and cigarettes. They examined here many war-relics, and smoked and chatted in a manner that placed every one at his ease.

Two Japanese noblemen were present, and paid their respects, and were questioned concerning their country.

The hour of one o'clock having arrived, the Grand-duke and suite took leave of Mrs. Fox and the other ladies, and departed. As his Imperial Highness appeared on the steps, he found himself surrounded by a great crowd, in the midst of which a photographic artist had planted his apparatus. As soon as the Grand-duke perceived his object, he paused for a moment, to allow the agitated artist to succeed; then, entering his carriage, they drove rapidly through the crowd to the Merrimack-Street station. The chimes of St. Anne's and all the bells of the city were ringing, and the immense assemblage of people at the depot gave him enthusiastic cheers. Through the careful arrangements of the police, no disturbance occurred, and the whole party were soon in the Pullman car and off for Boston.

The visit seems to have given much satisfaction to the distinguished strangers, and our citizens are pleased that every thing was conducted so well, and that they had an opportunity to see, very near, this unaffected youth, son of so noble a sire. The absence of speeches, of hand-shaking, of processions, of bands of music, and of soldiers, was appreciated. The Grand-duke saw labor and capital happily combined in establishments which have been models for the world. We cordially wish good health and long life to our handsome visitor, who came and left in sunshine.

THE END.

www.ingramcontent.com/pod-product-compliance
Lightning Source LLC
Chambersburg PA
CBHW021316020526
44114CB00052B/795